RADICAL CARIBBEAN

To Dirk,
with Regards,
May, 96

Brian Meeks

RADICAL
CARIBBEAN
From Black Power to Abu Bakr

Brian Meeks

with a foreword by

Rupert Lewis

The Press University of the West Indies

Barbados ● Jamaica ● Trinidad & Tobago

Permission is acknowledged to reprint the following essays by the author, several of which have been revised for publication in this volume:

- "The 1970 revolution: chronology and documentation". In *The Black Power Revolution 1970: A Retrospective*, edited by S. Ryan and T. Stewart. Trinidad: ISER, 1995. Reprinted by permission of Selwyn Ryan.
- "C. Y. Thomas, the authoritarian state and revolutionary democracy", *Social and Economic Studies* 38, no. 1 (1989). Reprinted by permission of *Social and Economic Studies*.
- "Reviewing Rod Aya's *Rethinking Revolutions and Collective Violence*", *Social and Economic Studies* 41, no. 1 (1992). Reprinted by permission of *Social and Economic Studies*.
- "Re-reading *The Black Jacobins*: James, the dialectic and the revolutionary conjuncture", *Social and Economic Studies* 43, no. 3 (1994). Reprinted by permission of *Social and Economic Studies*.
- Quotations from *The Black Jacobins* used in this article reprinted by permission of Robert Hill.
- "The Imam, the return of Napoleon and the end of history". In *Colors of the Diaspora*, edited by M. Marable. Boulder: Westview, in press. Reprinted by permission of Manning Marable.
- "Caribbean insurrections", *The European Journal of Development Research*, 5, no. 1 (1993). Reprinted by permission of Frank Cass.

The Press University of the West Indies
1A Aqueduct Flats Kingston 7
Jamaica   W I

00 99 98 97 96   5 4 3 2 1

CATALOGUING IN PUBLICATION DATA
Meeks, Brian
    Radical Caribbean : from black power to Abu Bakr / Brian Meeks.

    p. cm.
    Includes bibliographical references and index.
    ISBN 976-640-023-7

    1. Government, Resistance to—Caribbean,
    English-speaking—History—20th century.
    2. Caribbean, English-speaking—Politics and
    government. 3. Radicalism—Caribbean,
    English-speaking. 4. Nationalism—Caribbean,
    English-speaking. I. Title.
    F1621.M43 1996   972.9 dc—20

Book design by Prodesign Ltd
Set in 9/13pt Cheltenham ITC

For
Neto and Anya

Contents

Foreword

There is a common thread running through Brian Meeks' political biography and that is the link between his political activism in Trinidad, Jamaica, and in the Grenada revolution (1979-1983) and his intellectual efforts to theorize the praxis of Caribbean radicalism. Meeks is concerned with the role of political revolutionaries, the ambit of political action and the complex of relations between agency and the material context of Caribbean societies. This collection of seven essays continues his reflections on issues he has probed in his book *Caribbean Revolutions and Revolutionary Theory: an Assessment of Cuba, Nicaragua and Grenada* (1993). This volume brings together conjunctural analyses of the 1970 revolution in Trinidad, the 1990 Muslimeen assault led by Abu Bakr on the Trinidadian state, and Jamaica in the mid nineties, along with review articles on C. Y. Thomas' work *The Rise of the Authoritarian State in Peripheral Societies*, Rod Aya's *Rethinking Revolutions and Collective Violence* and a political re-reading of C. L. R. James' classic 1938 volume *Black Jacobins*. The conjunctural analyses have rich and fresh insights into political behaviour, social relations, the erosion of hegemonic values, and the role of the state in the English-speaking Caribbean. In the review essays on comparative revolutions, Meeks battles with theories of revolutions – from the volcanic theories through to the structuralist interpretations of Theda Skocpol, rational choice Marxism, and the economic determinism of some Marxist writing and scholarship.

All of this is the backdrop to his preoccupation with the role of human intervention. The matter of agency is a theme that crops up explicitly in all the theoretical essays and implicitly in the conjunctural analyses. Brian Meeks' political narratives of Trinidadian politics twenty-five years ago and today, Jamaica in the 1990s, and the Grenada revolution enable us to go beyond the formal characterizations of politics in the English-speaking Caribbean as a relatively stable democratic area with periodic elections and Westminster-type political systems.

Readers of *Caribbean Revolutions and Revolutionary Theory* will be familiar with the identification of the state-building middle class revolutionaries and his rejection of economic determinism. In *Radical Caribbean: from Black Power to Abu Bakr* he shifts the focus from the state to the problem of how to transform hegemonic values. He writes:

> One hundred and sixty years after emancipation, the culture of slavery still casts its shadow over the entire Caribbean. Middle class tempers still run hot in Jamaica when children come home speaking 'bad' English. Very dark persons still experience snubs in schools, restaurants and nightclubs and beauty queens are still predominantly, if not overwhelmingly, of fairer colour. Despite significant advances in educational levels, employment policies and, to a degree, ownership patterns, the African heritage is still largely devalued in a region with a population – with the exception of Trinidad and Guyana – which is overwhelmingly of African descent. At one level then, the history of post independence revolt in the anglophone Caribbean has not been so much an attempt to seize state power as it has been an endeavour to transform the hegemonic values which, with modifications, have dominated the Caribbean for four centuries (p. 3).

Meeks goes on to point out that

> In the seventies, middle class, potential state-builders inspired by socialism were the means for attempting to assert personhood and identity. With the retreat of the radical middle classes, that same assertion is continuing apace through the informal economy, the music, on the burgeoning talk programmes which have accompanied the liberalization of the electronic media, and through countless interpersonal encounters, in which the old norms of hierarchy and deference are being questioned and deconstructed. This study is an attempt – by no means comprehensive – to trace some of the main contours of that process of assertion of selfhood which began in the late sixties and is continuing today (p. 3).

The author has shifted focus to issues of hegemonic creation and erosion in the Caribbean, leaning on Antonio Gramsci's discussion of hegemony.

Agency is a major issue in Meeks' work. In the essay reviewing C. L. R. James we get the restatement of historical materialism: "In the final count, social consciousness is determined by social being; human agency is underwritten by material context" (p. 114).

The dialectics of the relationship between subject and prevailing conditions and the potency of human agency preoccupy the author in the Haitian revolution where he argues that James "elevates the individual and agency to levels unprecedented in classical Marxism" (p. 105) but draws no conclusions for Marxist theory in general. James therefore has problems in coping with his materialism and the independent will of Toussaint and the other revolutionaries. Meeks had concluded *Caribbean Revolutions* with the statement that

> Revolutions, like life in all its multiple dimensions, are like multi-level chess games, with incalculable options and choices at any single moment. There is no deterministic explanation which can account for Fidel Castro's chance survival

of the 'Granma' landing; or Fonseca's death two years before the triumph of the Nicaraguan revolution; or Maurice Bishop's decision to march to the fort instead of meeting with the throngs waiting in the market square; nor to explain adequately the 'gridlock of events' in Grenada, with purposeful and chance occurrences piling one on top of the other, until a traffic-jam of consequences forces history in a particular direction; nor is there an explanation which can say with certainty how these revolutions would have unfolded if these events had gone differently. Much of the study of revolutions and indeed, life, is a matter of chance and cannot be reduced to simple formulae (p.187).

For me the political narratives which Meeks calls conjunctural analyses are richer than the reviews and critique of the theoretical literature in that they are closer to the complexities of life and activities of men and women than the abstractions of volcanic and structural theories of change.

In "The Imam, the Return of Napoleon and the End of History" Meeks undertakes a sophisticated analysis of the state in Jamaica, Trinidad, and Grenada. First, he finds inadequate Carl Stone's characterization of the Jamaican political system "as based on clientelistic relations where patrons dominate, but in which the clients, not infrequently, get their way" (p. 90), as well as Obika Gray's notion of authoritarian democracy. The author advances the view of the strength and resiliency of the Jamaican state. He argues that

> a state is resilient in the face of threats to its continued authority and dominance. Dominance is here used as a modified version of the Gramscian notion of hegemony, or the ability of the state, and the alliance of social groups who normally dominate in it, to exercise effective intellectual, moral and political leadership. A resilient state is one which is able to absorb, incorporate, head off in advance or, if necessary, crush effectively significant threats to its survival, integrity and coherence (p. 90).

On the other hand the state in Trinidad and Tobago is said to be fragile. "A fragile state is one in which the nature of its domination is such that it is often unable to respond adequately to tests to its survival" (p. 90). His case here is Abu Bakr's assault on the Trinidad state in 1990 and the arguments in Jamaica that had it happened in Jamaica Abu Bakr and his activists would have been killed. Anyone familiar with the Jamaican state knows the complex truth embodied in this statement. The political role of violence in Jamaica is a fertile route for research. The author argues:

> The critical feature which explains the notion of fragility is the indecisiveness of the Trinidadian state. Indecisiveness emerges from a society in which the ruling party depends for its electoral survival on the loyalty given to it by an alliance of ethnic groups. When members of the core group protest, even violently, against the government, care has to be taken with how they are handled (pp. 93-94).

He then turns to his third characterization which is the 'fractured state' and the case is Grenada. He argues that the Trinidadian state is not

> a consolidated hegemonic bloc as is the case with Jamaica. It is shot through with communal loyalties which fracture that possibility and create instead a Byzantine marketplace, where bargaining and jostling are the order of the day. But it is not a fractured state in the Grenadian sense, in which the fissures are so great, that reconciliation and hegemony, are almost impossible (p. 95).

Is there hegemonic dissolution in Jamaica?

> Counter-hegemonic forces are constantly at work, and never more so than in today's Jamaica, but the established and flexible system of élite hegemony is far from moribund (p. 95).

He fleshes out this proposition in the essay on Jamaica entitled "The Political Moment in Jamaica: the Dimensions of Hegemonic Dissolution". The Jamaican political system, he argues, has been characterized "by the existence of one of the tightest, most impermeable and consistent two party systems in the hemisphere" (p. 127). The constitutional system cannot explain the strength of its underpinnings and the system has both legal and extra-legal underpinnings or Jamaican conventions.

> Its success and relative longevity can be said to have derived from a series of unwritten pacts and compromises between the largely brown-skinned and educated upper middle classes who actually controlled state power and the black working and lower classes who voted for them and occasionally engaged in internecine warfare in the rank and file of either party (p. 127).

The three conventions are patron-clientelism; the acceptance of the principle of succession every decade; an accessible and charismatic type leader who

> would not simply rule according to bureaucratic and constitutional norms, but would maintain an extensive level of contact with his supporters – not only to facilitate the distribution of benefits, but to strengthen the notion of a unified and popular party with common national interests (p. 128).

The conventions also include codes of understanding between the two parties as well as within the parties. This system is falling apart and the author suggests three reasons: structural adjustment and the erosion of the resource base to maintain patron-client relations; the natural exhaustion of the two-party cycle; and the end of charismatic leadership with Manley's retirement in 1993.

> But if the moment is characterized by the collapse of support for the two tra-
> ditional parties, it is also one in which a radical alternative has failed to assert
> itself in the popular imagination. An effective, organized left does not exist in

Jamaica today, nor is there any other radical force of a populist, or religious, kind on the immediate horizon (p. 129).

Of the significance of Abu Bakr, Meeks writes

Bakr emerges at the end of a long narrative of failures. It is the failure of the Rhodes scholars and the university graduates – of 1970 – and of NJAC; the failure of the PNM to capitalize on the oil boom and of the 'one love' strategy of Robinson's NAR to bring the society together. It is all of these things and the falling living standards, growing anomie, increasing communalism and disillusionment which helped to bring the Muslimeen to the fore . . . Bakr is Janus-faced. He represents simultaneously the future and the past. His organization, in its genuine if controversial attempts to solve the drug problem by direct action against the pushers and by rehabilitation programmes, represents an Anglo-Caribbean variant of the Latin American *basismo* tradition . . . While Bakr sought (and seeks) to break the statist bond, to redefine the relationship between civil society and the state, he does so with medieval attitudes on the question of women's rights; a highly authoritarian and disciplinarian structure; a fundamentalist and prophetic sense of destiny and leadership; and an implicit distrust for democracy, evident in his praxis of 'direct action' (p. 96).

Meeks analyses the failure of the Workers Party of Jamaica and the retreat of the middle class. I would have liked to see some more on the retreat of the middle class and the forms this has taken. I think there is an assertion of sections of the middle class on the political front in the PNP and the JLP, and most significantly in the formation of the National Democratic Movement (NDM) led by Bruce Golding, former chairman of the Jamaica Labour Party.

On the economic front there is the entrepreneurial thrust of a new generation in the middle class. Granted this does not change the political retreat from the masses that the author is talking about, but the masses themselves have changed in ways that correspond to the thrust in the middle class. They too have become more entrepreneurial as is evident in the growth in the informal traders as they struggle with increasing impoverishment. These issues need further enquiry.

The author's argument for hegemonic dissolution takes up dance hall culture, the erosion of the middle class and its hegemonic values over the masses. He notes the contradictory character of this erosion:

. . . the collapse of middle class hegemony has meant the collapse of the reflexive deference to persons of a fairer complexion, but it has also meant the collapse of deeper universalistic norms of respect for other individuals which are the underpinnings of any functioning civilization. The baby is in danger of being thrown out with the bath water. The glue which held Jamaica together is in the process of terminal meltdown (p. 134).

Meeks concludes:

> The old hegemonic alliance is unable to rule in the accustomed way, but equally, alternative and competitive modes of hegemony from below are unable to decisively place their stamp on the new and fluid situation. What is definitely absent is an effective populist political organization, which might provide leadership though, perhaps, also steer the people in the direction of more traditional, hierarchical channels. There is, also, in the new unipolar world order no permissive world context, or international conjuncture which would facilitate the success of a national revolutionary upsurge, so in this critical respect also, the present moment is different (p. 134).

The author concludes with the statement of three alternatives in the Jamaican situation: an authoritarian government; democratic renewal; or common ruin of the contending classes.

Through his theoretical work on Caribbean revolutions and insurrections Brian Meeks has posed some key issues that will shape the agenda for political theory research well into the twenty-first century.

Rupert Lewis
Reader in Political Thought
Department of Government
University of the West Indies
November 1995

Acknowledgements

It is difficult to disentangle personal from political, and both from intellectual debts, and in a study which spans more than two decades of intense involvement and observation of Caribbean politics. I wish to thank Gordon Rohlehr and Kamau Brathwaite for, in their own ways, teaching me the importance of the rigorous study and appreciation of popular culture as both central cause and effect of the political process. To the late Maurice Bishop and to Bernard Coard, I belatedly acknowledge my gratitude for their offer of a job in 'the People's Revolution' in those dark days in 1980 after the Seaga government had come to power in Jamaica when I, along with many other news and current affairs workers, had been made redundant at the government owned Jamaica Broadcasting Corporation. My life and ideas would have been completely different in many respects had I observed the unfolding drama of Grenada from a distance; instead, I was among the privileged few to be a part of an event which was profoundly edifying, yet ultimately bitter and sobering in its tragic outcome.

To my colleagues at the University of the West Indies, there are many debts. I thank Rupert Lewis and Hubert Devonish for their willingness to read, listen and encourage, but also for the less tangible gift of friendship. I thank both the late Carl Stone and Trevor Munroe for, in their quite distinct ways, setting examples of what commitment, scholarship and hard work really mean. Many others have in various ways contributed to the realization of the ideas expressed in this volume. Among them, I want to thank Manning Marable, Jan Carew, Louis Lindsay, Tony Bogues, Nadi Edwards, Charles Mills, Carolyn Cooper, Rhoda Reddock, Kim Johnson, Folke Lindahl, Obika Gray, Christine Cummings, Norman Girvan, Claremont Kirton, David Lehmann, Gladstone Mills, Anthony Payne, Edwin Jones, Mark Figueroa, Barry Chevannes, Winston Suite, Lloyd Best, Kari Levitt and the late Derek Gordon. None of this would have been possible, of course, without my parents Corina and Charlie Meeks who gave me stability and taught me how to think, and my wife Patsy Lewis who in the darkest moments encourages, and never fails to ask the question 'why'.

Chapter One

Introduction

On October 16, 1968, Walter Rodney, Guyanese lecturer in history at the Mona campus of the University of the West Indies, was declared *persona non grata* by the Jamaican government headed by Hugh Shearer. On his return from the recently concluded Black Writers' Conference in Montreal, Rodney was not even allowed to leave the plane to pack his bags and make interim arrangements for his future and that of his family. Incensed by what they considered as the arbitrary and high-handed action of the government, hundreds of students at the University, led by the traditionally cautious Guild of Undergraduates, staged a demonstration[1] from the campus to the National Heroes' Park in the heart of the capital city, Kingston. On the way, the students were met by armed police who repeatedly attempted to disperse the demonstrators using tear gas and the occasional baton charge. Faced with daunting odds, the marchers – overwhelmingly composed of middle class teenagers who had never considered confronting the law – eventually dispersed, but not before hundreds of largely unemployed young men who had joined the protest, began to riot. The destruction which followed – compressed into a brief six-hour period – was the worst in the country's history since the 1938 labour riots, generally considered as the turning point on the road towards a modern and independent Jamaica.

Many commentators regard the 'Rodney Riots' as the symbolic beginning of the anglophone Caribbean Black Power movement. Caribbean Black Power, inspired though not guided by the North American movement, was a loose coalition of intellectuals, unemployed young persons and some workers, united around anti-imperialist slogans of 'freedom' and 'power'.[2] It reached its apogee in Trinidad and Tobago two years after the Rodney events, where massive, largely urban street demonstrations eventually culminated in an abortive coup led by junior officers in the army. The 1970 events signalled the beginning of a tumultuous decade, with the high points[3] being the six-year-long Manley experiment in democratic socialism in Jamaica and the 'People's Revolution' led by the Marxist New Jewel Movement (NJM) in Grenada in 1979.

But the initial euphoria felt by the radical intelligentsia and their popular constituency proved to be short-lived. Manley's People's National Party (PNP) was defeated in the brutal and traumatic general elections of 1980 and three years later, the NJM government, which had shown so much promise in building the Grenadian economy and introducing innovative social and cultural policies, collapsed in a bitter and murderous feud between its leaders.

For most people, the US-led invasion of Grenada – hot on the heels of the killing of Prime Minister Bishop and a number of his colleagues – signalled the decisive defeat of the radical movement in the Caribbean. Indeed, within six years of the collapse of the Grenada revolution, the PNP was reelected in Jamaica, this time, however, on a platform which rejected in all but name the anti-imperialist policies of the late seventies.[4] Few of the nascent, left wing movements[5] survived the traumatic shock waves of the Grenada events, and those that did – with the possible exception of the resilient progressive trade union movement in Trinidad and Tobago – were to flounder a few years later with the collapse of the Soviet Union and the subsequent crippling of the Cuban social and political project. With Grenada as the worst kind of example as to the likely outcome of Leninist policies; with no Soviet Union as an alternative pole for military assistance, aid and trade; with the defeat of the Sandinistas in the 1990 Nicaraguan elections; and with the economic example of Cuba as a constant reminder of what was likely to happen to any state which opposed American policies in a unipolar world, the left – certainly its Marxist-Leninist component – shorn of credibility, all but withered away.

Events since 1983, however, suggest that in the absence of its middle class leadership (which has largely retreated into private concerns) and without its enabling and, also, potentially crippling worldview of Marxism, Leninism and Socialism, the popular movement has continued to develop in its own peculiar way. Flowing in uncharted channels, occasionally throwing up unorthodox and often quixotic leaders, but inexorably advancing in a sort of flanking manoeuvre, a widespread movement of social and cultural resistance to hegemonic forms has continued to grow. The Abu Bakr events of 1990 in Trinidad; the flourishing of Rastafarianism in the Eastern Caribbean, Britain[6] and the United States long after its apparent eclipse in its country of origin, Jamaica; the growth of dance hall culture with its myriad linguistic, musical and social implications in Jamaica and, remarkably, throughout the entire Caribbean diaspora and beyond, are all cumulative parts of a linked universe of resistance. At the root of this resistance lies the harsh reality of small societies severely divided against themselves. The juxtaposition of conspicuous wealth beside desperate poverty has been definitive of the West Indies since the time of the earliest travel writers. Gordon Lewis is right when he generalises on ". . . the remarkable unanimity with which travellers to the region, almost from the very beginning, remarked on the stark contrast everywhere between the beauty of its natural habitat and the Gothic horrors of its social scene: where every prospect pleases and only man is vile".[7]

Much has changed since then, but a great deal remains the same. It remains statistically true to say that social policies and infrastructure, despite 'structurally adjusted' deterioration, remain among the best in the developing world;[8] that educational opportunities are still open to a wide cross-section of the people; and that health facilities, while severely overburdened are, comparatively speaking, fairly accessible. Nevertheless, the broad, secular trends point to a worsening rather than an improvement in the standards of living of the majority of people. But even as it is affirmed that most of the region's problems are attributable to economic structures, it has been evident for a long time that others lie at a deeper, psychological level.[9] One hundred and sixty years after emancipation, the culture of slavery still casts its shadow over the entire Caribbean. Middle class tempers still run hot in Jamaica when children come home speaking 'bad' English or, worse yet, when university academics 'who should know better', suggest that Jamaican patois should be recognized as a language in its own right. Persons with very dark skin still experience snubs in schools, restaurants and nightclubs, and beauty queens are still predominantly, if not overwhelmingly, of fairer colour. Despite significant advances in educational levels, employment policies and, to some degree, ownership patterns, the African heritage is still largely devalued in a region with a population – with the exceptions of Trinidad and Guyana – which is overwhelmingly of African descent. At one level then, the history of postindependence revolt in the anglophone Caribbean has been not so much an attempt to seize state power in order to transform the economic substructure, as it has been an endeavour to transform the hegemonic values which, with modifications, have dominated the Caribbean for four centuries.

From this perspective, the transient vehicle has been less significant than the intransigent message. In the seventies, middle class, potential state builders inspired by socialism were the means for attempting to assert personhood and identity. With the retreat of the radical middle classes, that same assertion is continuing apace through the informal economy, the music, on the burgeoning talk programmes which have accompanied the liberalization of the electronic media, and through countless interpersonal encounters, in which the old norms of hierarchy and deference are being questioned and deconstructed.

This study is an attempt – by no means comprehensive – to trace some of the main contours of that process of assertion of selfhood which began in the late sixties and is continuing today. There are two types of essay in the collection. The first consists of conjunctural analyses of specific and significant events which have helped to shape and define the character of the radical movement in the last quarter century. The second type seeks to comprehend and flesh out a theory of revolt, in an attempt to understand why revolts occur and to critically interrogate various methodologies used to explain how history is made.

The second chapter, "The 1970 Revolution: Chronology and Documentation", traces the course of the 1970 Black Power uprising in Trinidad and Tobago. Written as a series of diary entries, it seeks to understand the dynamics of the actual moment of revolt as, at the same time, it adopts Leninist positions popular in the nascent Caribbean left in the early seventies. Thus, implicit in the explanation of the failure of the revolt is the lack of ideological clarity of the leading organizations, including an appreciation of the pivotal role of the working class in revolutionary mobilization and the need for a tight, centralist organization, as opposed to the loose, 'spontaneist' approach adopted by the National Joint Action Committee (NJAC).

Chapter three, "C. Y. Thomas, the Authoritarian State and Revolutionary Democracy", is based primarily on a critique of Thomas' book, *The Rise of the Authoritarian State in Peripheral Societies* (1984). Written in its first draft in the mid eighties, in many respects it represents a transitional phase in this writer's development. A leading member of the Guyanese Working People's Alliance (WPA), Thomas had been among the most scathing of the leftwing critics of the Grenada revolution. In the book, he sought to identify with a libertarian Marxist perspective including, most prominently, that of Rosa Luxemburg. He argues that socialism is impossible without broad, liberal democratic rights, which are not to be seen as 'bourgeois rights', but rights won from the bourgeoisie by the working people. While agreeing with Thomas' general conclusions on the need for democracy, the chapter, basing itself on the experience of the Grenadian débâcle, asserts, from what is still essentially a Leninist perspective, that in revolutionary situations it may not be possible to concede liberal democratic rights all at once. There is evident sympathy for the need to rethink the notion of democracy at all stages of the revolutionary process, but there is still an unwillingness to abandon a certain reading of the 'dictatorship of the proletariat' and of vanguardism as a strategy.

Chapter four is a critique of Rod Aya's fairly obscure but important book *Rethinking Revolutions and Collective Violence*. Aya, in attempting to understand the underlying causes of revolutions, adopts rational choice methodology while rejecting economic and structural determinism. This approach provides an important extension to the social science debate on revolutions, which carries it beyond Theda Skocpol's 'state structuralist' approach. By 'bringing people back in' as subjects rather than objects in the making of revolutions, Aya helps to provide a more textured explanation. However, it is argued that while the elevation of the human agent is significant, Aya deprives him of the necessary cultural and ideological baggage which is critical in appreciating his role in the revolutionary matrix.

Chapter five, "Caribbean Insurrections", represents this writer's developed critique of Caribbean Leninism and the first attempt to go beyond Aya's approach and more thoroughly incorporate ideas and cultural values into a conjunctural analysis. It returns to the 1970 Black Power uprising in Trinidad and Tobago and compares it with the Grenada revolution and the 1990 abortive overthrow of the Trinidad government by Abu Bakr. It suggests that Leninism played a central role in the 1979 Grenadian victory, while its absence as a tactical guide contributed to the defeat of the two movements in Trinidad and Tobago. While, however, Leninism contributed immensely to the New Jewel Movement's success, it lay the basis for the isolation of the vanguard and the ultimate collapse of the revolution.

Chapter six, "The Imam, the Return of Napoleon and the End of History", focuses more specifically on the Abu Bakr uprising of 1990 in order to initiate a comparative analysis of the character of the Caribbean state. Borrowing from Jean François Bayart, it argues that the occurrence of armed insurrection and the eventual outcome in which an amnesty was granted to the insurrectionists cannot be understood without a close reading of Trinidadian history and culture. The central proposal is that the Trinidadian state – riven by ethnic and other historical divisions – is an example of a fragile state. Insurrections are more likely to occur in a weak state because the potential insurrectionists know that there is no united hegemonic bloc in opposition to them. Revolutions and insurrections cannot be properly analysed if there is a concentration on structures without, simul-taneously, a detailed understanding of the 'political trajectory' and the human agents who inhabit it. Abu Bakr's enigmatic career raises many issues about the character of 'postmodernist' radical movements. Equally, the course of recent Trinidadian events raises fundamental questions as to whether any totalizing ideology can hope to grasp the complexity of ever-unravelling human history, much less accurately predict its future course.

Chapter seven, "Rereading *The Black Jacobins*: James, the Dialectic and the Revolutionary Conjuncture", critically examines C. L. R. James' classic study of the Haitian Revolution in order to better understand his own interpretation of Marxist methodology. Relying on contemporary postmodernist and Marxist critiques, it traces the sequence of events as interpreted by James and asks the question as to whether even James' creative application of the Marxist method is sufficient to account for the peculiar role of the individual in the making of the Haitian Revolution. Determinism and the subordination of the human agent, it is argued, have profound implications not only for historical analysis, but for the likelihood of democracy emerging when applied to practical politics.

The final chapter, "The Political Moment in Jamaica: the Dimensions of Hegemonic Dissolution", focuses on the counter-example of Jamaica, a country fraught with sharp social and political divisions, but which has not so far taken the route of insurrectionary confrontation. Despite this, the sharpening clashes between the traditional élites and the insurgent majority across the gamut of social activities, has brought, it is proposed, a moment of 'hegemonic dissolution'. Jamaica may proceed in a number of possible directions, but the old order, deriving out of the postwar social and political arrangements, is moribund. The chapter concludes by proposing a number of possible options, including elements of a minimum programme of social and political reform in what is a critical and difficult juncture with no easy answers in Caribbean history.

If there is any single thread which runs through the entire collection, it is the attempt to move away from faceless, structuralist analyses of historical conjunctures towards an approach which is able to locate and highlight the role of the separate and disparate human agents who really make history.

There is also another, somewhat hidden dimension to the study. As with any collection which includes essays written over a period of two decades, it also reflects the personal development of the author. My own, somewhat checquered political career[10] has been decisively on the Caribbean left. As a middle class high school student at Jamaica College, I read Frantz Fanon and Eldridge Cleaver, and our small group of 'radicals' published our own Black Power pamphlets. Some of us travelled the short distance from Hope Road to the University to participate in the 1970 occupation of the Creative Arts Centre for its insufficient attention to black culture. As an undergraduate at the St Augustine campus of the UWI, in the heady politicized atmosphere in the months after the defeated 'revolution', I learnt about 'Mao Tse Tung Thought' and criticized 'Soviet revisionism'. Back in Jamaica, as a postgraduate student at Mona in 1974, I was eventually converted to a more orthodox Marxist-Leninist position under the influence of Trevor Munroe and the Workers Liberation League, through study groups which examined works like Lenin's "Two Tactics of Social Democracy in the Democratic Revolution".

As a loyal cadre of the Workers Party of Jamaica, I worked as a television producer at the Jamaica Broadcasting Corporation and gave 'critical support' to the Michael Manley government (1976), only to be made redundant along with the entire news and current affairs department when Edward Seaga's Jamaica Labour Party came to power in 1980. Invited the following year to help the Grenadian People's Revolutionary Government (PRG) set up its fledgling mass media, I worked 'in the revolution' until 1983 when, returning to Jamaica in September to take up a position as assistant lecturer at UWI, I soon discovered that the revolution was in terminal crisis and about to self- destruct.

The process of rethinking, which has necessarily occurred since the 1983 collapse, has been an attempt to rescue from the detritus of my Leninist inspired radicalism of the seventies a philosophical approach which would depart from the hierarchical and closed confines of orthodox dogma and simultaneously preserve my core concerns for human self-assertion and popular empowerment. This has operated both at the epistemological level as a questioning of the closed, essentialist and determinist elements in Marxism, and at the political level in a thorough questioning of the efficacy of the political party – particularly the vanguard party – in any genuine process of democratic renewal. An earlier stage of that process of self-examination and rethinking is captured in my comparative study of Cuba, Nicaragua and Grenada, *Caribbean Revolutions and Revolutionary Theory.*[11]

This collection of essays attempts to move beyond the limits of that study as it also seeks to look back on the rich experience of the recent past.

Notes

1 For an early and still relevant comment on the student demonstration and its implications for Jamaican politics, see Norman Girvan, "After Rodney: the politics of student protest in Jamaica", *New World Quarterly* 4, no. 3 (High Season 1968). For a more recent and gripping description of Rodney's role in the growth of a counter-hegemonic ideology in Jamaica in the late sixties, see Rupert Lewis, "Walter Rodney: 1968 revisited", *Social and Economic Studies* 43, no. 3 (September 1994).

2 For the political programme of the leading organization in the Trinidad movement, see National Joint Action Committee, *Conventional Politics or Revolution?* (Port of Spain: Vanguard, 1971), and for a compendium of some of the important debates within the regional Black Power movement, see "Special Issue on Black Power", *New World Quarterly* 5, no. 4 (1971).

3 The breadth of the radical movement and the extent to which it dominated the headlines, if not parliamentary politics in the mid seventies is still to be properly documented. Among the 'lesser' incidents which contributed to its cumulative effect were (i) the Union Island uprising of 1979, where Black Power advocates on the St Vincent ward of Union Island rose up against the central government; (ii) the ouster of the Dominican Government in May 1979, when strikes and street demonstrations forced the unpopular administration of Patrick John to step down and in which the radical Dominica Liberation Movement (DLM) played a central role; and (iii) the St Lucian transitional imbroglio, again in 1979, where the newly elected St Lucia Labour Party (SLP) Government was hobbled when right-leaning Prime Minister Allan Louisy refused to honour a pre-election agreement to allow his leftist comrades to take over leadership of the party and government. For the background to some of the Dominican issues, see Bill Riviere, "Reminiscences concerning mass work among farmers in Dominica 1976-1989", *Social and Economic Studies* 42, nos. 2 & 3 (1993); for a comment on the St Lucia events, see Anthony Payne, *The International Crisis in the Caribbean* (Baltimore: Johns Hopkins,1984); and on the Union Island rebellion, see Philip Nanton, "The changing patterns of state control in St Vincent and the Grenadines", in F. Ambursley and R. Cohen (eds), *Crisis in the Caribbean* (Kingston, Port of Spain: Heinneman, 1983).

RADICAL CARIBBEAN *From Black Power to Abu Bakr*

4 For an analysis of the transition of Manley's and the PNP's positions, see David Panton's *Jamaica's Michael Manley: the Great Transformation 1972-92* (Kingston: Kingston Publishers Limited, 1993).

5 Perhaps the most profound and soul-searching debate in the immediate post-Grenada period took place in the ranks of the Guyanese Working People's Alliance. By 1986 the WPA – never one of the hard core Leninist outfits – had proposed a new programme calling for an open party with diverse membership and room for critical debate at all levels (see Working People's Alliance, "Draft Programme for the Democratic Republic" (Mimeo, *c* 1986). And, for an important insight into the debate on the same issues in the Workers' Party of Jamaica – perhaps the most Leninist oriented of the Caribbbean contingent – see Workers Party of Jamaica, "Contribution to rethinking: issues in the Communist movement" (Mimeo, 1987).

6 Anna Marie Smith presents an interesting comment on the role of Rastafarianism in the metropole in "Rastafari as resistance and the ambiguities of essentialism in the 'New Social Movements'", in Ernesto Laclau (ed), *The Making of Political Identities* (London, New York: Verso, 1994).

7 Gordon Lewis, *Main Currents in Caribbean Thought: The Historical Evolution of Caribbean Society in its Ideological Aspects: 1492-1900* (Kingston, Port of Spain: Heinneman Caribbean, 1983), 15.

8 Important international statistics continue to rate the social performance of most of the Commonwealth Caribbean territories very favourably. See, for example, UNDP, *Human Development Report, 1994* (New York, Oxford: Oxford University Press, 1994).

9 For a continuation of his three-decade-long discussion of some of the critical issues of culture, race and class in contemporary Jamaica and the Wider Caribbean, see Rex Nettleford, *Inward Stretch, Outward Reach: A Voice From the Caribbean* (London and Basingstoke: Macmillan Caribbean, 1993).

10 I am convinced that Alasdair MacIntyre is absolutely right when he insists that while it may be impossible to be 'objective' in our social science writing and research, it is critical that we reveal to the reader who we are so that at least there is no pretension that we are not bringing our own predilections into the debate. MacIntyre asks: "What characterizes my situation as that of an agent *as such*, and what characterizes it as that of an agent *of a particular kind*, so providing me with an understanding of others as well as of myself?" See Alasdair MacIntyre, "Ideology, social science and revolution", *Comparative Politics* 5, no. 3 (April 1973).

11 Brian Meeks, *Caribbean Revolutions and Revolutionary Theory: an Assessment of Cuba, Nicragua and Grenada* (London and Basingstoke: Macmillan, 1993).

8

Chapter Two

The 1970 Revolution: Chronology and Documentation[1]

The initial proposal is that 1970 is an example of an aborted revolution. Fundamental to both state structuralist[2] and Marxist[3] definitions is the idea of political power passing from the hands of the defeated ruling class or coalition, into the hands of the emergent revolutionary alliance. The critical factor is that revolution at one point or another brings on to the historical agenda the question of state power as an issue. Whether or not the state is in fact wrested from the hands of the ruling classes, is an indicator of the success or failure of a critical, indeed, definitive, stage of the revolution.

An intense nationwide battle that ends with the defeat of the revolutionary forces, with the old ruling coalition still in control of the state, can still be considered revolutionary in its scope, but one which is not completed. The Black Power revolt of February to April 1970 in Trinidad and Tobago was a revolutionary struggle which was not completed, where state power at the end of the upsurge still lay in the hands of the old social forces – a broad alliance of merchants landed and foreign interests and in the political sphere, state bureaucrats and the governing People's National Movement (PNM).

It is during the course of revolutionary struggles that social interests become most well defined, express their outlooks both in theory and in actual practice in the clearest perspective, and thus reveal their character to the mobilized, revolutionary population for them to judge where they stand. Lenin effectively advances this 'teaching' dimension of a revolutionary struggle:

> During a revolution, millions and tens of millions of people learn in a week more than they do in a year of ordinary somnolent life. For at the time of a sharp turn in the life of an entire people, it becomes particularly clear what aims the various classes of people are pursuing, what strengths they possess and what methods they use.[4]

The aim of this essay is to try to chronologize the events from February 26 to

April 21, 1970, with the presentation of the necessary documentary evidence; to examine some of the strategies and tactics of the main social forces; and to suggest the critical turning points in the process.

In its first phase, the struggle was carried primarily by unemployed persons and students. The popular character of the demonstrations became more evident and the slogan of 'revolution' was taken up by the demonstrators as a whole. This period was also one in which reformist elements sought to divert the struggle from its increasingly independent line and bring it under their hegemony, as, concurrently, the threat of counter-revolutionary violence was hinted at. The critical turning point of this phase was Eric Williams' Address to the Nation, which attempted to win over the revolutionary forces by making a number of concessions. The resounding negative response with which this was greeted, signalled a clear break with the PNM and carried the struggle decisively into a new stage.

The second period, which lasted from March 23 to April 17, began with the rejection of Williams' speech and saw an all round intensification of the contradictions between the government and the demonstrators. During this period, sections of the population historically close to the ruling PNM joined the revolutionary forces, as an important element in the leadership eventually split with the party. This phase climaxed on April 17 with the entry of the organized working class on a grand scale – qualitatively increasing the size and power of the revolutionary alliance and setting off a chain of events, including the declaration of a state of emergency, the mutiny of pro-revolutionary soldiers in response to this, the overt involvement of the United States of America and then, with the capitulation of the rebel soldiers, the decisive defeat of the movement.

The Prelude

Seventeen days before the start of the February Revolution, Trinidad and Tobago celebrated Carnival. Traditionally seen as an annual moment of national reconciliation, Carnival 1970 started on a fundamentally different note. The appearance of Black Power and protest bands alongside the traditional fantasy and historical costumes, hinted at the new mood. Commenting on the qualitatively new content of Carnival, the *Express* reported:

> There was just one little fly in the ointment, or perhaps it was really three flies in the ointment, or perhaps it was really three flies masquerading as one or vice versa.
>
> It was the advent of the protest groups among the masqueraders both on Monday and Tuesday. Using the unlimited license granted to carnival revellers,

three groups made slashing comments on the social and political conditions in the country as they saw them.

We were warned about the band coming to town from Cedros to dramatize the plight of the people in that area. But the J'Ouvert crowd in Independence Square was taken by surprise, first by the presentation of 'The Truth About Blacks' from Pinetoppers Inc., and then by 'King Sugar' put out by the UWI. 'Truth' has been described as a band put out by Black Power militants in Port of Spain to voice their protest against the harassment of militant black leaders abroad and the banning of Stokely Carmichael by the Trinidad and Tobago government from entering the country where he was born. The marchers carried huge portraits of Eldridge Cleaver, the Black Panther leader, the late Malcolm X, Carmichael and others. There was also a caricature of Prime Minister Dr. Eric Williams, looking somewhat like a pig.

. . . 'King Sugar' recreated the hardships suffered by the workers in the sugar industry from slavery and indentureship up to the present day. The message the band was trying to put over was scrawled on its banner. 'Black blood, black sweat, black tears – white profits'.

. . . But the one thing in common about these three bands is that they may have started a trend and if we are to have another carnival before elections, we may find politics more strongly represented on both days than ever before . . .[5]

The government, aware of the historical importance of these events, but insufficiently cognizant of the urgency of the situation, attempted to 'look into' a programme of reforms, to reincorporate what it saw as the now more independent popular movement under its leadership. The *Express* of February 16, in an article entitled "New PNM search on for black dignity", listed the main elements of the government's initiative:

The PNM has started work toward black dignity, pride and equal opportunity in Trinidad and Tobago. The Party's General Council appointed Prime Minister Dr Eric Williams yesterday to a committee that will do the groundwork . . . Their job will be to find people to formulate a programme to achieve dignity and self-respect for the numerically dominant groups in the community and seize anew the opportunity to lead our nation and the region to a higher sense of nationalism and integration. This is to be achieved specifically by:
  – researching and publishing the historical and cultural background of the Indian and Negro in the community
  – equating the economic potential of the various ethnic groups
  – educating the worker in sound investment practices
  – promoting business enterprises through the cooperative movement
  – developing respect for security in investment among the new investing class.[6]

The proposed strategy suggested at least two of the main considerations of the governing party. First, its relatively comprehensive nature, stressing community-based, educational and economic programmes, indicated a recognition of the breadth of the opposition the government now faced. Secondly, that although the protest during Carnival had been made by a rural community in one case, university students in another and with the possibility of working class participation only in the third group (Pinetoppers), the majority of the concessions were granted to the working class. This suggests that while the PNM recognized a growing alliance against it, they considered the latent working class opposition as potentially the most dangerous. Even before the formal demonstrations had begun, then, it is evident that the government was preparing to outmanoeuvre the traditionally most independent and least reliable component of the national movement.

Phase One: The Demonstrations Begin

February 26, 1970 marked the anniversary of the Sir George Williams incident. In Montreal one year before, a number of mainly West Indian black students had been arrested after seriously damaging the University's computer system. This was the culminating event in a series of demonstrations against what was considered as the racist policies of the administration and some professors at Sir George. In Port of Spain, university students and supporters, led by the National Joint Action Committee (NJAC), staged a solidarity march for the Sir George students, many of whom were still facing trial in Montreal. The *Express* of February 27 recalls the main events of what would in fact be the first day of the revolution:

> Some 200 demonstrators entered the Roman Catholic Cathedral of the Immaculate Conception yesterday and staged a sit-in which lasted just under an hour. Chanting 'Power, Power', and other revolutionary slogans, the marchers swarmed into the Independence Square Cathedral, occupied the pews, the pulpit and other chairs near and around the altar.
>
> The demonstrators had begun their march at the Railway Building, South Quay, to mark international solidarity day, protesting the trial in Canada of West Indian students.
>
> Last night, Guild President Carl Blackwood, one of the three persons who improvised a public address system at the Cathedral, said: 'As president of the Guild of Undergraduates, I would like to inform the public that the Guild Council decided on Wednesday to support and take part in today's demonstrations against the miscarriage of justice at the trial of students involved in the Sir George Williams University issue.'

From the old railway building the demonstrators had marched to the Canadian High Commission on South Quay where there was a scuffle involving police and some of the marchers. The next stop was at the Royal Bank of Canada on Independence Square where some of the demonstrators attempted to enter but were blocked by policemen. At this point, the march was just under 100 strong. They comprised mostly members of the National Joint Action Committee, elements of revolutionary organizations in the Port of Spain area and a handful of students. After leaving the Cathedral the demonstrators headed up Henry street and down Park Street where there was a short stop at the Park Street branch of the Royal Bank of Canada. Then the marchers turned into Frederick Street, loudspeakers blasting business places as 'exploiters'.

When they attempted to enter certain stores, the doors were shut. By 3.30 pm, when the march got on to the stores between Queen Street and Independence Square on Frederick Street, the doors were all shut, except those of Woolworth and Company.

Into Broadway and South Quay and a pause at the offices of the Trinidad Chamber of Commerce for a tirade against the business community, the demonstration went back across Independence Square to the Furness Withy Building. There, with the riot squad bus nearby, and the police blocking the entrance to the building, two black American students addressed the demonstrators, urging solidarity. Afterwards they went to Woodford Square where a meeting was held. This was 4.10 pm.[7]

While of minor importance to the whole process which was to follow, the Sir George Williams incident was by no means completely divorced from it. Racialism in Canada, though somewhat different in form, was seen as connected to the proposition that in Trinidad, skewed ownership of the means of production still underpinned white domination of that society. The fact, too, that the country involved had been Canada, one of the chief sources of foreign investment in Trinidad and Tobago, made the connection more explicit, as did the common black power slogans used there and, increasingly, by the disparate Trinidadian movement.

The early political outlook of the demonstrators can best be illustrated by looking at their targets of focus. The Roman Catholic cathedral suggested an anticlerical trend, linked closely, perhaps, to the fact that white French creoles remained influential in its ranks. The Canadian High Commission and Royal Bank of Canada, while clearly targeted as visible representatives of the country in question, also suggested an anti-imperialist approach, while the Chamber of Commerce indicated opposition to big national capital. The common denominator in all of this of course, at least from the perspective of the black urban unemployed of 1970, was that all these institutions were 'white' or at least, white dominated.

Immediately after this first demonstration, two trends were evident in the national media. A liberal trend, expressed by Deputy Prime Minister A. N. R. Robinson, sought to reincorporate the slogans and content of Black Power under PNM leadership. His approach was to largely support Black Power, but isolate the extremists. In the *Guardian* of February 27, there was a report of Robinson's position:

> Minister of External Affairs and Deputy Prime Minister, Mr A. N. R. Robinson, is in support of the new mood of questioning of traditions, habits and customs which the younger generation has undertaken nowadays. Delivering the feature address at the annual speech-day and prize-giving function of the St François Girl's College held at Queen's Hall, the Minister said yesterday that he did not regard this new mood as anything to be disquieted about:
>
> 'Nothing has caused me personally greater faith in the future than this new mood; nothing has given me greater pride in our young people than this new awareness of themselves', Mr Robinson said.
>
> He said, however, that there were always those who might have been used by others as well as those who, for their own reasons, adopted extreme positions before they had adequate reflection or experience: 'These fortunately are by far the minority', he declared. He claimed that they were not typical, but there were people who were anxious to exploit the activities of the few in order to impose by force their own patterns of thought and behaviour. '. . . Many, while not intending to impose their own views and ways of behaving on others, will be quite prepared in certain circumstances, to allow someone to impose these patterns in their name . . . This is often how dictatorships arise', he warned, explaining that the most favourable circumstances for such an event were conditions of confusion . . . [8]

Benedict Wight, one of the more liberal commentators, expressed views similar to Robinson's, while being more explicit in his criticism of the actions of the demonstrators:

> The history of Youth shows a tendency to revolt, but I cannot believe that last Thursday's band of demonstrators achieved any freedom by storming into a cathedral unless it is the freedom to do as one pleases. But this has always been the impertinent right of prostitutes and criminals in every society. However, the sudden scurry of protests exposes in fact our hypocrisy and error and the despicable lie that Massa day is done. But the insolent cry of 'Power!' which alone seemed to find a response in the dull faces of Thursday's young demonstrators, precipitates a judgement that all these protests are mere mimicry, alienating at the same time any sympathy with these demonstrators as senseless and romanticism. [9]

More cautious than both Robinson and Wight was the position taken by the largely East Indian Democratic Labour Party (DLP), the parliamentary opposition in Trinidad and Tobago. While attacking the 'desecration' of the Cathedral by the demonstrators, the DLP also opposed the position of the demonstrators toward Canada and the United States:

> Enoch Powell's England can be called many names, for England, the former mother of the Empire, has closed her doors to Negroes and to Asians – even those who hold British passports.
>
> Canada and the United States of America, on the other hand, have still kept their doors opened and are taking in our unemployed.
>
> We believe our students ought to recognize this. We believe that our students should align themselves with protest against social injustices but that they should do so responsibly. [10]

Although Prime Minister Eric Williams himself had sniped at demonstrators, referring to them as 'hooligans' in a March 2 speech, [11] he remained largely silent. The most vitriolic opposition came, not surprisingly, from the traditionally conservative *Guardian*. Without conceding any historical justification for the demonstrations – as Wight and Robinson had done – the editorial of February 27 roundly attacked the demonstrators for their abusiveness and anarchy:

> Yesterday's marathon demonstration through the streets of Port of Spain has brought lessons for everyone, not the least of whom would be the demonstrators themselves. In making their point, the demonstrators succeeded in causing considerable disruption to normal activities in downtown Port of Spain, showed disrespect to the Roman Catholic Church and its followers and quite probably did their own cause considerable disservice in the process. What started off as a demonstration to protest alleged discrimination against West Indian students on trial in Canada snowballed into wholesale denunciation of everyone for wrongs real and imagined and very nearly ended up in serious chaos. This degree of disorder can find favour with no one.
>
> . . . No demonstration anywhere has a right to degenerate into the level of desecration and disorder which was in evidence yesterday. In our society there is room for dissent and protest and in this context, we uphold people's right to demonstrate. But somebody has to draw the line between legitimate demonstration and disruption of everything . . .
>
> No self-respecting citizen relishes the thought of an unruly mob wandering around town at random from place to place. Which is what, in effect happened yesterday . . . if there are to be demonstrations then one expects that both the demonstrators and the police would want to ensure that such processions take place along prescribed routes where they are not likely to cause disruption to persons who may not be involved, or interested for that matter.

This was a most inauspicious start to the search for black dignity and respect which the Prime Minister has insisted that all West Indians must seek.[12]

It should be recalled that at this point all of this reaction was in response to a small demonstration, which numbered at the most optimistic estimates some two hundred persons which, further, many people considered had committed political suicide by entering and 'desecrating' the Cathedral. Clearly, there was an underlying sense that more was at stake and that the society was close to some sort of breaking point. This was proven true in the following days, as the demonstrations suddenly mushroomed from a small clique of students to incorporate tens of thousands of unemployed persons and later, increasing numbers of workers.

March 4: The Escalation

On March 4 the NJAC leaders who had been detained in custody after the February 27 march were released, and that day, the first of a series of really large street demonstrations to 'Shanty Town' – one of the worst slums in Port of Spain – took place. Raoul Pantin, then a young reporter with the *Guardian*, captured the scale and spirit of the sudden escalation:

> More than 10,000 people marched through Port of Spain yesterday in a tightly disciplined demonstration in protest against the arrest of nine of their leaders. The arrests arose out of last Thursday's downtown demonstration, which included the occupation of the Roman Catholic Cathedral of the Immaculate Conception.
>
> Black Power groups from several areas in Trinidad and Tobago came to Woodford Square around 3.00 pm yesterday to join others in the march, which continued in the form of a meeting in the square until past 9 o'clock last night.
>
> Geddes Granger, leader of the National Joint Action Committee (NJAC) and one of the nine who face charges varying from disturbing a public place of worship, to conspiring to commit a breach of the peace, was again the main figure in yesterday's demonstration.
>
> From the start in Woodford Square, Granger and the leaders of various groups, organized a silent, disciplined demonstration. It was exactly that for most of the afternoon, with the exception of some singing and drum beating as the evening settled.
>
> Groups taking part in the march included the Black Panthers, the African Unity Brothers of St Ann, the African Cultural Association of St James, the Afro-turf limers from San Juan, the National Freedom Organization from Arouca and the Southern Liberation Movement from San Fernando. Black Power leaders also came in from Sangre Grande and other far flung areas.

The demonstration came together in Woodford Square but formally began outside Parliament where the thousands of the mostly young marchers joined shouting 'power' accompanied by the Black Power salute.

. . . They then moved up Richmond Street, across Park Street and down Frederick Street, where, as they did last Thursday, various business places came under attack. But there was no attempt at entering stores although some locked their doors anyway.

. . . When the front of the demonstration stood in front of the Trinidad Chamber of Commerce building on South Quay, the marchers extended back up Chacon Street across Independence Square and halfway up Frederick Street. The route then followed was up Broadway, across the fly-over bridge and up the Beetham Highway to Shanty Town. 'We are going to Shanty Town', Granger told the crowd, 'because every black man in this country is a Shanty Town!'

. . . Throughout the demonstration the theme was constant. An attack upon the 'White racist power structure and its black tools' oppressing black people. The need for black unity, demonstrated by thousands yesterday was also heavily emphasized . . . [13]

A similar report carried in the *Express*, made an important point when it said:

In fact the entire political and economic system of Trinidad received its share of the protests, with a trembling voice warning in the midst of it all of the confrontation to come. The aim of last Thursday's march (protesting the arrest of the West Indian students in the Sir George Williams University incident in Canada) seemed lost in the resolve of the youths. [14]

From an examination of the main participants in the march, one conclusion is immediately clear. In this, the first genuinely 'mass' demonstration, the vast majority of the participants did not, strictly speaking, come from the working class movement. Apart from the loose alliance that existed between NJAC and the Transport and Industrial Workers Union (TIWU) which, in the period immediately after February 26, was not translated into active support, there was no trade union presence in the march. The names of the groups suggested that they were overwhelmingly community based and, as in the obvious case of 'Afro Turf Limers', that they were unemployed. Franklin Harvey is thus on target when he argues that: "It was the unemployed youth movement that started and carried the 1970 social explosion for almost two months. They marched from area to area, organized demonstrations and public meetings and carried out other tasks." [15]

Further, the names of these loosely knit groups of unemployed young people and the general slogans which Granger and the NJAC leadership used indicated that some definition of 'Black Power' was already the dominant ideological form long before the first demonstrations had been held. The content of NJAC's interpretation of 'Black Power' was evident in an interview which Dave Darbeau and David Murray, two of the University of the West Indies student leaders of the movement, gave to the Canadian media in the following year:

> *Interviewer:* I understand that the beginning of the heightening of the political climate in Trinidad began last year February, partially as the result of a march which was organized in connection with the Sir George Williams affair, but that it really sparked off developments in Trinidad which were not related at all. Would you, Dave, like to outline some of those developments that the Sir George Williams march really acted as a catalyst for, but were the real issues in that series of events that began last year?
>
> *Dave Darbeau:* Our society suffers from some very serious problems. If you take something like unemployment which concerns people directly, 15 percent of the labour force is unemployed and you have another 20 percent who are underemployed; so you have the material conditions in the society for Revolution. In addition the society is very much controlled by a very small white minority and we suffer from the domination of societies like Canada, the US and Britain, in particular.
>
> *Interviewer:* Would you like to outline a little more how the society is under the domination of these countries as you see it?
>
> *Dave Darbeau:* The economic resources of the society are almost completely controlled from abroad. Canada controls our banking system, the United States controls our minerals and Britain controls a lot of our export agriculture. So that almost the whole economy of Trinidad and Tobago is in foreign hands – and the system which they have organized – well, for one thing, they have to control our tastes, because if we are to be consumers of products that these societies produce then they have to brainwash us to determine our tastes.[16]

NJAC's early version of Black Power was unambiguously revolutionary and 'anti-imperialist' in content. The persistent ills of Trinidadian society one decade after independence – growing unemployment, vast income inequality and white or fair-skinned domination of the economy, were interpreted as resulting ultimately from foreign economic domination. As Ian Belgrave, another important leader, confirms: "Principally, the category that the ideology of the outlook that NJAC would fall into in 1970 was anti-imperialist. It was anti-imperialist to the core. All their programmes, all their policies, their propaganda was totally and actively anti-imperialist, against foreign domination of the society."[17]

It was this perspective of a totally corrupt, comprador government in bed with foreign 'white' interests which needed to be removed by any means necessary in order to facilitate the progress of the black majority, which would guide the movement throughout the months of the active 'street' phase of the struggle.

March 5: Intensification

By March 5 the situation had escalated one stage further. At the trial of the nine NJAC leaders, a crowd of supporters had gathered and was dispersed by the police with baton charges. The fleeing and incensed demonstrators destroyed shop windows in the commercial area of downtown Port of Spain. On the night of March 5, a molotov cocktail was thrown into the home of Minister of Education and Culture, Senator Donald Pierre. On March 6, a crowd estimated as being between 14,000 and 20,000 strong, marched under NJAC leadership to San Juan, some five miles to the east of Port of Spain. On March 8, various banks, business places and the home of the United States Vice Consul were hit by molotov cocktails. Moving beyond the tactic of demonstration, isolated members of the loosely defined body of marchers who virtually all considered themselves as members of NJAC, had begun random attacks on symbols of white power.

The responses to this new phase can again be divided into both liberal and conservative camps. The Tapia House Movement's special newspaper on "The Current National Crisis" suggested the approach of the liberal left. Tapia, headed by UWI economics lecturer and intellectual guru Lloyd Best, associated itself with the cause of the demonstrators with one caveat. Despite the reality of upward of 20,000 people demonstrating daily in the streets, Tapia urged that the time was not ripe for such action:

> To the extent that the 'black power movement' opposes the regime of corruption and privilege, we are at one with it. To the extent that the movement fails to think and understand the nature of its frustrations and its motivations, we cannot support it without at the same time insisting on the rest of the work needed to provide the nation with positive ideas for the reconstruction of society.
>
> The Tapia House group is a body inducing people to stand up and throw off the Yoke law of colonialism by the constant discipline of increasing our insights into the realities of our situation. Any abandonment of this empirical, imaginative search for the truths behind the sham, any departure toward the kind of impulsiveness that can lead to misplaced insult and injury, would be from our point of view, a retrograde step. The weakness of the black solidarity movement here is its tendency to oversimplify issues and to see things in terms of black vs. white, we vs. they, capitalist vs. workers, intellectual discussion vs. direct action.
>
> . . . Revolution is not achieved simply by feeling the fraudulence and the brutality of the regime and reacting against it. Revolution, that is to say, fundamental change, is achieved when we also see so clearly through the regime that we can take the steps required, not to replace it with another tyranny, but to displace it with a better order.

Protest and demonstration are certainly essential. Indeed they are vitally necessary for those (and there are many of them) who, precisely because of the brutality of the regime, are left no other medium of expression.

Yet demonstration and protest are not enough. To hope that 'ideas and technical direction' will come from elsewhere is too dangerously random a procedure. We cannot risk destroying more than we create.

. . . This is not to say that a time might well come when guns and violence may be necessary to overthrow those who have dispossessed us, in the last resort, by guns and violence. We know this very well, and our strong sympathies with the current revolt arises from precisely this understanding. But we know, too, that the revolt must be reinforced by its thought, must be informed by its own ideas. This blend between thought and action must be organic – which is quite a different thing from merely imposing plausible sounding 'technical solutions'. That procedure can only lead to the strongman, the maximum leader.

The present crisis with its threat of utter breakdown and chaos shows disturbing signs of taking just that turn. For Tapia to join the revolt in the role of technical advisor, would mean a betrayal of our integrity and our convictions. It would be helping to create precisely the kind of power structure to which we are fundamentally opposed.

We know very well and feel very deeply the cruel injustices that have been and are being perpetrated on the people, the acts of commission and omission that are the whiplash on the backs of the country . . . We are not afraid to identify the Church as an evil incubus on our society or to expose the shabby expediency which Williams has spuriously dignified with the name 'pragmatism'. We have to say these things so that when the genuine social revolution comes it will not have to ask anybody for ideas. It will know what it is destroying and why and it will know what is needed to displace the old regime. In short, we are seeking to avoid the kind of revolution which by taking a 'leap in the dark' succeeds only in replacing one tyranny with another.[18]

Tapia's objections to the 'spontaneity' of the movement was roundly criticized by those to the left of it as an attempt to pour cold water on the independent popular initiative, without any clear alternative proposal as to how to confront governmental corruption and mismanagement. Speaking from self-imposed exile in Britain, C. L. R. James, the most well known of the left-leaning Trinidadian intellectuals, in an interview with Ivor Oxaal, stated this perspective most clearly:

[Oxaal] 'What about Tapia House Group?' I asked. His [C L R James'] reply was outspokenly critical. There had been a genuinely popular revolutionary movement in Trinidad, he pointed out. The duty of those who sought basic change, he implied, was plain. It was to join the movement in however humble a capacity.[19]

On the other side of the fence, the alarmed and alerted conservative position was eminently expressed in a speech to the nation by the Attorney General, Karl Hudson-Phillips, on March 11. For the first time, a government spokesman was forthrightly threatening repression of the entire movement, on the basis of the outbreaks of violence which had occurred at intervals over the preceding days. In an article entitled "You Can Talk or March but Government Won't Stand Violence", the *Express* reported the Attorney General's speech.

> 'Anarchy or repression', the government has said at last, 'can be the only results of disrespect of fundamental rights.'
>
> Attorney General Karl Hudson-Phillips broke government's silence on the situation last night in a radio-television broadcast.
>
> '. . . While accepting the right of freedom of speech and the freedom to demonstrate peacefully, the government cannot condone the use of these rights or the pretended use of these rights, as an excuse for violence, intimidation, fire setting, or indeed brutality in any form whatsoever.
>
> '. . . Disrespect of fundamental rights can only result in either anarchy or repression. Violence and brutality by anybody cannot therefore be condoned and indeed must be condemned.
>
> 'I therefore appeal to all citizens of this nation and indeed to those in our midst to respect the rights of themselves and others.'[20]

Positions were obviously polarizing, as in the next phase both camps sought to consolidate political support for the ultimate, and increasingly evident, confrontation.

March 12: The March to Caroni – Searching for Alliances

The scope of the movement, its increasingly nationwide scale, and the vanguard position of the NJAC became more apparent after the Caroni march. On that day, March 12, over 6,000 Afro-Trinidadians marched into the heart of the largely Indian sugar belt of Caroni in Central Trinidad, to actively demonstrate for racial unity between African and Indian 'black people'. Despite the active opposition of Bhadase Maraj, Indian strongman, head of the All Trinidad Sugar Workers Union (ATSEFWTU), and the DLP leader, who had threatened violence once the marchers had entered the sugar belt, there were no major incidents during the march. The *Express* reporter captured the substantial themes of the march:

> The march on Caroni to make clear in the minds of its residents that Black Power meant unity between Indian and African brothers, was peaceful and that was the most important thing. Another important thing was whether it succeeded in winning Caroni people over to the idea of committing themselves to Black Power.

> There were no shows of over-enthusiasm, no welcoming of liberation troops type of sympathy. But there were the significant gestures, one of which was women of the villages coming to the aid of thirsty men and women who had marched so many miles from Port of Spain. Buckets of water were placed at gateways as the marchers passed. Front yards with running water were open to the demonstrators. 'Welcome' was written on the village notice board in LaPaille: 'We are asking the people of LaPaille to come out and give their support to Black Power for our rights'. In place of a street name on a corner sign post were the words 'Welcome to Power'.
>
> There was little involvement by the people of Caroni beyond the evidence that the marchers were not unwelcome.[21]

At minimum the march had served to breach a psychological barrier, in that large numbers of Afro-Trinidadians had entered Caroni without Maraj's dire predictions coming to pass. However, while the Indian villagers were not hostile, neither did they join the demonstrators in numbers as the urban unemployed had done over the preceding weeks. But then, NJAC's drive had been directed at the 'community', broadly speaking, in Central, as it had been in Northern Trinidad. The subsequent, far more bullish response of the Indian sugar workers to the movement, would suggest that NJAC's initial tactics had been misdirected. An earlier appeal to the trade union movement in the sugar belt might have led to organized, consolidated support at the beginning of the process, instead of the vague expressions of sympathy which the Caroni march gained.

Further, despite NJAC's broad definition of 'black' to include Africans and Indians, many Indians refused to identify with the slogan of Black Power, and ended up being even further alienated from the movement. The very name the movement gave itself was, to this extent, often a liability in the specific ethnic complexity of Trinidad and Tobago. Brinsley Samaroo effectively brings out this point:

> Another important reason for the Trinidad Indians' reluctance to join the power movement is that they do not regard themselves as black. Most national commentators for example, automatically equate negro with black, and since newspapers carry considerable authority in the West Indies, such identification becomes readily accepted.
>
> Reinforcing the Trinidad Indian belief that the black power movement is really a Negro one, are certain symbols used by the advocates of Black Power. The Trinidad Indian feels hardly welcome in a power demonstration when he knows that the clenched fist is really borrowed from the Black Panthers of the US, a purely negro group, or when he sees the local advocates of power wearing Dashikis, a symbol of identification with Africa.[22]

These were some of the evident limitations of NJAC's variant of Black Power.

However, within these confines, the movement had shown some flexibility in addressing the specific contours of the society. Trinidadian born but US-based Black Power advocate Stokely Carmichael would, a few months later, make the gravest error in neighbouring Guyana by suggesting that black power was exclusively for Afro-Guyanese, excluding the majority Indian population. NJAC, at least, had stood for a broad cross-racial platform, whereas Carmichael's position was potentially divisive and catered to the racial antagonisms already deeply entrenched in Guyanese as in Trinidadian society.

NJAC's more considered position appears in a pamphlet published after the end of the revolutionary upsurge. Entitled "Conventional Politics or Revolution?", it states:

> Great emphasis was placed on uniting the two major Black races, the Indians and Africans, during the revolutionary months. African-Indian unity must be the basis for a new society. We knew that . . . only deliberately created barriers could prevent two suffering Black people from uniting to fight the common enemy. Our history indicated the potential for the two groups to struggle together. What was done in 1919, when a young Indian brother, Beharrysingh, was killed mobilizing his Indian brothers to fight along with the Africans, and again in 1937 when Butler appealed to the sugar workers, was done again, even more effectively in 1970.
>
> Black people went through a process of re-education which made it quite clear that the Indian's oppression did not come from the African neither did the African's come from the Indian. We are all kept down by the white man in a vicious system created by him for the protection of his economic interests.[23]

If the Caroni march did achieve anything, it was to send a signal to the Indian community of Central Trinidad that the Black Power leadership and its supporters wanted to build bridges. This would serve the movement well in the critical, if abortive, trade union mobilization which was soon to follow.

March 12 to March 22: Consolidation and Momentum

In this period, NJAC consolidated its early successes with meetings in Arima in the East and in Southern Trinidad along with the Universal Movement for the Reconstruction of Black Identity (UMROBI). Further momentum was gained with the return on March 22 of some of the students who had been tried and fined over the Sir George Williams incident. The metaphorical replenishment of the student core of the movement was cause for celebration, but also helped to emphasize how far events had moved from the first march in February. This was no longer a student affair, but a full scale mobilization of tens of thousands of young people against a government which had purportedly come to power in defence of the black, poor and young. Then, on March 23, Eric Williams for the first time since the start of the demonstrations, spoke to the nation and the content of his speech as well as the response of the people signalled the beginning of a new and more radical stage of the process.

March 23: Radicalization

Before March 23, it would be fair to suggest that only a small minority of the demonstrators fully appreciated the revolutionary potential of the movement. While, objectively, the huge demonstrations with their accompanying acts of incendiarism and sabotage were moving in the direction of confrontation with the government, many individuals had continued to support the ruling PNM and looked beyond the foibles of individual ministers to Eric Williams for direction and salvation. Aldwyn Primus, head of the tiny Trinidad Black Panther Movement, expressed the view in a 'white paper' in early March that the demonstrators were to be seen primarily as a pressure group which would encourage the government to carry out its own programme of reforms:

> The four-page document includes repeal of the Industrial Stabilization Act, removal of certain government ministers and redistribution of land in Trinidad and Tobago. Summing up his demands, Primus said that 'an effective team must be set up to deal with their implementation over the next three months'. But, he warns, 'during this time, the movement will continue to march'.[24]

This persistent belief that the PNM government could be the vehicle for radical reform was largely shattered after Williams' speech. While praising his government's achievements in seeking to establish a multiracial society, promoting "black economic power, free secondary education and black presence in the civil service", Williams suggested that the reason for the demonstrations was that the people were ignorant as to what the government was doing for them:

> The demonstrations, however, suggested that neither the policy of the government nor the measures taken to implement that policy are sufficiently known. I get a feeling that there is not sufficient awareness of our policy statement in the Third Five-Year Plan to strengthen local decision making where investment is concerned and to achieve a larger national share in the principal enterprises.[25]

Williams agreed that the pace of change had been too slow over the past years and that it had now to be speeded up. On the question of Black Power itself, he, like A. N. R. Robinson, sought to emphasize the small proprietor dimension of the movement in an attempt to channel its revolutionary content in a direction more acceptable to the status quo. Williams noted:

. . . the fundamental feature of the demonstrators was the insistence on black dignity, the manifestation of black consciousness and the demand for black economic power. The entire population must understand that these demands are perfectly legitimate and are entirely in the interest of the community as a whole. If this is Black Power then I am for Black Power.[26]

To this end, Williams' main tactic to appease the demonstrators took the form of a series of concessions. The first was a 5 percent tax on Pioneer companies, which was to generate some ten million dollars to pay for an employment relief programme. The second, to address the charge of persistent white domination of the private sector, was the appointment of a commission to examine the charge of racial discrimination in businesses. The third, to address the charge of foreign control of the economy, was the purchase of 51 percent shares in the Bank of London and Montreal.

For the increasingly militant demonstrators, this response, which might have been looked on favourably in February, led instead to further militancy and a gathering hostility towards Williams and his party. James Millette of the United National Independence Party – not by any means one of the more radical of the organizations – captures the general mood which followed Williams' speech:

> The Prime Minister's broadcast on Monday last has merely emphasized the gravity of the continuing national crisis. Not only did it offer far too little, and that too late, but the spectacle of the government, 14 years in office and innocent of a strategy with which to right our country's ills, must have rammed home the extreme seriousness of our situation. Ten million dollars to be spent on unemployment is, to use the Prime Minister's own phrase apropos the marketing of Trinidad-Tesoro's oil, 'a mere bagatelle' compared with what is really required . . .
>
> The government's response to the month-old national crisis precipitated by the arrest of the leaders of the solidarity day demonstration of February 26 is interesting too, for two other reasons. In the first place, it put the PNM where it should be – that is – on the side of the international corporations and at odds with the people . . .
>
> Clearly after 14 years in office the PNM is intrinsically a part of the vested interests with which the country is at odds. It is no surprise that it shrinks from the task of dealing with those interests.
>
> . . . In the circumstances it was to be expected, we suppose that the speech should have abounded with half truths and vapid prophesies. But was it really to be expected that the government would continue to pretend that it had the right to govern?[27]

The possibility of using reforms to bridge the contradictions between those on the streets and those in power had passed. The popular movement, albeit with a leadership not absolutely clear as to the correct slogans and tactics with which to direct the struggle, nonetheless moved leftward. Lloyd Best, in a later analysis, also sensed that this was a critical turning point: "In this third phase [after Williams' speech] it was quite clear, or it became crystal clear as the days passed that the new movement was looking for a confrontation to bring the regime down as quickly as possible. There is no question about that."[28]

March 25 to April 9: The Crisis Ripens

During this period, the NJAC leadership found itself at something of an impasse. The extent and effectiveness of the community-based 'street' support appeared to have reached its limits. The government had responded with concessions which, if anything, had served to stoke the flames of revolt, but, at the same time, NJAC had failed to qualitatively increase its mass support, particularly after the lukewarm response from the Indians of Central Trinidad. Nevertheless, the period between March 25 and April 4 saw the NJAC leadership working assiduously to forge new alliances in order to find the formula which would give the movement sufficient strength to confront the government.

Three events suggested that NJAC had been largely successful. On April 1, NJAC met with the National Association of Steelbandsmen and the following day the *Express* reported an alliance between Black Power and the steelband movement:

> The Black Power and steelband movements found common ground for an alliance during a two hour meeting of leaders yesterday. The Steelband Association said after the meeting, its leaders felt it 'could not divorce or disassociate itself from the Black Power movement since the aims and objectives of Black Power are the same as that of the steelband movement'.
> A statement said steelband leaders also dispelled rumors that there are plans afoot to organize anti-Black Power activities with steelbandsmen. 'If we find any section of the community using steelbandsmen for anti-Black Power activities,' the Association said, 'we will instruct members not to take part.'[29]

The significance of this is inestimable. For many years the steelband movement – a critical cultural and political, if loosely organized force – had given its support to the PNM. Despite Williams' mention of the steelband movement as a special recipient of funds in his speech, it nonetheless chose to break with him at a critical moment. This, more than anything, indicates how rapidly the society had polarized.

Then, on April 4, the anticipated expansion in social forces bore fruit with the declaration of open support for the movement by the militant, strategic and highly organized Oilfield Workers Trade Union (OWTU), followed four days later by a pro-Black Power demonstration by OWTU workers at the Trinidad and Tobago Electricity Commission (T&TEC). A new coalition, including for the first time significant contingents of the organized working class, was gathering and this was evident on April 9. That day, a political funeral was held for Basil Davis, a young demonstrator who had been shot by the police and was considered the first 'martyr of the revolution'. Some 30,000 to 100,000 persons (depending on the estimators) – by far the largest mass event of the entire period – followed the funeral entourage from Port of Spain to San Juan. This was the clearest indicator of a new alignment of forces, which served to precipitate an internal crisis in the ruling PNM, as it also drew new contingents from among the unemployed and, critically, the working class, towards NJAC and the movement.

By April 8, too, the position of the conservatives had hardened. The Hudson-Phillips tendency, which had hinted at repression even in the early phases of the struggle, became more strident, even as the liberal approach which had advocated concessions, moved increasingly towards repressive positions. As the popular movement veered left, in a phenomenon common to all revolutionary situations, the defenders of the status quo moved to the right. Commenting on the developments of the preceding weeks, in particular, an NJAC sponsored march which had taken place in Tobago, the hitherto conciliatory *Express* editorial sounded the trumpet of law and order:

> It is almost naïve to hope now that it will end well. Violence breeds violence. This is obvious whether it is the subtle violence of unemployment, discrimination or the open violence of window smashing or molotov cocktails. People are not always able to turn the other cheek or to believe when they lose confidence in brotherhood that vengeance belongs to the Lord.
>
> And yet, it is all very sad because the solution of Trinidad and Tobago's problems does not require the useless shedding of blood and the unnecessary pitting of brother against brother, sister against sister. In spite of the hysterical railing of George Weekes and the *Vanguard*, we do not need an armed revolution in these islands to win from the Government and the Establishment a better deal for black Trinidadians. What we need is determination and direction.[30]

But it was the growing support for the mass movement, so evident after April 9, which led to the critical split within the PNM, between its liberal wing led by A. N. R. Robinson and the more conservative right and centrist trends within the party. The *Express* inadvertently captured one of the important points of Robinson's resignation from the Cabinet: "It is a display of no-confidence in the Prime Minister and his handling of current events, and it represents as well a challenge to the Prime Minister and his leadership and authority in the government and his party."[31]

Robinson's position within the PNM in many respects paralleled Lloyd Best's in Tapia, in that they both sought to push the movement away from its radical, 'spontaneist' direction. But since neither Best nor Robinson could happily associate themselves with the repressive trends in the country, they were at the same time out of favour with conservatives and radicals. On the one hand, the burgeoning movement rejected the reformists as it searched for men of action with the appropriate slogans to increase its momentum. On the other, the defenders of law and order increasingly considered the reformists as dangerous, in that they gave more room for 'anarchism' to grow and prosper. This pincer movement would lead to the increasing marginalization of both personalities, who would play insignificant roles in the few remaining, though turbulent, days of the open struggle.

April 17: The Workers Stir

On April 17, the organized working class movement of Trinidad and Tobago decisively entered the national struggle, tilting momentarily the delicate balance of social forces in favour of the revolutionary alliance and precipitating the last stage of the revolution. In the loose alliance that was the early NJAC of 1969,[32] the 'progressive' trade unions had played an important role. Furthermore, members of the nascent NJAC, had cooperated with the Transport and Industrial Workers Union in April 1969 during the important bus workers strike. Thus, it was not entirely surprising that from the very early days of the demonstrations, Clive Nunez of TIWU became an important leader of NJAC and that on the Caroni march, Weekes of the OWTU, and both Nunez and Joe Young of the TIWU were present. Further, from the very early days of the demonstrations, the OWTU, through its newspaper *The Vanguard*, had placed its imprint on the character of the demonstrations. *The Vanguard* editorial of March 21 was a clear indication of the position of the minority of 'progressive' trade unionists:

> The Black Power movement has placed the whole society on trial, and every member of the establishment, the bourgeoisie and the neo-bourgeoisie and the pseudo-bourgeoisie has got to stand up and declare himself a friend or an enemy, and stand by the consequences. No attempt to define or contain the movement will succeed. From now on the movement makes its own rules, and defines its own terms, and that is the only way we can ever hope to achieve any kind of real democracy in this society. For democracy as we understand it has always been about the majority which means in this society, the black majority.[33]

In early April, furthermore, NJAC had rejected the call of the more conservative unions in the Labour Congress to celebrate May Day with them, firmly placing their allegiance alongside the progressive unions. *The Express* reported Clive Nunez's response on behalf of NJAC:

> Clive Nunez, Public Relations Officer of NJAC, commenting on the news of Congress' decision in a statement last night, said Congress leaders are aware that NJAC, which is the Black Power Movement, demonstrated with 'true progressive trade unions' in the country last May Day and will do so again this year. He charged, 'Congress leaders are dishonest when they say that Congress always stood for Black Power, when it has not up to today seriously fought for the repeal of the ISA.' Mr Nunez asked, 'As long as it remains on the statute books can Congress morally speak for the Black Man?'[34]

The growing influence of the movement among the workers is evident in the willingness, indeed, urgency with which even the conservative unions sought to associate themselves with it. This influence achieved critical mass after April 17, with the decisive intervention of broad sections of the organized working class, including industrial and agricultural workers on the political scene on the side of NJAC and the demonstrators.

On April 17, there was a pro-Black Power work stoppage at the Water and Sewerage Authority (WASA); on April 19, workers at Brechin Castle sugar estate downed tools; then on April 21 the TIWU called for a general work stoppage. Franklin Harvey suggests, appropriately, that these strikes were not economic, but political:

> The black working class did not play an important role at the beginning of the social explosion in 1970. But by March 15th, three weeks after the beginning of the explosion, the black working class began to intervene independently on the political scene. Undoubtedly, they were influenced and stirred by the Black Power agitation of NJAC and the unemployed, but when they began to act they did so as an independent social force. Between March 15th and April 21st almost every single manufacturing and industrial enterprise (including government services) was hit by a strike at least once. The strikes were over all kinds of issues – higher wages, better conditions, overtime, firing of a worker, shifting of a worker, insult by a manager. In almost all the workers' demonstrations the slogan 'power to the people' was clearly displayed. These strikes were not simply economic but highly political. By April 21st it was clear that a spontaneous national general strike was imminent.[35]

Of greatest import to the rapidly unravelling process was the strike of the largely Indian sugar workers and what it meant for the possibility of a broader, antigovernment unity of the two racial groups. Harvey again captures the possible meaning of this development:

> By mid-April the East Indian sugar workers began to act, and by April 21st four

factories and three of the largest estates were on strike and the strike was spreading. The East Indian workers held a huge demonstration in Couva and who did they call to come and speak, but George Weekes and Geddes Granger (NJAC's chairman). Many observers have not recorded this fact, but this act on the part of the East Indian workers was very significant. It was precisely because of the spreading strike in sugar, and the emerging link between the East Indian sugar workers and the Black Power movement that Williams decided to declare a State of Emergency, rather than allow the unity of the two racial groupings on a class basis, because that would have meant the end of Williams and the PNM.[36]

On the eve of the State of Emergency on April 21, the social forces in Trinidad were perhaps as polarized as they had never been before. Standing for Black Power and some notion of revolution were the urban, black unemployed, many students and increasing numbers of the clerical workers and civil servants in Port of Spain, San Fernando and other centres. Alongside them, were newly arrived battalions of urban workers as well as strategically and politically important divisions from the oil and sugar sectors. On the other side of the fence were the forces of order and stability in the PNM and the opposition DLP, the private sector and the official religious organizations as well as, critically, the traditional defensive arms of the state in the military and the police. While the political survival of the PNM was threatened by the developments in the streets and the factories, the security of the state remained unquestioned so long as the security forces remained loyal, because there was no credible or conceivable military threat from the NJAC or its allied organizations. But would the security forces remain loyal to the state? The State of Emergency answered this question at once and suggested the extent to which the revolutionary mood had penetrated all sections of the society as, at the same time, it revealed the inherent weaknesses in the Black Power movement.

April 21: Confrontation, Coup and Collapse

On April 21, a State of Emergency was declared, and the majority of NJAC and other Black Power leaders were arrested. After a brief stone throwing incident in Port of Spain and a notable attempt by Brechin Castle sugar workers to defy the state of emergency and march into the capital, the mass movement crumbled. There was, however, to be one more chapter in the revolutionary drama. When the 750-man Trinidad regiment was called into Port of Spain to enforce the emergency, an important section, headed by militant junior officers, refused to take up arms against their 'black brothers' and took over the army base at Teteron Bay on the north-western tip of the island. Commenting on the reasons behind the rebellion, Raffique Shah, then a lieutenant and one of the three main rebel leaders, reflects in a 1974 interview on the thinking behind the decision to mutiny:

> We realized that we controlled a very serious arm of the establishment, the army, the arms and ammunition. And this army was meant to be the oppressive arm, to keep the mass movement down. Trained as soldiers, one of our duties would have been to quell uprisings. But we felt that the Government had reached to the point where they no longer commanded a majority [of support] by 1970. We felt that more so, they could not order the army to suppress the people, because our loyalty is to the people and if they elect a government and the government is popular then we are loyal to that government. But when the government becomes unpopular we are not supposed to go out and oppress people on behalf of the government. So we took a stand, that we were making the army a negative force. We would take over the army and ensure that it would not go out and terrorize our people and this is why we had the uprising on April 21st.[37]

It is important to note that Shah clearly states that the aim of the soldiers was not to seize state power or even permanently to take over control of the regiment, but simply to act as a negative force, to prevent the soldiers being used to enforce the State of Emergency. This, together with a number of reforms within the structure of the regiment, had been the main goals of the rebel leaders, as evident in the demands made at the first negotiations between themselves and loyalist elements within the army:

> The first meeting did not actually begin until after eleven that morning and it lasted until around five that afternoon. Mr Karl Hudson-Phillips, the Attorney General, Mr Doddridge Alleyne, Permanent Secretary in the Ministry of Finance, and Mr Jim Rodriquez, acting Deputy Police commissioner represented the Government. Lieutenant Rex LaSalle was the main negotiator for the soldiers at Teteron Bay. When the negotiations got under way, the soldiers asked for a general amnesty, release of the soldiers who had been arrested after the Camp Ogden fire that morning, retirement of all short term officers, promotion to captain of Lieutenant LaSalle and Lt Rafique Shah, an enquiry into the Regiment and the return of Lt Colonel Joffre Serrette as Commanding Officer. The soldiers also wanted to be allowed to travel to Port of Spain with their arms. The government team was adamant on this point.[38]

The political naïvety of the soldiers who felt that once their demands had been met all would be forgiven and things return to normal, is evident. Indeed, after the appointment of Lt Colonel Serrette – the rebels' choice – they were all immediately arrested on charges of mutiny and treason. To find some historical parallel it is not at all inappropriate to recall Lenin's insightful "Lecture on the 1905

Revolution", which suggests many similarities with the situation in 1970. Lenin describes a similar inexperience, naïvety and lack of resolution which accompanied the nascent revolutionary spirit in the first of the three Russian revolutionary waves:

> The revolutionary fervour among the people could not but spread to the armed forces. It is indicative that the leaders of the movement came from those elements in the army and navy who had been recruited mainly from among the industrial workers, and of whom more technical training was required, for instance the sappers. The broad masses however, were still too naive, their mood was too passive, too good natured, too Christian. They flared up rather quickly; any instance of injustice, bad food, et cetera, could lead to revolt. But what they lacked was persistence, a clear perception of aim, a clear understanding that only the most vigorous continuation of the armed struggle, only a victory over all the military and civil authorities, only the overthrow of the government and the seizure of power throughout the country could guarantee the success of the revolution. The broad masses of sailors and soldiers were easily roused to revolt. But with equal lightheartedness they foolishly released arrested officers. They allowed the officers to pacify them by promises and persuasion; in this way the officers gained precious time, brought in reinforcements, broke the strength of the rebels and then followed the most brutal suppression of the movement and the execution of its leaders.[39]

Raffique Shah reflecting on his own actions in 1970, arrived at remarkably similar conclusions:

> To my mind [the reason why we did not remove the government in 1970] was because of a lack of political consciousness. Because on the morning when we were coming out of Teteron and the Coast Guard fired upon us, if we had been politically conscious to the point to understand revolution, to understand what it's all about, that it means life or death, it means making tremendous sacrifices, we would have blown those two boats out of the water, but we did not do this. We felt that there were innocent people on those boats. In a revolution you do not have innocent people.[40]

At the critical moment in the revolutionary upsurge, young officers, faced with a decision to detain young university students many of whom were personally known to them, balked. At the same time, young soldiers in the ranks, drawn from urban working class communities like Laventille and Belmont, were deeply influenced by the same Black Power movement under which their brothers and sisters marched only a few miles away. While the very trajectory and crest of the revolutionary upsurge demanded a leadership with clear tactics and an alternative programme to carry the movement to victory, neither the leadership of the NJAC nor the rebel officers possessed the experience or theoretical foundation to provide that clarity.

However, had that clarity existed and had the rebels seized the power, they might have achieved some initial success, but they would not have been able to hold it with an international balance of forces clearly tilted against them. Even as negotiations had begun between the government forces and the rebel soldiers, two Venezuelan warships were seen in Trinidadian waters. Raoul Pantin reported on the sighting of the ships:

> What almost broke down the negotiations completely, however, was the sudden appearance of two ships, reported to be Venezuelan, which were heading for Port of Spain. They could be clearly seen from Chaguaramas. Lt LaSalle said that the negotiations would end right there and then. And a report from the main gate at Chaguaramas also said that the feeling of the [loyal] soldiers there was that they would not fight against the rebels if foreign troops landed. The Coast Guard sped out to head off the ships and succeeded in getting them to go back out of the territorial waters.[41]

The Venezuelans, weary of the instability in Trinidad, on hearing of the mutiny had decided to act, quite probably on their own initiative but also, possibly, on the request of other forces. Far more significant, was the overt military entrance of the United States of America. On receiving information of the army mutiny, US warships and troops had immediately set sail from Puerto Rico. An article by Ralph Harris in the *Express* of April 23 describes the scope of the American intervention and captures the views of the US State Department on the importance of the 1970 uprising:

> US Navy and Marine Units sailed at top speed for Trinidad yesterday, ready to evacuate more than one thousand Americans if an army mutiny and Black Power rioting gets out of hand.
>
> An airlift of small arms and ammunition was also on its way from the United States to help the Trinidad and Tobago Government of Prime Minister Dr Eric Williams stem the violence of the past two days.
>
> The moves were announced by the State and Defence departments here (Washington), but a late report from the US Embassy in Port of Spain, the Trinidad capital, said the government believed the violence was easing and its police forces had gained control of the situation.
>
> . . . The six US warships sailing across the Caribbean towards Trinidad left from Puerto Rico and were believed to be carrying 2,000 marines and a number of helicopters. State Department spokesman, Carl Bartch, said the ships were ordered to Trinidad with the approval of Dr Williams' government strictly as a precaution in case US citizens were endangered and had to be evacuated.

There were more than 1,000 US citizens living in Trinidad and an unknown number of American tourists . . . The naval vessels ordered to the vicinity of Trinidad are the amphibious assault ship *Guadalcanal*, the guided missile frigate *Biddle*, three smaller landing ships – the *Spiegel Grove*, *Suffolk County* and *Terrebonne Parish* – and the cargo ship *Vermillion* . . . At the White House, presidential spokesman, Ronald L. Ziegler said there was no intention that the US warships should become involved in the emergency situation in Trinidad.

He stressed that their mission was to stand by in case it became necessary to evacuate Americans. The arms airlift was organized at the request of the Government of Trinidad and Tobago, which was said to be short of fire power in view of the army mutiny. The shipment consists of sidearms and rifles and automatic weapons, the State Department said. Asked why the United States was furnishing arms if the island government had regained control of the situation, Bartch replied: 'Because we are not sure the situation will remain under control.'[42]

The call of the United States to supply arms, Williams' quick approval of the clearly excessive figure of *2,000* marines to evacuate *1,000* American citizens, and Bartch's comment in the last paragraph all suggest that the State Department's real motives were to prevent the emergence of a radical government in strategically important Trinidad and Tobago and confirm the position of the United States of America as the critical force-of-last-resort in preventing the emergence or survival of revolutionary regimes. In the end, the first case of US intervention in the English-speaking Caribbean was averted only because of the acquiescence of the rebel soldiers and the subsequent consolidation of the Williams regime. It would take another two decades before the safety of US citizens abroad would be invoked as the cover for US intervention. The second time around, it would be ninety miles to the north of Trinidad in the spice island of Grenada where, ironically, the revolutionary process was, at least in part, sparked by the 1970 Black Power movement in Trinidad.

After the arrest of the mutineers and the prolonged dusk to dawn curfew which followed, the revolutionary movement, demoralized and without leadership, seemed to crumble and disintegrate as though it had never really existed. The daily stream of thousands of people along Frederick Street and the Eastern Main Road, accompanied by the resounding shouts of "Power!", passed rapidly into the collective unconscious.

But frequent events in the following decades suggest that the emotional issues which fuelled the movement in those epic months have not been adequately resolved. Thus, the brief and tragic campaign of the National Union of Freedom Fighters in the months following the State of Emergency; the oil and sugar workers' mobilization just prior to the oil boom of the mid 1970s; and, not least of all, Abu Bakr's bizarre coup attempt almost on the twentieth anniversary of the Black Power movement, all point to the unresolved antagonisms of a small island state, in which many feel excluded from the wealth of the oil-rich economy and marginalized on the fringes of real power.

Notes

1 This essay is based on a chapter from my Master's thesis submitted to the Department of Government at UWI Mona in 1976 and entitled "The Development of the 1970 Revolution in Trinidad and Tobago". Rereading the original after an hiatus of many years was, in its own right, a profound revelation. Dogmatic determinism competed with mechanical 'workerist' positions in equal measure. My first response was that the dissertation was so flawed, that any attempt to sketch the main sequence of the 1970 events would require a total abandonment of that piece of work. On further reflection, however, I chose to take the route of sticking with the original chapter, though with significant editing. Despite its crude historicism, it stands up, on its own, as an element of history, reflecting in part the naïve optimism which young, middle class intellectuals like myself felt with regard to the imminent possibility of social revolution in the Caribbean in that seminal decade.

2 See, for example, Theda Skocpol, States and Social Revolutions: A Comparative Analysis of France, Russia and China (Cambridge: Cambridge University Press, 1979), and Ellen Kay Trimberger, Revolution From Above: Military Bureaucrats and Development in Japan, Turkey, Egypt and Peru (New Jersey: Transaction Books, 1978).

3 See Maurice Cornforth, Historical Materialism (New York: International Publishers, 1972), and Jack Woddis, New Theories of Revolution (New York: International Publishers, 1974).

4 V. I. Lenin, "Lessons of the Revolution", in *Between the Two Revolutions* (Moscow: Progress Publishers, 1971), 346.

5 *Daily Express* (February 15, 1970),1.

6 *Daily Express* (February 16, 1970),1.

7 *Daily Express* (February 2, 1970).

8 *Trinidad Guardian* (March 27, 1970).

9 *Daily Express* (B. Wight), "Finding a way out of this gutter of abuse" (March 2, 1970).

10 *Daily Express*, "The march – what the DLP had to say" (February 28, 1970).

11 *Daily Express*, "Williams hits at hooliganism in the church" (March 2, 1970).

12 *Trinidad Guardian* (Editorial), "How many can now feel proud?" (February 27, 1970).

13 *Trinidad Guardian* (March 5, 1970), 6.

14 *Daily Express* (March 5, 1970).

15 F. Harvey, "The rise and fall of party politics in Trinidad and Tobago" (Toronto: New Beginning, February 1974), 45.

16 D. Darbeau and D. Murray, Interview by the Canadian media (1971).

17 Ian Belgrave, Interview by author (August 1974).

18 *Tapia*, "Special on the Current National Crisis" (March 1970).

19 Ivor Oxaal, *Race and Revolutionary Consciousness* (Cambridge, London: Schenkman, 1971), 25.

20 *Daily Express* (March 12, 1970).

21 *Daily Express* (March 13, 1970).

22 Brinsley Samaroo, "Afro/Indian solidarity", *The Vanguard* (March 21, 1970).

23 NJAC, *Conventional Politics of Revolution?* (Trinidad: Vanguard Press, 1971).

24 *Daily Express*, "The Black Panthers have come up with a White Paper" (March 1970).

25 Eric Williams, "Speech to the nation", *Daily Express* (March 24, 1970).

26 Williams, "Speech to the nation".

27 James Millette, *Daily Express* (April 1, 1970).

28 "The February revolution", *Tapia*, no. 12 (December 1970).

29 *Daily Express*, "Black Power and pan: reason for alliance" (April 1970).

30 *Daily Express*, "Our opinion" (April 8, 1970).

31 *Daily Express* (April 4, 1970).

32 For a discussion of the formation and development of NJAC, see Meeks, "The development of the 1970 revolution".

33 *The Vanguard* (Editorial) (March 21, 1970).

34 *Daily Express* (April 1970).

35 Harvey, "Party politics", 46.

36 Harvey, "Party politics", 47.

37 Raffique Shah, Interview by author (Port of Spain, August 1974).

38 *Trinidad Guardian* (April 30, 1970).

39 V. I. Lenin, "Lecture on the 1905 revolution", in V. I. Lenin, *Selected Works*, Vol. I (Moscow: Progress Publishers, 1971), 786.

40 Shah, Interview.

41 *Trinidad Guardian* (April 22, 1970).

42 *Daily Express* (April 22, 1970).

Chapter Three

C. Y. Thomas, the Authoritarian State and Revolutionary Democracy

The appearance of C. Y. Thomas' *The Rise of the Authoritarian State in Peripheral Societies* (1984)[1] has significantly advanced the blossoming debate on the role of the political in the Third World. Following in the path of Saul,[2] Shivji,[3] and Leys[4] in Africa, Alavi[5] in Asia, and Cardoso[6] and others in Latin America, Thomas, while surveying the Third World as a whole, anchors his study on the experience of the Caribbean region. This in itself is a major breakthrough but, even more critically, he attempts and in the main succeeds in bringing together the strands of the debate being conducted on the periphery with the rich discussion on the state in developed capitalist formations.[7]

The Authoritarian State as a Historical Materialist Category

Thomas' immediate concern is the prevalence of repression and terror in the periphery. From a Marxist perspective he seeks to answer three questions:

- Why have repression and state violence been increasing so rapidly?
- What is the correct relationship between the struggles for the emancipation of the working class and the peasantry and the struggle for so-called bourgeois democratic reforms?
- Can Marxism be indifferent to the forms of the state or the state of legality in the periphery?[8]

To achieve this objective, he begins with three theoretical premises. First, he suggests that the state in peripheral societies cannot be understood simply by 'deduction' from the theories on developed capitalism. Rather, relevant theory ". . . must root itself in the concrete conditions of the periphery".[9] Secondly, he posits that the state must be seen as a historical materialist category: ". . . the authoritarian state cannot be reduced to the existence of a dictator or to authoritarian or dictatorial forms of rule, although these accompany it. We must look at the state as a historical materialist category and understand its social and material basis".[10]

Thirdly, he proposes that the state develops in response to both national and international factors as the peripheral capitalist state is inevitably a part of the global system of capitalism.[11] Thomas, in using this methodology, establishes his clear advance over the 'development school'[12] with its ahistorical approach to political development and its failure to appreciate the importance of the economic base, in favour of a generalized description of the structural features in the political sphere. However, as is now increasingly more popular, he also seeks to avoid 'economism', the approach often adopted by 'Marxist' thinkers which places all importance on the economic, to the virtual exclusion of the political as an actor in its own right.[13]

Economism may take the form of 'historical determinism' where economic forces are always seen as the ultimate determinants of events, leading in practice to fatalism and political complacency. It may also take the form of a tendency to over-generalize, or insufficiently appreciate the critical differences between state forms within the same mode of production.[14] The qualitative differences between bourgeois democratic and authoritarian versions of the capitalist state are vital, as Thomas correctly identifies, in the strategy of any anti-imperialist or anti-authoritarian project.

Thomas traces the development of the peripheral (West Indian) state through its colonial stages up to independence. The details of this journey are not within the scope of this paper except, perhaps, to touch on three of his conclusions. The first is that the origins of the colonial state are to be found in the process of colonialism itself. The state is set up as a 'public power' to ensure the reproduction of the relations of production under slavery and later, under 'freedom'. The state, he then argues, can clearly be seen as arising out of the needs of the dominant social classes. The second point, following from this, is that the character of the state can only be fully appreciated if it is recognized that its formation is both internally and externally determined. Internally, it is constructed by the local planters, to mediate between themselves and the slaves and later the free workforce; and externally by the wider needs of the colonial power which requires an institution to maintain control over the entire colony.[15]

Approaching independence, this relationship is transformed. The state, while retaining its primary function, begins to play a bigger role in the reproduction of capitalist relations. Concomitantly, its *relative* role as a repressive apparatus decreases. The state grows rapidly and, along with it, the power of the class which manages it – the 'bureaucratic petty bourgeoisie'.

The results of this, in the postindependence era, are twofold. First, a disjuncture occurs between those who wield political power and those who traditionally possess economic power, *ie* between the merchants and plantation oligarchy on the one hand and the state petty bourgeoisie on the other. Secondly, there is a dramatic increase in the scope and activity of the state. We then have, in Thomas' words, a "reversal of the classic relation of economic power to political power".[16] This reversal and consequent 'autonomization' form the background to the rise of the authoritarian state.

However, as mentioned previously, Thomas sees the authoritarian state as a historical materialist category, not just 'any' repressive or dictatorial system. Its material basis has therefore to be located, and Thomas does this by identifying eight necessary historical and structural conditions. These can be roughly summarized as follows:

- The existence in the country of underdeveloped productive forces and multistructured modes of production with little capacity for autonomous accumulation.

- A system of economic reproduction linked historically and currently to the 'centre' imperialist countries in a 'chain of capitalist domination'.

- The consequent underdevelopment of the major classes of the capitalist era, with the dominant classes (petty bourgeoisie, military elements, bourgeoisie) allied with the bourgeoisie of the centre. Contradictions exist in this alliance, but everywhere it is characterized by the exclusion of the masses (workers and peasants) from power.

- The results include a leading role for one or more sections of the petty bourgeoisie.

- The general underdevelopment of capitalist relations also means the under-development of bourgeois norms of legality.

- State property increases dramatically, not in order to regulate economic crises, as in developed capitalism, but to stimulate accumulation.

- The growth of state property expands the general coercive ability of the state which is now a significant, if not the major, employer of persons.

- Finally, and of most immediate importance for the timing of the emergence of the authoritarian state, is that it emerges in the present era where there is a structural crisis of world capitalism.[17]

Further, and critical to his argument, Thomas asserts that to maintain existing patterns of domination in the face of world recession the state must "win a reduction in the growth of real wages and the standard of living of the masses, along with increased worker productivity".[18] The authoritarian state is therefore the specific late twentieth century response of the ruling class in the periphery to the crisis confronting the society.

One additional point relevant to our analysis comes out in Thomas' description of the emergent state form. He observes that the authoritarian state can develop with either a 'left' or 'right' posture. While he recognizes the "different lines of development implicit in the two ideological rationalizations",[19] he argues that the roots of the authoritarian state form "go deeper than the level of ideology or the consciousness of the rulers."[20] This seems to weaken his analysis somewhat, because there is a tendency here to ignore the very historical approach which, prior to this, is so consistently utilized. There is an insufficient appreciation of the world balance of forces, of the historical shifts away from capitalism, and the role even repressive authoritarian states with a 'left posture' play on the global/historical field.[21] While this overcorrection of the acknowledged tendency to underestimate the political is understandable, it leads to dire consequences particularly when Thomas carries the discussion over to that of the state in the transition to socialism.

Further on, Thomas makes the important proposal that there are five minimum practices necessary for political democracy to exist. They are:

- the absence of any discrimination on the grounds of race, religion, tribe, property/income, political party affiliation and the like in the exercise of political opinion, whether expressed directly or through an elected representative

- except for stipulations on the legal age for voting, all citizens should have an equal vote

- all political parties should have equal status before the law, so that a contest between organized political groups is a real contest, representing real alternatives

- the principles of majority rule should hold in the election of representatives and in the legislative process; a majority decision, however, should not limit the minority's right to become a legal and constitutional majority

- due process should operate in the legal system to ensure that the above rights are enforced[22]

It is noteworthy that he deliberately excludes economic rights, other specific democratic rights such as worker self-management and, most pointedly, the Leninist notion of 'soviets' or worker councils. In relation to the latter, he justifies their exclusion because: "They are impossible within the framework of capitalist relations and in any case, while they may be complementary to representative democratic institutions, they can be no substitute for them."[23]

The next stage of the analysis is central. He proposes that while there is some truth in the argument that political democracy masks the reality of the economic and social domination of workers by capitalists, there is none in the next step which is that "the dictatorship of the proletariat is essential for socialist development and that this dictatorship can encompass [supposedly intermediate] dictatorial forms of rule".[24]

Thomas, in this pivotal statement, seems to elevate the principles of 'political democracy' to the point of becoming fetishistic without addressing its obvious and inherent dangers. Representative democracy has been used, at least since the ancient Greeks, as a useful form of the state for a particular class in the society over and above other classes. At minimum, a more thorough discussion of the pitfalls along its path is required. Elsewhere in the book, for example, he suggests that 'political democracy' where it exists is only maintained as a result of popular struggles and where the popular forces are strong enough to keep it in place. While this may be true, it seems to ignore the issues subsumed in the argument that the bourgeoisie has the most to gain from a form which on the surface obscures class domination, but in reality, preserves it. Fascism, for example, the most extreme authoritarian form of the capitalist state, has historically occurred at a moment of severe capitalist crisis and therefore suggests, by implication, the advantages which might exist for the bourgeoisie in having representative democracy in 'normal' times.

Additionally, as has been suggested, Thomas gives very little importance to the various forms of direct or 'participatory' democracy. This, despite their importance as the main ideological and practical alternatives to liberal democratic forms in the twentieth century. If the Soviet inspired notion of participatory democracy is only, at best, complementary to representative democracy as Thomas suggests, then at least a thorough analysis of its inadequacies is necessary. This he does not provide. Finally, Thomas appears to distort Marx in his characterization of the dictatorship of the proletariat as 'sociological domination' of the working class. The concept of 'proletarian dictatorship' is at the very centre of the whole debate surrounding the state in transition. What will the attitude of the defeated ruling class be to the transcendent revolutionary alliance? What, in turn, will the attitude of the victorious alliance be to the defeated ruling class? This, at least in the Caribbean, is not an abstract question, as the issue was and still is being raised by the Cuban, Nicaraguan and late Grenadian revolutions.

Political Democracy and the Dictatorship of the Proletariat

The Marxist approach on which the book is based and Thomas' own assertive statements on the issue of the dictatorship of the proletariat require a closer analysis of what the classic Marxist texts had to say on this issue.[25] Perhaps the best exposition of Marx and Engels' views on the state in transition and the dictatorship of the proletariat is to be found in the Civil War in France.[26] This is to be expected because here, for the first time, the practical issue of state power was placed on the agenda. Writing on the tasks facing the Paris proletariat which had seized power and declared the Commune in March 1871, Marx asserted: ". . . the working class cannot simply lay hold of the ready made state machinery and wield it for its own purposes".[27] Rather, the task as Engels outlined in a later introduction, was the "shattering (Sprengung) of the former state power and its replacement by a new and truly democratic one . . ."[28] As to why the old state had to be shattered, Engels develops a position which specifically identifies the bourgeois democratic state as a form of class rule:

> In reality, however, the state is nothing but a machine for the oppression of one class by another, and indeed in the democratic republic, no less than in the monarchy; and at best an evil inherited by the proletariat after its victorious struggle for class supremacy, whose worst sides the victorious proletariat, just like the Commune, cannot avoid having to lop off at once . . .[29]

And what about the form of the new state? Marx in an extremely rich passage, describes the main elements of the Commune state and, at the same time, generalizing from the Paris experience, suggests some of the critical features necessary for the state in transition:

> The Commune was formed of the municipal councillors chosen by universal suffrage in the various wards of the town, responsible and revocable at short terms. The majority of its members were naturally working men, or acknowledged representatives of the working class. The Commune was to be a working, not a parliamentary body, executive and legislative at the same time. Instead of continuing to be the agent of the central government, the police was at once stripped of its political attributes and turned into the responsible and at all times revocable agents of the Commune. So were the officials of all other branches of the administration. From the members of the Commune downwards, the public service had to be done at workmen's wages.[30]

A number of criticisms of the old parliamentary form and a description of the main elements of the new state emerge clearly here. First, it should be noted that the concept of representative democracy itself is not rejected. Rather, an attempt is made to strengthen or transcend it with the introduction of the principle of recall. Perhaps the central feature of the bourgeois parliamentary state which Marx and Engels continually criticized was the inability to mandate elected representatives and to revoke their appointment if they failed to carry out their mandate. Under parliamentary democracy, society had created the parliament to look after its interests. However, in the course of time, the servants had become the masters. Hence, the workers' state, learning from this, had to "safeguard itself against its own deputies and officials by declaring them all, without exception, subject to recall at any moment".[31]

A second feature relates to the class character of the state. The majority of its members were naturally working men or their 'acknowledged representatives'. This point deserves further discussion in light of Thomas' second criterion for 'political democracy', *ie* no discrimination, including on income/property grounds. Marx, while not calling for class discrimination in the election of representatives, recognized that the state is class-based and must have in it significant representation of the dominant class. This is reinforced by his obvious support of the Commune's decision to pay its members and the administration as a whole 'workmen's wages'. This measure would immediately make the state less attractive to the bourgeoisie as a 'career path' and it would, by implication, strengthen the state's working class character.

A third feature, the 'working' as opposed to 'talking' character of the Commune, related to another Marxist criticism of parliamentary democracy. Instead of a talking-shop where members debated while decisions were made elsewhere, giving the electorate the illusion of power, the Commune combined both executive and legislative functions. Those who talked actually carried out decisions and therefore, combined with the principle of recall, the electorate would have a far more direct line into the decision making process. This would undermine the potential power of the bureaucracy, which leads to what seems to be Marx's most important point. By disconnecting the police and administration from a monolithic central governmental apparatus and making them directly responsible to the elected representatives in the Commune, Marx saw the beginning of the end of bureaucratic power. By making the bureaucracy responsible to the people (through the Commune), the state as a power over the people would be broken. The state as *state* would begin to 'wither away'.

The debate on the extent to which the Russian Revolution and subsequent revolutionary movements achieved these aims is, of course, extensive and will be addressed briefly in relation to one case study from the Caribbean. The germane issue, though, is that Marx on the basis of his observation of the Commune experience, presents a thoroughgoing critique of bourgeois democracy and goes on to suggest many elements of what the dictatorship of the proletariat might look like. Thomas hints at disagreements with bourgeois democracy but provides us with no such thoroughgoing critique. Rather, he leaves us with little vision beyond the narrow confines of his five constraining criteria for political democracy.

With special reference to Thomas' interpretation of the dictatorship of the proletariat as 'sociological domination', it would seem that this differs substantially from the positions adopted by both Marx and Engels.[32] Ten years after the Commune, in a letter to F. Domela-Niewenhuis, Marx wrote:

> One thing you can at any rate be sure of: a socialist government does not come into power in a country unless conditions are so developed that it can

immediately take the necessary measures for intimidating the mass of the bourgeoisie sufficiently to gain time – the first desideratum – for permanent action.[33]

This point is developed further and from the perspective of defeating Thomas' contention, decisively, in Engels' "Letter to Bebel" of March 18-25, 1875. Proposing that the Commune was no longer a 'state' in the old sense of the word, he elaborates on the form of the state in the transitional period:

Since the state is only a transitional institution which is used in the struggle during the revolution to hold down one's adversaries by force, it is pure nonsense to talk of a free people's state: so long as the proletariat still uses the state it does not use it in the interest of freedom but in order to hold down its adversaries and as soon as it becomes possible to speak of freedom, the state as such ceases to exist.[34]

The Lenin-Kautsky Debate and Rosa Luxemburg

The victory of the Russian Revolution in 1917 forms the next natural point of departure for debate on the character of the transitional state. Kautsky, in his pamphlet "The Dictatorship of the Proletariat"[35] polemicized against the newly established Soviet state. He opposed the closure of the Constituent Assembly by the Bolsheviks as the clear indicator that the Leninist approach was undemocratic. He further regarded the soviets (class-based institutions) as limited from a democratic perspective because they excluded wide sections of the population. Further, he attacked the decision to disenfranchise the bourgeoisie as an entire social group as unwarranted and saw it as the crowning undemocratic act of the dictatorial Bolshevik project. Lenin's response on this last point was that the act of disenfranchisement was specific to the Russian conjuncture and not an indispensable characteristic of the proletarian dictatorship: "The indispensable characteristic, the necessary condition of the dictatorship, is the forcible repression of the exploiters as a class, and con-sequently, the infringement of 'pure democracy', *ie* of equality and freedom, in regard to that class."[36]

Rosa Luxemburg, whom Thomas, appropriately, quotes at length also disagreed with Lenin on the dispersal of the Constituent Assembly and the elevation of the soviets as the supreme governing body. She called for a free press, full adult suffrage and the return of representative, as opposed to soviet forms of democracy.[37] Interestingly, Luxemburg differs fundamentally from Kautsky (and Thomas) in recognizing the almost inevitable need for repressive measures against the counter-revolution:

These included the deprivation of political rights, of economic means of existence, etc. in order to break their resistance with an iron fist. It was precisely in this way that the socialist dictatorship expressed itself, for it cannot shrink away from any use of force to secure or prevent certain measures involving the interests of the whole.[38]

However, it is precisely Luxemburg's recognition of the need for 'socialist' dictatorship that makes her subsequent support for 'representative' democracy all the more important. In defending the dispersed Russian Constituent Assembly as the truly legitimate form of rule, she criticized the Leninist view that representatives, once elected, only reflected the view of the electorate at the time of the election and were probably disconnected from them thereafter. The organization of the people outside of parliament constantly flowed around it, Luxemburg felt, and this "living fluid of the popular mood"[39] penetrated and guided the representatives. Luxemburg's real fear was that the soviet representative forms would not allow the free flow of debate and interchange of opinions which existed under parliamentary democracy.[40] Indeed, this is the constant danger, particularly in a situation where the revolutionary classes are led by one party which naturally dominates the workers' councils or soviets.

But Luxemburg fails to point to any specific structural features of the new state form which were inherently antidemocratic or bureaucratic. The point, rather, seems to relate to the dangers present in any one-party system, whether liberal democratic or 'soviet', where the single party becomes complacent, loses contact with the people and where, inevitably, corruption becomes institutionalized.

In a different vein, Lenin, while not debating the superiority of representative democracy *per se*, suggested that the soviets embodied a higher form of democracy: "The way out of parliamentarianism is not, of course, the abolition of representative institutions and the electoral principle, but the conversion of representative institutions from talking-shops into working bodies."[41]

Gramsci in his 'L'Ordine Nuovo' period added a novel and important dimension to the debate. The institutions of the capitalist state develop out of the capitalist mode of production and are suited to capitalism. The proletariat cannot simply use these instruments, because they are suited to competition, not a 'communal' way of life:

> ... merely to change the personnel in these institutions is hardly going to change the direction of their activity. The socialist state is not yet communism, *ie* the establishment and practice of a way of life that is communal, but it is the transitional state whose mission is to suppress competition via the suppression of private property, classes and national economies. This mission cannot be accomplished by parliamentary democracy. So the formula 'conquest of the state' should be understood in the following sense: replacement of the

democratic parliamentary state by a new type of state, one that is generated by the associative experience of the proletarian class.[42]

Gramsci's attempt to apply the dialectic to the new emergent transitional state form possesses many subtle implications, which cannot be elaborated here. The most immediate question is: can a state based upon the majority, particularly an associative class like the proletariat, still utilize the old forms of multiparty competitive elections which emerged (Gramsci would argue) because the bourgeoisie is split into its industrial, financial, petit and grand fractions? This is a debatable point but it underlines the inadequacies of Thomas' fixed and frozen five criteria for political democracy.

There is one final issue which needs to be addressed, and that is the question of hegemony. Gramsci, of course, plays a pivotal role in introducing this element into the debate on the state. Hegemony refers to the extent to which the dominant class has achieved a consensus within civil society and is opposed to the concept of 'domination', which implies rule by force. Only weak states need to use the threat or use of force. Strong states rule almost exclusively through hegemony.[43] This helps to illuminate many things. It explains, for example, why nascent revolutions must resort to force. It is at its birth that the revolutionary state is weakest and least able to exercise hegemony. It also explains why established states during periods of intense crisis (such as the rise of European fascism during the depression) abandon hegemonic forms of rule and substitute naked force. These crises weaken confidence in the state because they facilitate the disjuncture between the ideological view which the state propagates and people's real life experiences. The concept of hegemony also assists in an understanding of why liberal democracy in its mature form in, say, the United Kingdom, can (relatively speaking) abandon internal shows of force while newly emergent revolutions cannot. Hence, hegemony is a process; and any study of the state in transition cannot approach it as either democratic or dictatorial, black or white, but the stage in the continuum from insurrection to hegemony on which it is located.

The following stages, with all the reservations implicit in any schematic approach of this type, can be suggested.

The first stage, for the purposes of the approach taken here, is the *revolutionary overthrow*. The old state form, or at least its greatest retarding features are 'lopped off'. A government is established which by its very nature must be provisional. Only under very specific circumstances could the question of elections be on the agenda. Rule in this phase would invariably be imposed by decree and order enforced by the armed forces of the revolutionary alliance, with attempts at counter-revolutionary resistance put down by force. This is clearly not a feature specific to the transition to socialism, but common to virtually all revolutionary transfers.

The second stage can be called the period of *initial consolidation*. Rule by decree is relaxed and new representative organs are fleshed out. In the state in transition from capitalism to socialism, democratic involvement would be extended throughout the society. Obvious areas would include the involvement of the entire workforce in the trade union movement; women in women's organizations; the growth and development of local government assemblies and the voluntary involvement of citizens in the running of the state apparatus including, as a central factor, voluntary military duty and voluntary work on infrastructural programmes. This, while being a period of intense training in new forms of democracy, would have as its counterpoint – to the extent that it was necessary – continued repression of counter-revolution.

Stage three could be seen as the period of *institutionalization*. It is usually marked by the discussion and ratification of a revolutionary constitution. Elections are regularized and the repressive or dictatorial aspect of the state is significantly de-emphasized. The extent to which this aspect remains a prominent feature would depend on the extent of external resistance to the process, with further democratization in converse relationship to the existence of an external threat.

Stage four can simply be called *hegemony*. This is both a national as well as an international feature and depends, ultimately, on the extent to which the new formation is dominant in global terms. The degree of global dominance will help to determine the extent to which the emergent, now consolidated state form can relax security measures and rule with limited reference to the use of force. Naturally, in any of these broadly defined stages, crises of one form or another could precipitate emergency measures which might lead to the reassertion of levels of force associated with earlier stages.

The Grenadian Experience

The Grenadian experience, at least, would seem to support the view that transitional revolutionary governments cannot simply, and at once, adopt Thomas' five principles of democracy. At the time of the seizure of power,[44] the revolutionary alliance[45] headed by the New Jewel Movement (NJM) had as its immediate priority the suppression of the counter-revolution.

This issue, it would seem, is impatient of debate. Without the arrest and detention of members of Gairy's 'mongoose gang' and other members of his security forces, the counter-revolution would almost certainly have regained the initiative. An important question, however, is: why was there no election called in the first few weeks after the overthrow?[46] From a strategic point of view, the answer has to be that it was inappropriate. The NJM had waged a seven-year struggle precisely because parliamentarianism under Gairy had served to institutionalize dictatorship. As early as 1973, the NJM had envisaged the following stages in 'restructuring' the government:

- appointment of a provisional government made up of representatives of main stratas [*sic*] of society.
- development of a system of people's assemblies at village and parish levels as well as workers' assemblies, as mechanisms for self-government.[47]

For this to be accomplished, the old constitution had to be abolished and experience in new forms of self-management/government would have to be gained. This was particularly so, given the low level of organization and experience in even parliamentary representative democracy amongst the largely rural and semi-rural population, subject as they had been to corrupt electoral practices under the Gairy regime. Further, almost immediately following the defeat of the Gairy forces, the revolution faced the ominous threat of US intervention. Much has been published detailing aspects of this threat;[48] thus, only the most illustrative examples need be mentioned:

- The June 1980 bombing of the grandstand at Queen's Park, where the entire leadership of the Revolution was present to celebrate Heroes' Day. The blast missed the leaders but killed three women and injured 90 others.

- The repeated attempts by the US to use its influence in the World Bank and IMF to lobby against loans for Grenada. In 1981, for example, when Grenada applied for an IMF loan of 8.17 million US dollars under the Extended Fund Facility, the US representative blocked the loan.

- The mounting psychological pressure exerted on the Grenada government by the holding of military manoeuvres in the Caribbean with thinly veiled references to Grenada, Nicaragua and Cuba. In the *Ocean Venture '81* manoeuvres, for example, the small Puerto Rican island of Vieques was code named 'Amber' (Grenada) and its sister islands 'the Amberines' (Grenadines). The object of the exercise was to capture Amber, hold US-style elections and install a government friendly to America.[49]

In this context, with an extremely adverse international situation, the People's Revolutionary Government (PRG) was never able to move from a stage of initial consolidation to institutionalization. A preventive detention law was passed (Peoples Law No. 8 of 1979) and action was taken against counter-revolutionary newspapers such as the *Grenada Voice* and others such as the *Torchlight*, which were seen as threatening national security. By January 1982, some 183 persons had been detained.[50] Despite this, the revolutionary government, without having reached the stage of institutionalized elections, was able to make significant democratic advances in the following areas:

1. The growth of mass organizations involving significant sections of the adult population, the most important being the phenomenal growth in trade union representation. As a result of Peoples Law No 29 of 1979 (The Trades Union Recognition Act), union membership moved from less than 30 percent of the workforce in 1979 to some 80 percent in 1982. In addition, the trade unions, women and youth organizations found representation on all state bodies and parastatal enterprises.

2. The growth of an embryonic zonal and parish assembly system for the whole population and, parallel to it, a class-based workers' assembly system called the Workers Parish Councils. Within their experimental limits, these councils incorporated the right to summon political leaders and administrators who were held accountable at monthly meetings of the Council.[51]

3. Other forms of consultation included the annual budget debate in which thousands participated in the formulation of the national budget plan; the 1979 Consultation on Education, involving hundreds of educators in an exercise to overhaul the educational system; and the 1981 and 1982 national conferences on unemployment, which sought to address the decreasing but still significantly high unemployment rates at the national level.

The final act of this stage of the process which would have signalled the transition to the *institutional* stage was the drafting of the new Constitution which was to take the form of the budget debate, but on a more elaborate scale.[52]

Why then, did the Revolution fail? The primary reason was essentially a failure of the leadership to fulfil the people's expectations. Following Gramsci, we accept the position that a party is "only the nomenclature for a class".[53] However, parties may represent alliances between classes or fractions of classes. This is further complicated when the classes represented (as Thomas correctly points out) are underdeveloped. Gramsci further recognizes that parties can become disconnected from their social base. This may occur for numerous reasons, but is essentially dangerous, particularly if the party represents a class alliance which holds power:

> At a certain point in their historical life social groups detach themselves from their traditional parties, *ie* the political parties in that given organizational form, when the men who constitute, represent and lead them, are no longer recognized as the proper representation of their class or fraction of a class. When these crises occur, the immediate situation becomes delicate and dangerous, since the field is open to solutions of force, to the activity of obscure powers represented by 'men of destiny' or 'divine men'.[54]

The events surrounding the collapse of the People's Revolutionary Government in October 1983 in Grenada represented one of these occasions in history when the party, the vast majority of whose members had disagreed with the leader's views on the question of joint leadership, became separated from the class (or more correctly, class alliance) which remained loyal to their leader until the end. The result was a historical disjuncture between vanguard and masses with the creation, as Gramsci put it, "of a delicate and dangerous situation, opening up the field to solutions of force".[55] Critical to any revolutionary project therefore, along with the necessary institutional transformation of the state, is the maintenance of the vital link between the vanguard organization and its class base.

This brings us to the final criticism of Thomas and this concerns the question of alliances. Thomas calls for the broadest possible alliance against the authoritarian state, including all the major classes, strata and social groups that are directly affected by this system of state domination.[56] I agree with this and his further conclusion that the aim of the alliance is to bring about fundamental political changes: "The task of the alliance therefore goes further than bringing about a change of government, with the state structure remaining more or less intact and with a bourgeois democratic path resumed."[57] But what is to prevent this? He has no answer, except to warn that the "greatest danger" is that the strategy "might degenerate into a social democratic path."[58] Indeed, apart from this appropriate warning, there are no suggested strategies to guard against this occurrence. The effect is not unlike driving rapidly around a corner and seeing a sign saying 'danger: 50 feet to end of road'. The danger is apparent, but the end is inevitable.

While no simple solution can be pulled out of a hat, the direction would seem to lie in the character of the alliance and whether the forces in the driver's seat have an interest in transcending or deepening bourgeois democracy, or whether for them, that is the end of the road. In this connection, the noncapitalist school provides a useful solution when they suggest that what is at stake is not the existence of an alliance, but the displacement of the bourgeoisie from domination within it: "The decisive aspect of noncapitalist development in which lies its historic importance is the fact that the national bourgeois elements within this bloc are deprived of a monopoly of political power."[59]

I agree with Thomas that noncapitalist theory tends to limit discussion of the 'political' in the transitional state and tends to see economic change as the main plank of democratic development.[60] But in the political sphere, the real question is not a Manichean divide between political democracy, as Thomas defines it, and dictatorship, but the extent to which the revolutionary democratic dictatorship *which is inevitable* is able to hold power and at same time begin the process of democratic transformations in favour of the new class alliance.

Conclusion

Critical to an appreciation of C. Y. Thomas' *Rise of the Authoritarian State*, is his firm placement of the question of the state on Marxist terrain. This places him far ahead of those structuralists who have lost sight of the historical and fail to see the state as the product, albeit with its own dialectical autonomy, of a particular time and place. Thomas' commandeering of the familiar historical material to identify the authoritarian state as a peculiar late-twentieth-century development in the periphery, is refreshing and on target.

Even here, though, the seeds of later weaknesses are present. While seeking to avoid an economistic approach to the state and while recognizing similarities in authoritarian structures in both 'left' and 'right' states in the periphery, he under-estimates the epochal and global changes which these variations represent. There may be little difference to the beleaguered citizen between a Guyana with its leftist rhetoric (at least until Burnham's death) and a Honduras, for example. However, in relation to the South African liberation struggle, the issue of support for the New International Economic Order, the struggle inside UNESCO for a new information order, relations with the socialist world and other similar issues, there is a marked and important distinction.

Thomas' main error, though, is of another kind. He fails to draw a distinction between 'left-rhetorical' states – Guyanese-type formations, which nonetheless still reflect deep global shifts – and revolutionary democratic states where the project appears to be more genuinely in the direction of a transition to socialism. While the petty bourgeoisie and revolutionary intelligentsia play key roles in both, the question is whether or not their project is one of building up the bureaucratic petty bourgeoisie as a new statist ruling class (as in Guyana), or drawing the workers, peasants and unemployed into the state without building a material base for the petty bourgeois intelligentsia itself, as I suggest was the case in Grenada. Here, the particular fraction of the petty bourgeoisie concerned, its ideological approach and the character of the party's relationship with the international working class movement are all important variables.

In the revolutionary democratic project then, the question cannot be one of authoritarianism *per se*, but against whom and for how long this authority is directed. Engels' discussion of this question merits further attention:

> Have these gentlemen ever seen a revolution? A revolution is certainly the most authoritarian thing there is; it is the act whereby one part of the population imposes its will upon the other part by means of rifles, bayonets and cannons – authoritarian means – if such there be at all; and if the victorious party does not want to have fought in vain, it must maintain this rule by means of the terror which its arms inspires in the reactionaries.[61]

To what extent does the revolution then proceed to broaden democracy for the vast majority, to involve them in public life and through the process of institutionalization in a more thoroughly democratic electoral and representative system? This seems to be the relevant concern. The dangers are many. The least is not the Grenadian case where the party becomes alienated and disconnected from the masses. This constantly needs to be struggled against, particularly if the revolution throws up one party instead of a number in alliance. The danger of complacency and corruption is greater, though not inevitable by any means, in one-party formations, if there are no checks and balances within the alliance to keep the leadership alert and on its toes.

There are no fail-safe solutions. One thing which is apparent is that a path which seeks to avoid the authoritarian aspect of revolutionary democracy is likely to return to liberal democracy, with the power in the hands of those who have the wealth, traditional contacts and other structures to manipulate the parliamentary system in well-known ways.

Notes

1 C. Y. Thomas, *The Rise of the Authoritarian State in Peripheral Societies* (New York, London: Monthly Review Press, 1984). Henceforth abbreviated as *RASPS*.

2 See, for example, "African socialism in one country: Tanzania", in G. Arrighi and J. Saul (eds), *Essays on the Political Economy of Africa* (New York and London: Monthly Review Press, 1973).

3 See I. Shivji, *Class Struggles in Tanzania* (London: Heinemann, 1982).

4 See, for example, Colin Leys (ed), *Politics and Change in Developing Countries, Studies in the Theory and Practice of Development* (Sussex, Cambridge: IDS, 1967).

5 See H. Alavi, "The state in postcolonial societies: Pakistan and Bangladesh", *New Left Review*, no. 74 (July/August 1972).

6 See F. H. Cardoso, "Associated dependent development: theoretical and practical implications", in A. Stepan (ed), *Authoritarian Brazil: Origins, Policies and Future* (New Haven: Yale University Press, 1973).

7 Harry Goulbourne makes a plea for the 'coming together' of the debate on the state in postcolonial societies and in Europe in his book *Politics and State in The Third World* (London: Macmillan, 1983). See also Ralph Miliband, *Marxism and Politics* (Oxford: Oxford University Press, 1977) and Nicos Poulantzas, *State, Power, Socialism* (London: NLB, 1978).

8 *RASPS*, xv.

9 *RASPS*, xviii.

10 *RASPS*, xx.

11 *RASPS*, xx.

12 See, for example, Goulbourne's cogent critique of this school in "Some problems of analysis of the political in backward capitalist social formations", in Goulbourne, *Politics and State,* 18.

13 Thomas makes the point that "There is instead a dialectical relationship between the development of the state and the material relations of society, and because of this, the state has been able at times to operate relatively independent of the existing material conditions of social reproduction" [Thomas 1984: 7]. Also, for a 'classical' Marxian reference, see Engels' "Letter to Joseph Bloch, September 21-22 1890", in K. Marx and F. Engels, *Marx-Engels, Selected Correspondence* (Moscow: Progress Publishers, 1975), 394-95.

14 *RASPS*, xxi.

15 *RASPS*, 17.

16 *RASPS*, 62.

17 *RASPS*, 37.

18 *RASPS*, 88.

19 *RASPS*, 95.

20 *RASPS*, 95.

21 The positions of the 'non-capitalist path' theoreticians serve as a useful point of departure for a discussion of the role of the global balance of forces and its dialectical relationship with the national. See, for example, K. N. Brutents, *National Liberation Revolutions Today,* Vol 1 (Moscow: Progress Publishers, 1977).

22 See *RASPS*, 98-99.

23 *RASPS*, 99.

24 *RASPS*, 100.

25 See, for example, Marx's discussion of the role of the parliament in "The Eighteenth Brumaire of Louis Bonaparte", in L. Feuer (ed), *Marx and Engels Basic Writings on Politics and Philosophy* (Glasgow: Collins, 1974).

26 The version used here is from Feuer, *Basic Writings.*

27 Feuer, *Basic Writings,* 402.

28 Feuer, *Basic Writings,* 401.

29 Feuer, *Basic Writings,* 401.

30 Feuer, *Basic Writings,* 405.

31 Feuer, *Basic Writings,* 400.

32 The actual term 'dictatorship of the proletariat' is most famously used in "The Critique of The Gotha Programme" in K. Marx and F. Engels, *Marx-Engels Selected Works,* Vol. II (Moscow: Progress Publishers, 1973): "Between capitalist and communist society lies the period of the revolutionary transformation of the one into the other. Corresponding to this is also a political transition period in which the state can be nothing but the revolutionary dictatorship of the proletariat."

33 Feuer, *Basic Writings,* 429.

34 Marx-Engels, *Selected Correspondence,* 276.

35 See relevant passages from Kautsky in "The proletarian revolution and the renegade Kautsky", in V.I. Lenin, *Selected Works,* Vol. 3 (Moscow: Progress Publishers, 1971).

36 Lenin, "The proletarian revolution", 91.

37 See Rosa Luxemburg, *The Russian Revolution and Leninism or Marxism?* (Ann Arbor, Michigan: University of Michigan Press, 1970), 64-67.

38 Luxemburg, *Russian Revolution,* 65.

38 Luxemburg, *Russian Revolution,* 60.

40 Her forceful defence of liberal democratic rights is worth quoting: "Without general elections, without unrestricted freedom of press and assembly, without a free struggle of opinion, life dies out in every public institution, becomes a mere semblance of life, in which only the bureaucracy remains as the active element". Ibid., 17.

41 See V. I. Lenin, *The State and Revolution* (Moscow: Foreign Languages Publishing House, nd), 79.

42 Antonio Gramsci, "The conquest of the state", in A. Gramsci, *Selections from the Prison Notebooks* (London: Lawrence and Wishart, 1977), 76.

43 The process of achieving hegemony begins prior to the seizure of power. The activities of the emergent hegemonic alliance must already have been in the process of gaining ascendancy long before the insurrection. See, for example, W. L. Adamson, *Hegemony and Revolution* (Los Angeles and London: University of California Press, 1980).

44 For a description of the seizure of power, see Ian Jacobs and Richard Jacobs, *Grenada: The Route to Revolution* (Havana: Casa de las Americas, 1980).

45 The class composition of the alliance is an important issue in understanding both the economic direction of the process and its political character. I disagree with Fitzroy Ambursley's definition of the process as having been an 'interrupted' popular revolution. The implication is that the petty bourgeoisie played a 'Bonapartist' role in managing class conflict ultimately in favour of the bourgeoisie. The petty bourgeoisie, or more succinctly, a section of the intelligentsia, undoubtedly played a critical role, but largely on the side of the workers, peasants and unemployed. See F. Ambursley, "Grenada: the New Jewel revolution", in F. Ambursley and R. Cohen (eds), *Crisis in the Caribbean* (London: Heinemann, 1983).

46 There were many arguments both within and outside the region in favour of an early tactical election in order to neutralize regional and international countries which were not implacably hostile to the revolution, but remained wary, so long as elections were not held. The NJM's error was on this tactical terrain and not out of failure to hold elections as early as possible and at any cost.

47 "NJM Manifesto for Power to the People and Achieving Real Independence" (1973), 9.

48 See, for example, Chris Searle, *Grenada: The Struggle against Destabilization* (London: Writers and Readers, 1984).

49 See Searle, *Struggle against Destabilization,* 7.

50 It might be instructive to note that while these acts of the PRG may be considered repressive, if the historical record is examined then it is evident that most countries reserve the right to abrogate liberal democratic rights in emergency situations. It was not until 1931, for example, that the US Supreme Court ruled that states were prohibited from suppressing newspapers in anticipation of wrongful printing. During the Second World War, US newspapers were prohibited under the espionage act and even today, the Federal Communications Commission has the right to refuse licenses to stations that do not broadcast in the public interest. See Rossett and Vandermeer (eds), *The Nicaragua Reader* (New York: Grove Press, 1983).

51 See Chris Searle and Merle Hodge, *Is Freedom We Making* (St Georges, 1981) and *Report on Human Rights Developments in Grenada* (St Georges, November 1982):

> The NJM showed a good understanding of the need for alliance and breadth in its incorporation of sections of the bourgeoisie in the People's Revolutionary Government and its numerous consultations with the private sector on the national budget, unemployment, etc. Where the NJM failed decisively was in the areas of the relationship of the party to the Grenadian people and their involvement and knowledge of the party, both within and outside of its structures.

See Brian Meeks "Some Reflections on the Grenadian Revolution Two Years after its Defeat" (Mimeo, 1986).

52 Nicaragua went over to the 'institutional' stage five years after the revolution in November 1984 with the holding of general elections. For those who supported the need for 'tactical' elections in Grenada, including myself, it is a point of consideration that this did not halt but intensified the hostility of the United States towards the Revolution.

53 See Adamson, *Hegemony and Revolution*, 209.

54 Antonio Gramsci, *The Modern Prince and Other Writings* (New York: International Publishers, 1970), 174.

55 Antonio Gramsci, *The Modern Prince*, 174.

56 *RASPS*, 130.

57 *RASPS*, 135. In this, Thomas echoes Poulantzas (*State, Power, Socialism,* 262) whose "democratic road to socialism" requires a swing to the side of the popular masses as a result of "a change in the relationship of forces on the terrain of the state". How is the new state to be held? Poulantzas is very vague on this. Force is inevitable, but backed by a broad popular movement. How is this going to differ from the Leninist interpretation of the dictatorship of the proletariat? This vital question is not asked and not answered.

58 *RASPS*, 130.

59 R. Ulyanovsky, *Socialism and the Newly Independent Nations* (Moscow: Progress Publishers, 1974), 83.

60 Ulyanovsky recognizes that in states of socialist orientation political aspects of democracy are "lacking or not functioning to the full extent they should", but no serious analysis is attempted to suggest why this is so. See Ulyanovsky, *Newly Independent Nations*, 103.

61 F. Engels, "On authority", in L. Feuer, *Basic Writings*.

Chapter Four

Reviewing Rod Aya's *Rethinking Revolutions and Collective Violence*

Twentieth-century social scientific thinking on the subject of revolution can perhaps be categorized as a series of four successive waves.[1] The first, best exemplified in the works of Crane Brinton, George Pettee, G. LeBon[2] and others, adopted ad hoc anatomical or psychological schema to suggest that revolutions were essentially violent illnesses on the body politic, aberrations from the norm which needed to be avoided, or if acquired, eliminated as urgently as possible. Hurried responses to the post-World War I European revolutionary wave, these theories were rooted in thin methodological soil. While making pointed observations on the tendency of revolutions to follow a typical routine, usually with a Thermidorian outcome, such observations were considered inadequate to address the post-World War II revolutionary wave, which was concentrated for the most part in the newly independent countries of the 'Third World'. For this task, a new school of largely American social scientists emerged to do battle.

Rooted in a positivist and quantitative tradition, scholars such as Ted Gurr, James Davies, the Feierabends and Chalmers Johnson,[3] travelling through anthropological, sociological and political science streams, sought to understand revolutions, which were often equated with collective violence. Behind the flashing lights of massive data collection techniques, this wave came to a remarkably similar set of conclusions: revolutions were caused by accumulated frustrations. When these frustrations reached a certain critical mass, they burst out in revolutionary upheavals. The point was how to prevent the volcano from exploding. Out of a series of trenchant criticisms of these hypotheses, a third school emerged gradually, beginning with Barrington Moore's *Social Origins of Dictatorship and Democracy* and Eric Wolf's *Peasant Wars of the Twentieth Century* and ending at its high point in Theda Skocpol's *States and Social*

Revolutions, first appearing in 1979.[4] In short, Skocpol represented a qualitative advance over the earlier wave because she shifted focus from the notion of diffuse, frustrated masses as the engine of revolt to the state. She emphasized the position of the state in a competitive world of nation states and focused on the competition between elites in charge of and around the state apparatus. She asserted that it was at the conjuncture where old regimes faced unprecedented pressures from both outside and within, that revolutionary situations emerged. Further, Skocpol proceeded beyond the second wave theorists' primary concern with the causes of revolutions to look also at their outcomes. The character of popular uprisings which accompanied the revolutionary crisis, and the degree of autonomy of these forces from the revolutionary vanguard were factors which came together to help dictate the character of the post-revolutionary regime.

However, while Skocpol was regarded as making significant advances over the earlier school, nagging problems remained with her analysis. Dunn, for example, argued that it placed too much emphasis on structural factors;[5] Hermassi thought that it focused too narrowly on the so-called Great Revolutions;[6] and Farhi and Goldfrank argued that it placed insufficient importance on the role of ideological and cultural factors in understanding the phenomenon.[7] Beyond Skocpol, we might suggest, a fourth wave is emerging which is trying to adopt the methodological lessons learnt from the Skocpolian *œuvre,* while at the same time incorporating the role of agency, ideology and culture in a less positivist and determinist approach to the subject.

Rod Aya's book *Rethinking Revolutions and Collective Violence* is a product of this fourth wave of thought. Designed primarily for the social historian or specialist political scientist student of revolution, it is nonetheless an eminently readable commentary on the subject – witty and biting in parts, if somewhat belaboured by excessive footnotes. In attempting to construct his alternative approach to the understanding of revolutions, Aya goes through three stages. He begins by attempting to redefine revolutions; he then engages in a dismissive critique of what he calls the 'volcano' theorists; finally, he presents an alternative metho- dological approach based on a 'political' model, utilizing the notion of 'vicarious problem solving'. In this, he is largely successful in throwing light on the tactics of revolutionary elites in revolutionary situations, but falls short insofar as he provides little help for an understanding of the occurrence of revolutions in the sweep of history or the recurrence of revolution as myth, symbolizing change and progress.

Aya begins by recognizing that there are serious conceptual problems inherent in the generic definition of revolution. Many studies have rushed headlong into the factual evidence of specific 'revolutions' without a clear conceptualization of the phenomenon. The concept, he suggests, can be broken down into three distinct areas: first, revolutionary intentions, where the aim of the primary actors is to radically transform; secondly, revolutionary outcomes, or the fact of radical transformation; thirdly, revolutionary situations, where 'dual power' exists and contending forces battle for state power. None of these, he argues, can be reduced into the others:

> Revolutionary situations often do not owe to revolutionary intentions or lead to revolutionary outcomes. Those who do much to bring such situations and outcomes about often do not mean to. And those who do most to transform society often do so only after the revolutionary situation in which they take power is past.[8]

This disconnection in the three aspects of revolution is equally captured in the disconnection in the stages of any revolutionary process. Revolutions are not predetermined, one-track 'locomotives' Aya posits, but rather they develop to the extent that a tentative and cumulative sequence of events fits together to yield what is usually an unprecedented outcome. What is needed is a way of defining revolutions which "sensitizes one to the causes and effects of contingent steps in a cumulative sequence rather than [tramples] them down under a forced march of historical inevitability."[9] With this initial fusillade, he launches a campaign against all macrodeterminists, with the most successful engagement waged against those he identifies as 'volcano theorists'.

Ted Gurr, Chalmers Johnson and others of the American 'new school' theorists based their extensive statistical research on the simplistic assumption that in societies undergoing stress, people get frustrated and when they are sufficiently mad, revolutions break out. Rapid change, the argument went, led inevitably to discontent and discontent eventually to revolution.

Aya, at his theoretical best, showed in his study that this approach suffered from serious errors of reductionism. It assumed that specific grievances automatically led to general discontent. It ignored the presence of identifiable action groups in real revolutionary situations and substituted instead the abstract notion of anonymous, discontented masses. Further, it assumed that discontent inevitably led to revolt, when apathy or anomie might have been equally possible alternatives. It was not that grievances and discontent are not prerequisites for revolt as, in his metaphor, oxygen is for a fire; but it is unsupportable to say that they are the cause of the fire. Thus, Aya dismisses the 'volcanic school' and, it should be mentioned, he does so with biting panache, as in his critique of Smelser's *Theory of Collective Behaviour*[10] (an all-encompassing attempt to understand why societies change) which he describes thus: "Tediously long-winded, soporifically repetitious, maddeningly opaque, yet impressively ingenious (with sporadic flashes of brilliant insight), Smelser's *Collective Behaviour* has got what it takes to be most influential in social theory."[11] It is on this field, constructed out of a redefinition of revolutions and a dismissal of one school of thought that Aya seeks to construct his own approach.

Borrowing political and state centred notions from Tilly,[12] Clauswitz[13] and Skocpol in that order, he argues essentially that revolutions can be understood, as in Clauswitz' well-known definition of war, as a continuation of politics by other means. Political actors go beyond diplomatic means to solve disputes and resort to violence only rarely. For this to happen, he argues, a number of conditions must be fulfilled. These include (i) the blocking of the avenues to peaceful resolution; (ii) the capability of the actors to act in concert, due to the possession of appropriate assets, organization and know-how; (iii) the feeling on the part of the actors that they could get away with the action, thanks to the existence of coalition partners, the collapse of central authority or both. Aya's rider, however, is that the intention of these actors was rarely to revolutionize society but to get (or keep) things they felt rightfully entitled to. At the heart of Aya's enterprise can be found his adaptation of rational choice theory.[14] It is via a methodology which he characterizes as one of 'vicarious problem solving' that we can understand revolutionary situations; then, having identified the crisis at the top, we might attempt to trace the passage of accumulated events until we arrive at the revolutionary outcome: "The combined result is a focus on political goals and constraints – the contenders' aims and tactical power chances, including the occurrence of power struggles in government that, without warning, may *open* the political arena to popular intervention . . ."[15]

By focusing on the activities of those players 'above' – on the power struggles of those in and around the state – Aya separates his outlook from that of the 'volcano theorists' and attains his closest proximity to Skocpol's state centred approach. However, while Skocpol's focus is on the tension between states in an international system and national class forces in and around the state – *ie* a profoundly *structuralist* analysis, with little room for agents – Aya bases his conclusion precisely on the rational or 'satisficing' choices real human players make in given conjunctural situations. While he admits that different economic epochs may determine the form of various revolutionary (and nonrevolutionary) struggles, the actual outbreak of revolution is to be determined by irreconcilable divisions at the top, understood through the methodology of vicarious problem solving.

My own study of three twentieth-century Caribbean revolutions[16] suggests that there is a great deal of validity to Aya's proposal. In Cuba, Nicaragua and Grenada, it was crisis up above which led to revolutionary situation. An aggressive faction or personality intervened to upset or take advantage of instability in a previously stable arrangement of power sharing between statal and economic élites. This occurred in a shifting international context which revealed weaknesses in the hegemonic relationship between the small state and the dominant power and provided opportunities for the reorganization of the national state and perhaps of the hegemonic relationship itself. In this window, excluded élites, *potential* state builders, who feel aggrieved because of what they consider their unwarranted and unjust exclusion from power, seek allies to violently unblock the blocked system of élite circulation and, in the international opening, move aggressively to take state power. The extent of popular intervention from below, fuelled by a largely different agenda of popular grievances and coupled to specific histories with varying degrees of relatively autonomous organization, helps to determine the potential for democracy and popular involvement in the revolutionary outcome. Popular intervention, however, appears to be far less important in the actual genesis of the revolutionary situation. One further factor of importance, and which is understated in Aya, is what I refer to as the 'cumulative and available ideological context', or the available political and state-building ideas which define the horizons within which the revolutionary élites operate. It is the cumulative and available ideological context which helps to dictate the tactics chosen for the seizure of power and thus the likelihood of initial success, and beyond that the possible democratic profile of the postrevolutionary regime.

However, while Aya's approach to rational choice steers clear of a certain mode of crass determinism and effectively captures the 'tentativeness' in revolutionary eventuation, it falls flat in a few critical areas. Most notably, he throws little light on what we might term the 'rhythm of revolution', or the recurrence of distinct revolutionary waves throughout modern history. Halliday,[17] for example, identifies an early-twentieth-century wave involving countries which had avoided outright colonization, but were subject to partial modernization by capital, including Persia, Egypt, Russia, the Ottoman Empire and Mexico. After the Second World War until 1954, a further wave saw revolutions occurring in Albania, Yugoslavia, China, Korea, Vietnam and Bolivia, and unsuccessful attempts in the Philippines, Malaya, Iran and Guatemala. A third wave between 1958 and 1962 led to successful revolutions in Iraq, North Yemen, Cuba, the Congo and Algeria and then there is a long break, until between 1974 and 1980 when some fourteen revolutions occurred, largely in the Third World. Perhaps Walter Goldfrank is closest to understanding the causal factor for these waves in identifying the 'permissive world context' – or a temporary lapse in the strength and/or vigilance of hegemonic powers – as a necessary condition for successful revolution. However this leaves unanswered the further question as to why these lapses occur. The person who seems to address this question frontally is Immanuel Wallerstein, whose World Systems analysis[18] with its long waves and economically determined crises attempts to reassert the Marxist vision of revolution driven, however, on a global and not on a national scale. All previous 'revolutions', Wallerstein argues, have been mere revolts, or signposts on the way to the possible, if not inevitable, world revolution. The irony is that Wallerstein's approach (which at least provides an explanation for revolutionary waves) is diametrically opposed in methodology and spirit to Aya's rational choice with its central emphasis on human intervention. While Aya's vicarious problem solving does seem to be a useful tool at the moment of revolutionary crisis to suggest the immediate course events might take, it does little to fill in the larger and obviously very important global/historical picture.

Further, in trying to divorce the study of revolution from what he calls the "hocus-pocus of classist dogma", Aya loses sight of what one might term the "myth of revolution". At least since the French Revolution, the word has been invoked either as a synonym for human progress and improvement, or as the ultimate descent into barbarism. The persistence of the 'progress' myth, despite the frustrations, defeats and Thermidorian outcomes of so many revolutions, merits further explanation. There is too little room in Aya's rational choice for this ethical/mythical dimension which, so often invoked, is a motivating force in its own right. The words of the Jamaican reggae hero Bob Marley, when he sings

> It takes a revolution
> to make a solution[19]

capture the popular myth as they suggest the power the myth might have to influence the policies of real men in revolutionary situations. Might not rational choice theory strengthen its analytical usefulness by recognizing that a powerful motivation of at least some revolutionaries in some situations is the ideal of making a better world? Might not the study of revolution, clinical and value free as we might strive to make it, be placed on a grid which would examine the extent to which such revolutionaries contributed to or retarded a historical tendency towards democracy and human liberation? Might not, in other words, the ethical question be introduced as a legitimate element in social analysis?

Aya successfully carries us away from sterile, mechanical interpretations of history to correctly focus on the human agent as the critical variable; but his is a human agent whose capacity for thought and action is itself narrowly defined by a limiting, mechanical notion of human imagination and possibility. Freedom and democracy are real human desires which help to explain why the myth of revolution has persisted. Aya misses this central mark in what is otherwise a thought-provoking book.

Notes

1   See Jack Goldstone, "Theories of revolution: the third generation", *World Politics*, no. 32 (1979), and Brian Meeks, *Caribbean Revolutions and Revolutionary Theory: an Assessment of Cuba, Nicaragua and Grenada* (London and Basingstoke: Macmillan, 1993).

2   See Crane Brinton, *The Anatomy of Revolution* (Great Britain: Jonathan Cape, 1953), George Pettee, *The Process of Revolution* (New York: Harper and Brothers, 1913), and G. LeBon, *The Psychology of Revolution* (New York: Putnam, 1913).

3 See Ted Gurr, *Why Men Rebel* (Princeton: Princeton University Press, 1971), James Davies (ed), *When Men Revolt and Why: a Reader in Political Violence and Revolution* (New York: Free Press, 1971), Ivo K. Feierabend & Rosalind Feierabend, "Aggressive behaviour within polities, 1948-1962: a cross national study", in Davies (ed), *When Men Revolt*, and Chalmers Johnson, *Revolutionary Change* (Boston: Little, Brown, 1966).

4 See Barrington Moore, *Social Origins of Dictatorship and Democracy: Lord and Peasantry in the Making of the Modern World* (Harmondsworth: Penguin, 1987), Eric Wolf, *Peasant Wars of the Twentieth Century* (New York: Harper and Row, 1969), and Theda Skocpol, *States and Social Revolutions: a Comparative Analysis of France, Russia and China* (Cambridge: Cambridge University Press, 1979).

5 John Dunn, *Modern Revolutions: an Introduction to the Analysis of a Political Phenomenon* (Cambridge: Cambridge University Press, 2d ed, 1989).

6 Elbaki Hermassi, "Toward a comparative study of revolutions", *Comparative Studies in Society and History* 18, no. 12 (April 1976).

7 See Farideh Farhi, "State disintegration and urban based revolutionary crisis: a comparative analysis of Iran and Nicaragua", *Comparative Political Studies* 1, no. 2 (July 1988), and Walter Golfrank, "Theories of revolution and revolution without theory", *Theory and Society* 7, nos. 1 & 2 (1979).

8 Rod Aya, *Rethinking Revolutions and Collective Violence: Studies on Concept, Theory and Method* (Amsterdam: Het Spinhuis, 1990), 5.

9 Aya, *Rethinking Revolutions*, 18.

10 See Neil Smelser, *Theory of Collective Behaviour* (Great Britain: Routledge and Kegan Paul, 1961).

11 Aya, *Rethinking Revolutions*, 34-35.

12 See, for example, Charles Tilly, *From Mobilization to Revolution* (Reading, Mass.: Addison-Wesley, 1978), and Charles Tilly, *Big Structures, Large Processes, Huge Comparisons* (New York: Russel Sage Foundation, 1984).

13 Carl von Clauswitz, *On War* (Princeton: Princeton University Press, 1976).

14 For a reasonable statement on rational choice theory see Jon Elster, *Ulysses and the Sirens: Studies in Rationality and Irrationality* (Cambridge: Cambridge University Press, 1979) and Jon Elster, *Making Sense of Marx* (Cambridge: Cambridge University Press, 1979). For a useful and recent critique, see Alex Callinicos, *Making History: Agency, Structure and Change in Social Theory* (Cambridge: Polity Press, 1989).

15 Aya, *Rethinking Revolutions*, 65.

16 Meeks, *Caribbean Revolutions*.

17 See Fred Halliday, *Cold War, Third World: an Essay on Soviet-US Relations* (London, Sydney: Hutchinson Radius, 1990).

18 See Immanuel Wallerstein, *The Politics of the World Economy* (Cambridge: Cambridge University Press, 1984).

19 Bob Marley, *Revolution* (Cayman Music, 1974).

Chapter Five

Caribbean Insurrections[1]

Theorizing on revolutions and revolutionary situations is generally accepted as having reached a watershed with the 1979 publication of Theda Skocpol's *States and Social Revolutions*.[2] Skocpol moved beyond both volcanic and economy-centred approaches[3] to focus on the role of the state. She examined it both as an actor within its own boundaries and as part of an international system of nation states as the crucial object of observation for an understanding of revolution. Many, however, regarded the major weakness in her otherwise innovative approach as being its too rigid structuralist determinism which appeared to leave little room for the intervention of human agency. Thus, John Dunn was typically on target when he suggested that:

> There is very little about the military or political activities of state agents which can be clearly understood except through the categories of human intervention and action. The military, diplomatic, economic, welfare and repressive ventures of states (the range of characteristics which makes and keeps a state a state) are all complicated – if often poorly integrated – human performances . . . the causal importance of imitation, obduracy and intellectual invention in the history of twentieth century revolution is very hard to overestimate.[4]

Indeed, Skocpol was aware of the weaknesses associated with a purely structuralist approach and sought to solve this with her concept of 'world time':

> One possibility is that actors in later revolutions may be influenced by developments in earlier ones; for example, the Chinese communists became conscious emulators of the Bolsheviks and received, for a time, direct advice and aid from the Russian revolutionary regime. Another possibility is that crucial world-historically significant breakthroughs – such as the industrial revolution or the innovation of the Leninist form of party organization – may intervene between the occurrence of one broadly similar revolution and another. As a result new opportunities or necessities are created for the development of the

later revolution that were not open to, or pressed upon, the former, because it occurred at an earlier phase of modern world history.[5]

But the world time variable ended up 'structuralizing the agent' by removing the human content from historically significant breakthroughs, which then appear as determined, almost inevitable, events and not the peculiar outcome of chance, contingency and human ingenuity.

Beyond Skocpol, a number of thinkers, including Farideh Farhi, Walter Goldfrank and Rod Aya have sought to combine the advantages to be gained from a state-centred focus with a greater appreciation of the role of the agent as a critical variable in the making of history.[6] Aya in particular, travelling a route well trod by rational choice theorists, suggests that the approach to be taken in understanding revolutionary situations should be one of 'vicarious problem solving':

> . . . to explain social action through Vicarious Problem Solving, you just assume the rationality principle that people do what they think will gain their goals under given constraints, place yourself 'vicariously' in the same situation, and figure out what you would do if you were they.[7]

But if Aya's approach sought to distance itself from overt determinism and historicism, it suffers precisely because it is too disconnected from the historical moment. By this is meant not just the social and economic structures which predominate, but the accumulation of ideas and values which inform the revolutionary agents providing the justification for their action and to some extent determining the contours and horizons of their intervention into history.

It is suggested, then, that a more fruitful approach to the understanding of revolutionary situations might emerge from the amalgamation of Skocpol's state-centred methodology with Aya's vicarious problem solving, wedded to an appreciation of the cumulative and available ideological context. With this, we might tentatively describe revolutionary situations in the following way: Due to a variety and combination of factors, including external threat, economic crisis and questions of succession, powerful and aggressive individuals or groups at the helm of the state close off traditional avenues by which young, ambitious state building élites might have access to state power. This fissure between the dominant and contending statal élites is usually compounded by other tensions, as the dominant élites concurrently use their position in the state apparatus to make inroads against the traditional oligarchy and the bourgeoisie. The economically dominant classes resist these incursions, but it is the enraged and excluded potential state builders, typically young and relatively highly educated, who form the bedrock of resistance to the dominant powers. In their quest to remove the roadblock which stands in the way of their accession to the political kingdom, they seek allies and an appropriate mix of strategy and tactics which will lead to victory. If there is resistance to their peaceful attempts at changing the status quo, as in this context there inevitably is, they resort to insurrectionary strategies. The strategies which young, potential state builders adopt are not, however, to be understood purely from the perspective of 'vicarious problem solving', but from an appreciation of the cumulative and available ideological context. Insurrection is translated into revolutionary triumph when revolutionary élites are able to forge effective alliances with aggrieved elements from below, among workers, peasants, the urban unemployed, or whatever other popular social forces are available, aggrieved, and willing to act, on the basis of an independent agenda, against the dominant, aggressive group/individual.

The extent and character of the intervention from below, together with the horizons for democracy and flexibility written into the cumulative and available ideological context, are decisive elements in determining not just the actual victory, but the profile of the postrevolutionary regime, and its potential for greater democracy and the reduction of hierarchy. Thus, it is suggested that a close examination of the prevalent ideas which guide and influence the revolutionary élites is not peripheral, but central to any study of revolution.

All of this, however, is in vain, if at the time of the seizure of power there does not exist, particularly in the case of small, peripheral countries, a permissive world context, or relaxation of the traditional vigilance and power of the dominant hegemonic powers.[8] It is primarily the battle between the various local forces which determines whether insurrection proceeds to revolutionary victory, but it is the existence of a permissive world context which will help to decide whether state power can be held by the newly victorious alliance.

In this exploratory essay, we examine three important insurrectionary events in the postindependence history of the Commonwealth Caribbean. While recognizing the broader palette of external and national accelerators, the aim is to focus primarily on the cumulative and available ideological context in order to better understand why these events occurred and why they had particular outcomes. The three are: the 1970 Black Power 'Revolution' in Trinidad and Tobago and the subsequent army uprising; the 1979 insurrection of the NJM against the Gairy government which led to its overthrow and the establishment of the short-lived People's Revolutionary Government; and the 1990 failed coup attempt led by Abu Bakr and the Jamaat al Muslimeen, again in Trinidad and Tobago.

The 'Black Power Revolution' and Army Coup: Trinidad 1970

On April 21, 1970, after two months of Black Power demonstrations led by the NJAC, a State of Emergency was declared in Trinidad and Tobago. As leaders of the protest movement were arrested and a dusk to dawn curfew declared in the twin island state, a section of the 750-man defence force mutinied. After minor confrontations between loyalists and mutineers, the rebel elements were contained in their base on the northwestern peninsula of Trinidad. Negotiations stretched on for several days, leading eventually to the surrender of hostages and arrest of the mutineers.[9]

The background to 1970 can be seen as resulting from a series of connected but relatively autonomous developments. Real wages, starting from a base of zero in 1956, at first increased, reaching a high of 14 percent in 1960 and then gradually decreased to the low point of -4 percent in 1968.[10] Unemployment, following a well established pattern evident in small countries attempting import substitution, increased steadily throughout the 1960s. In 1955, 6.4 percent of the labour force was unemployed; in September 1969 the figure was 15 percent.[11] This was most acutely felt in strategic sectors of the economy, including the critical oil and sugar sectors. Between 1960 and 1965, the number of workers in the petroleum industry declined by 15.5 percent and in sugar by 16.1 percent.[12] There were ample causes for popular dissatisfaction with the Eric Williams government, but the events of 1970 were not initiated by uprising from below. While there were distinct moments in the decade when trade union disputes dominated the national agenda, this was not the case in 1970. In 1965, the threatened unification of oil and sugar workers led to the government declaring a state of emergency and in the seminal transport workers strike of 1969, contacts were established between student and trade union organizers.[13] But the first major protest of 1970 was primarily a student affair, a demonstration to the Canadian High Commission and the Royal Bank of Canada against the trial of West Indian students who had been arrested in Montreal after a confrontation at the Sir George Williams University.[14]

The student march of February 26 was a tiny affair confined to radical undergraduates, eminently negligible but for the fact that a section of the marchers invaded the nearby Roman Catholic Cathedral and proceeded to give speeches and engage in dialogue with the resident priests. What happened a week later was therefore unprecedented and entirely unexpected. In support of five students and four nonstudents who had been arrested for "disorderly conduct in a place of worship", a mammoth Black Power demonstration of more than 10,000 persons was held in the streets of Port of Spain. Led by Geddes Granger, head of NJAC, they occupied Woodford Square, declared it the 'People's Parliament' and placed it in permanent session. Between March 4 and April 21, with distinct ebbs and flows, this popular movement grew in scope and intensity. On March 12, the 'long march' was held from the capital to the heart of the sugar belt as a show of solidarity and unity between the predominantly Afro-Trinidadian demonstrators of the city and the Indian populations of the sugar belt. On April 9 a massive demonstration – perhaps the largest of the entire period – was held for the funeral of Basil Davis, a young demonstrator who had been shot dead three days before by the police in Port of Spain. On April 13, serious splits began to appear in the PNM government as Minister of External Affairs A. N. R. Robinson quit the cabinet. Then on April 19, in what was from the government's perspective the most serious event, 600 daily paid workers at the Brechin Castle sugar factory went on strike as sugar, oil, transport and electricity workers planned to join Black Power groups for an April 21 general strike and march on Port of Spain.

It was fear of the likely results of a general strike that led the government to declare a State of Emergency on April 21, the act which precipitated the mutiny in the army. But before examining that signal event, we need to characterize the nature of the movement from February 26 to April 21.

Middle class university students had their own social and political agenda. The nationalist movement led by the PNM and Eric Williams was predominantly Afro-Trinidadian in its character. But there was a definite and justifiable perception that despite deep incursions into the state apparatus by black Trinidadians, the private sector was still predominantly under the control of foreign multinationals and local white or fair-skinned élites.[15] There was a further perception, again supported by evidence, that the People's National Movement had retreated from its more radical nationalist stance of 1956 and had made fundamental compromises with foreign powers and local élites. Thus, compromises made at the time of the Chaguaramas[16] agreement, the Mbanefo Commission into Subversive Activities of 1963, the State of Emergency of 1965 and the subsequent Industrial Stabilization Act, were all seen as part of the 'thunder on the right' which indicated the exhaustion of the PNM's potential as a genuinely nationalist movement.[17] For young, upwardly mobile potential state builders, there was also another problem. The PNM had been in power for fifteen years. It was the primary vehicle through which Afro-Trinidadian élites might enter the state. The door to that entry had not been decisively shut, but it certainly was not as open as it appeared to have been in 1956.

The events of 1970, then, can be seen as representing an 'incipient fissure' – a social and political movement led by young, black middle class potential state builders to reestablish a trajectory into the state and society which appeared to have been increasingly frustrated throughout the 1960s. Had these young élites acted alone, it may well have taken the form of an innocuous social and political reform movement; alternatively, had they been well organized and imbued with a clearly defined and hegemonic ideology, it is very likely that they may have directed the movement from above in their chosen direction. But there was little organization, and the cumulative and available ideological context was defined by flexibility, openness and the absence of hierarchy. As an outcome of this and, critically, because of the spontaneity, scope and size of the popular movement, NJAC – the organization most closely representative of the black, student middle class ethos – was never able to sculpt and define events in its own way. At best, it acted as a tribune, a sounding board for the mobilized crowd, now, through the People's parliament suggesting this or that direction, organizing marches and speakers, but always with an ear to the favoured tactic of the black urban unemployed, many of whom called themselves NJAC but acted on their own volition.

Ivor Oxaal is insightful when he writes that the popular movement in its methods and direction most closely fulfilled the Jamesian paradigm of spontaneous revolution: "In its emphasis on spontaneous action it could qualify as an eminently Jamesian revolutionary movement, resistant – probably more by instinct and action than by theoretical design – to ideological or organizational crystallization."[18]

The 'Jamesian' in Oxaal's passage refers to the political positions of the Trinidadian C. L. R. James, probably the most outstanding West Indian political thinker of the twentieth century. In a prolific career in which he could have been variously described as a novelist, historian, literary critic and sports analyst, James was perhaps less known for his central work as an original Marxist thinker. Never successful in activist politics at home – his short-lived Workers and Farmers Party was a failure in national elections – he nonetheless influenced a generation of young West Indian political activists who later played leading roles in regional politics. Joining the Fourth International in Britain in the 1930s, James eventually migrated to the USA as a speaker for the Trotskyite cause, but broke with the movement in 1940 to form his own tendency. Together with the talented theoretician Raya Dunayevskaya, the new movement (at first called the Johnson-Forrest Tendency) adopted political positions expressing implacable hostility to Stalinism together with deep distrust for Trotskyism and all forms of vanguardist politics.[19]

The mutiny of the soldiers in the Trinidad and Tobago regiment on May 21 can be seen as part of the broader spontaneous movement of which Oxaal speaks. Junior officers in the military had their own litany of complaints which mirrored those of young middle class potential state builders outside the army. Many had been trained at Sandhurst and other prestigious British institutions while their senior officers were often untrained political appointees who had variously been accused of nepotism, corruption and inefficiency.[20] When the State of Emergency was declared, some junior officers with support in the ranks acted spontaneously without any clear plan against their seniors. While some commentators have argued that there were plans to divide the island into military regions and rule under a draconian state of emergency, the limited, if still unrealistic demands of the leaders as described here, suggested a different agenda:

> When the negotiations got under way, the soldiers asked for a general amnesty; release of the soldiers that had been arrested after the Camp Ogden fire that morning; retirement of all the short term officers; promotion to Captain for Lt.

Lasalle and Lt. Rafique Shah; an Enquiry into the Regiment; and the return of Lt. Colonel Joffre Serrette as Commanding Officer. The soldiers also wanted to be allowed to travel to Port of Spain with their arms.[21]

In 1970, young state-building élites and their equivalents in the junior ranks of the military were possessed of an eclectic and incompletely developed political outlook which had no clear perspective on the necessary tactics for the taking of power. NJAC's Black Power was a loose amalgam of American Black Power themes, Guevarrist slogans, Walter Rodney's thoughts and traditional African cultural nationalism.[22] It provided the movement with a tribune from which long held grievances could be aired and political awareness stimulated. The differentiation between leaders and led, so critical to a vanguard type organization was absent, as Ian Belgrave, then an important member of the movement, suggests: "NJAC was a unique type of vanguard organization. There was no party and there was no set organizational structure. People became NJAC for very curious reasons. Anyone who marched was a member of NJAC."[23]

Most obvious in its absence was the Leninist notion of the vanguard, as was Marxism as a political guide to action. This can be partly accounted for in the failure of the Left in the Cold War period to establish a permanent base in Trinidadian politics, and the subsequent displacement of radical politics in a nationalist direction.[24] This freed the movement from the constricting and hierarchical structures inherent in the vanguard party without an alternative theory which, in revolutionary situations, would provide a strategy and the necessary tactics for the taking of power. Oxaal has described 1970 as Jamesian, so it might be useful to examine some of the essentials of the Jamesian position on revolutions and insurrections.

C. L. R. James' main argument is that in revolutionary situations it is the class that acts decisively and not the often self-appointed leaders. The leadership, composed of intellectuals with their distinct class interests, seeks to carry the revolutionary movement in directions contrary to those of the revolutionary class. It is therefore up to the revolutionary class to find the wherewithal to break the fetters of the intellectual vanguard, which restrains its true historical potential. These themes run throughout James' entire *œuvre*. Thus, in "Marxism and the Intellectuals" he argues for the self-activity of the workers: "What happens in a revolution is that the class for the first time finds itself free to think its own thoughts and give some concrete form to its own experience accumulated over the generations."[25]

And in *The Black Jacobins*, he develops his position against what he considers as the conservative constraints of the leaders in the Haitian Revolution:

> The dullness and inertia of revolutionary leaders should be one of the axioms of historical study, and their conservatism and moral cowardice have ruined

causes more often than the forces of reaction. The masses were fighting and dying as only revolutionary masses can, the French army was wasting away, despair was slowly choking Le Clerc. But still these black and mulatto generals continued to fight for Le Clerc against the 'brigands' . . .[26]

However, on closer examination of James' writings there is some unclarity on the relative roles to be played by class, party and leader in the revolutionary situation. Thus, in a well-known eulogy and critique of the Guyanese historian and activist Walter Rodney,[27] James begins with his usual assertion that it is the class which should lead, but ends up in a muddle as to the relative roles of parties and leaders:

> Walter went into that highly charged situation with people who were familiar with ideas but not with revolutionary organization, which has nothing to do with the party. A party may organize but that is not it. As Lenin says, the party can be in conflict. In 1937 and 1938 and in 1970, there was no party to organize the masses. The Stalinists and the rest of them have corrupted Marxist thinking and made the party everything. A party is useful. Many people think that when I say the party is not so necessary I mean the leader. There are always leaders.[28]

James seems here to retreat from the more purist positions on spontaneity to be found in *The Black Jacobins*. In the end, he presents not so much an alternative strategy of insurrection as one closely wedded to the traditional Marxist and Leninist framework. This, at the point of insurrection, is concerned not with the overall political situation, which it assumes as favourable, but rather with the specific military "order of battle", captured in this famous statement from Engels:

> Now, insurrection is an art quite as much as war or any other and subject to certain rules of proceeding which, when neglected, will produce the ruin of the party neglecting them . . . Firstly, never play with insurrection unless you are fully prepared to face the consequences of your play. Insurrection is a calculus with very definite magnitudes, the value of which may change every day; the forces opposed to you have all the advantage of organization, discipline and habitual authority; unless you bring strong odds against them, you are defeated and ruined. Secondly, the insurrectionary career once entered upon, act with the greatest determination, and on the offensive. The defensive is the death of every armed uprising . . . Surprise your antagonists while their forces are scattering, prepare new successes however small, but daily; keep up the moral ascendancy which the first successful rising has given to you; rally those vacillating elements to your side which always follow the strongest impulse . . . force your enemies to retreat before they can collect their strength against you; in the words of Danton, the greatest master of revolutionary policy yet known, *de l'audace, de l'audace, encore de l'audace!*[29]

The obvious requirement of direction and a centre, implicit in Engels' extract above, is brought out explicitly in Lenin's work. Thus, in *Marxism and Insurrection* Lenin recognizes the need for a popular uprising and the support of the "advanced class", but is equally unambiguous on the need for the establishment of a headquarters[30] for the pursuance of the insurrection and for the direction of the revolutionary detachment. James raises the issue of the negative consequences of middle class leadership, but fails to suggest an alternative to the Marxist tactic of concentration and the Leninist strategy of the vanguard – both potential vehicles for the dousing of popular initiative and the elevation of (middle class) specialists.

It was the absence of a Marxist and Leninist tradition that helped to determine the populist and open character of the 1970 movement. Ironically also, it was the absence of Marxist and Leninist insurrectionary tactics that contributed to the centre-less, indecisive and ultimately defensive character of the movement and therefore its defeat.

The New Jewel Movement (NJM) and the Grenada Revolution

In Grenada, Eric Gairy, the leader of the 1951 worker/peasant revolt against estate conditions,[31] had by the early 1960s made significant incursions against the traditional middle classes in the state and the economic base of the landholding oligarchy. By replacing white and brown-skinned civil servants with black people like himself, but more critically, by granting contracts and other favours to previously excluded black businessmen,[32] Gairy, within the limitations of late British colonialism, came to dominate the commanding heights of the state apparatus. And, in his 'land for the landless' programme carried out in the late sixties, he was able through legal means and force to break the back of the landed class and consolidate agriculture on a state farm basis under government control.[33] But, in making his incursions against the top, he also created many enemies below. As he sought to dominate the important cocoa and nutmeg associations, he undermined the power not only of the big planters, but also of the small growers who felt that they too had been disenfranchised.[34] Dissatisfaction below was further compounded by worsening living conditions in the early seventies. Increasing unemployment in 1973 was accompanied by serious inflation. The index of retail prices which stood at 130.7 in 1969, had risen to 189.5 in 1973 and by 1975 had moved to 269.4.[35]

Open hostility from above merged with dissatisfaction below when Gairy decided to use his victory in the 1972 general election to move to independence without having sought a distinct mandate from the people. The oligarchy and the middle classes resisted this move, which they saw as leading to the unchecked paramountcy of Gairy and his clique over them. Among young people, many workers and the unemployed, independence under Gairy was also perceived as against their interests, and likely to lead to increased police brutality and arbitrariness.

The organization that was to play the leading role in channelling the dissatisfaction of these forces was typically, however, not from below, but from the young, aggrieved middle classes. The Movement for the Assemblies of the Peoples (MAP) and the Joint Endeavour for Welfare Education and Liberation (JEWEL) had merged in 1973 to form the New Jewel Movement (NJM). The NJM filled the same niche as NJAC did in Trinidad in 1970, but its leadership, composed of lawyers and returning graduates fit far more neatly the notion of the state-building middle than the younger, student leadership of the Trinidadian organization.[36] But unlike NJAC, the NJM was, at least initially, self-consciously Jamesian in its outlook, opposing the notion of the vanguard, believing in spontaneous revolution and advocating 'assemblies of the people' instead of central planning.[37]

When resistance to Gairy grew to a climax after the November 1973 beating of Maurice Bishop and other NJM leaders, that organization was the leading, though not hegemonic force in the movement. Guided by Jamesian spontaneity however, the NJM was never able to carry the street struggle beyond the period of mass mobilization and demonstrations to take power from Gairy, and by March 1974 the struggle had been defeated.[38] By the middle of that year, then, the lesson had been learnt: if Eric Gairy was to be removed, new tactics would be needed. The answer, for the young, potential state builders, was to be found in Marxism-Leninism.

The consolidation of Marxism-Leninism in Grenada was the result of the defeat of the Jamesian position in 1974 as well as other regional and international conjunctures. The Cuban regime, after a decade in power had consolidated and, boosted by high prices for sugar, was able to carry out lavish infrastructure and social programmes. The Manley government in Jamaica and the Burnham regime in Guyana – neither yet in overt crisis – had legitimized 'socialism' by adopting this title to their respective programmes. In Vietnam and in the Portuguese African colonies, liberation movements 'guided' by Marxism-Leninism were making major advances against colonialism and imperialism. The shift from Bandung-styled, non-aligned nationalism was further confirmed as a result of the lessons drawn from every revolutionary victory and defeat in the seventies. The cumulative and available ideological context was informing the young, radicalized potential state-building élites that Marxism-Leninism was the 'correct' way. As a result, between 1974 and 1979, the NJM adopted all the Leninist organizational forms and methods, including centralism, élitism in the selection of cadres, clandestinity, and the need for prior military preparation.[39] Each of these tactics changed the nature of the NJM from being a flexible, popular tribune, to a far more rigid, hierarchical and centralized, Leninist type party. But at the same time it sharpened the cutting edge of the organization as a tool for insurrection.

When, in the face of a suspected Gairyite plot to eliminate the NJM leadership, the military wing acted on March 13, 1979, they were possessed of tactics and some weapons, which in the appropriate situation gave them the greatest possibility of victory. Clandestine planning; concentration of forces against the military barracks and the sole radio station; incremental victories throughout the day without going on the defensive; and audacious steps, such as calling on the people to assist in the takeover of the rural police stations, all helped to ensure the conquest of power. Ultimately, however, victory was consolidated because of a permissive world context which meant that after national power had been taken, an international mix of circumstances existed which stayed the hand of the hegemonic power. But on the day, national power was taken because the potential state-building élites were possessed of the requisite tools which allowed them to employ the most favourable tactics. It also left them with a legacy of hierarchy, of top-down commandism, and élitism, which would last throughout the revolution and contribute immeasurably to its ultimate fall.[40]

Abu Bakr and the 1990 Muslimeen Uprising in Trinidad and Tobago

Abu Bakr's attempted coup of 1990 was so different from the situation in 1970, yet so similar in many respects, in the underlying Trinidadian cultural and political themes.

The economic downturn of the eighties was, indeed, far more intense than that of 1970. According to the Central Bank, per capita GNP had fallen from US$7,560 in 1982 to US$3,480 in 1987. Between 1982 and 1990, structural adjustment policies carried out first by the PNM and then the National Alliance for Reconstruction (NAR) had led to an increase of 66,000 unemployed persons, taking the national figure to somewhere between 22 and 25 percent of the labour force.[41]

This combined with what Ryan describes as a legitimacy crisis – the withdrawal of support for the regime by a wide cross-section of organizations due to the perceived harshness of its austerity measures and the feeling that they were being implemented by an uncaring leadership. A poll carried out by Selwyn Ryan in June 1990, some three years after the NAR decisively defeated the PNM at the polls to end an unbroken thirty-year tenure, found that only 27 percent of the people wanted the government to have another five-year period in office. Only 29 percent felt that the NAR should retain its leader and Prime Minister A. N. R. Robinson for the next elections; 56 percent rated the ruling party's performance as 'poor' or 'very poor'.[42] Patience with the NAR government had grown thin by 1990.

The main issue which seems to have sparked the coup attempt surrounds the dispute which existed between the Jamaat al Muslimeen organization and successive governments over access to a piece of land on Mucurapo Road on the outskirts of Port of Spain. Abu Bakr and his supporters claimed that the land had been legitimately given to them by the Eric Williams PNM government. However, those in and around the government who opposed this position argued that the Muslimeen, who had transformed the property into their headquarters with mosque, shops and residences were, in effect, squatters.[43] Abu Bakr had gained increasing support, particularly among the black, urban dispossessed. He and his supporters had waged a somewhat brutal, if effective, campaign against drug dealers. Indeed, many fervent members of the movement had been reformed drug addicts. Bakr and his group had, for the most part, abandoned the traditional structure of party politics with its well established channels of clientelistic relations. His centre at Mucurapo Road had moved somewhat instinctively in the direction of Latin American *basismo*[44] – if on an Islamic foundation, with its emphasis on self-reliance and abandonment of traditional forms of dependence on the state.

As Bakr himself said in a 1985 interview: "We have an organization here that operates completely independent [*sic*] of any other organization and these things are not the norm for African people and such independence threatens those people who are used to having us depend on them."[45]

To many in the urban underclass, Abu Bakr was a larger than life Robin Hood-styled hero, but to the middle and upper classes, his flamboyant style and sometimes violent language was anathema.

A decision taken by Trinidadian High Court Justice Blackman, just two days before the insurrection, seemed to finally close the option of legal access to the land and appeared to have been interpreted as the last straw by Bakr.[46] The military wing of the organization, which operated clandestinely, had imported arms and made careful preparations for just such an eventuality. Moving boldly, some forty-two members seized the local parliament building (the Red House) and took the Prime Minister and most parliamentarians hostage. Another contingent of some seventy-one persons with Bakr himself as the leader seized the only television station, from which Bakr announced that the government had been overthrown.

Much controversy surrounds the question as to whether Bakr acted alone or as part of a wider conspiracy. In a series of interviews with this writer conducted in 1991, a range of public personalities, including then Prime Minister A. N. R.

Robinson supported some version of a conspiracy theory. It is true that Bakr had been a member of the Summit of People's Organizations (SOPO), a loose alliance of trade unions and small leftist groups which had been carrying out a programme of protest action against the austerity measures of the NAR government. But it is highly unlikely that SOPO could have been involved in the planning of the coup without compromising the critical element of surprise, which turned out to be the Muslimeen's main advantage. Bakr, until contrary evidence emerges, appears to have acted alone, though with insufficient political preparation and without the existence of a revolutionary fissure at the top. Thus, not only was he unable to gain the requisite support from *within* the army or other sections of the state, but when he called on the populace to rise up, they ignored him, instead using the opportunity of a distracted military to make up in a spree of looting the material goods they had foregone in the long and deep recession.[47]

Without active popular support, holed up in two exposed positions in the capital city, and with the army and police force regrouped, Bakr was, by the second day of the six-day siege,[48] forced on the defensive and could do nothing but ignominiously seek to negotiate the most favourable terms of surrender. This he did in a manner that was strikingly similar to that of the army rebels of 1970, with guarantees of amnesty for the insurrectionists.[49] These guarantees, as in the former incident (1970), were immediately ignored once arms had been laid down.

The growth and consolidation of the Jamaat al Muslimeen was a particularly Trinidadian response to the political conjuncture of the eighties. Indian Muslims, of course, comprised a distinct and important part of Trinidadian society, but Afro-Trinidadian Muslims have had a small but significant presence, particularly in the wake of the defeat of the 1970 movement. The growth of Abu Bakr's influence, can be seen in the context of the failure of secular 'progressive' organizations to gain an hegemonic position in Trinidadian politics. The defeat of NJAC, the fractured and tenuous nature of Marxist politics in Trinidad; the defeat of the revolution in neighbouring Grenada and with it the feasibility of a Marxist-led movement, coupled with the international collapse of 'really existing socialism' all contributed to a cumulative and available ideological context which could not be Marxist or even secular and, therefore, to the attractiveness of a militant but religious alternative.

Thus, the Muslimeen can be viewed as a postpolitical movement; an organization at the end of history where statism is abandoned along with secularism, but which Janus-faced, also looks back on an older more entrenched notion of authority and decisive leadership, personified in Abu Bakr, the charismatic leader writ large. I asked Abu Bakr in an interview in 1991 at the Royal Gaol why he acted and he answered "Simple. Overthrow!" Of course, there is more to it than that, but the statement does reflect a certain reality. It is almost a caricature of the well organized plans and methods of the Grenadian movement of 1979, at the same time as it must indeed reflect other currents so typical of Trinidadian society: the masque of carnival; the illusion and quality of 'grand charge' which is to be found, as sketched here, in such traditional carnival characters as the Midnight Robber:

> The Pierrots engaged in verbal battles before exchanging blows, but the midnight robbers do not fight and seldom converse with each other. Their speeches are monologues rattled off prospective victims who are harangued until they are payed [*sic*] a ransom to secure their release. The language of the robber is full of [such] empty threats and braggadocio that it has added to Trinidad vernacular the colloquial expression 'robber talk'.
>
> . . . For the day my mother gave birth to me, the sun refused to shine and the wind ceased blowing. Many mothers that day gave birth, but to deformed children. Plagues and pestilence pestered the cities, for atomic eruption raged in the mountains. Philosophers, scientists, professors said 'the world is come to an end' but no, it was me, a monarch was born. Master of all I survey and my right where none could dispute.[50]

These peculiarities of Trinidadian society cannot be seen as epiphenomena, but point towards a particular political culture on its own historical trajectory.[51] The regular threats against the government made by Abu Bakr with a feeling of impunity; the decision to attack without careful preparation of the mass base; the eventual retreat with amnesty in hand and the obvious feeling that it would be respected – all point to a sensitive understanding on Bakr's part of a certain state form and political culture which might, once again, tolerate insurrection without draconian consequences, as indeed, had occurred after 1970.

Bakr had done some of the right things for successful insurrection. He had obtained his weapons and trained his soldiers under a clandestine veil; on the day, he had followed many of the insurrectionary rules, including acting with audacity, striking where the enemy is weakest, and using superior force. However, in the end he suffered the consequences, as he had ignored the classical Marxist (and C. L. R. James') fundamental warning that the insurrection must ride on the back of the popular wave. He had mistaken what was a case of deep dissatisfaction with the policies of a government for a revolutionary fissure – a far rarer event – entailing a decisive, irreconcilable split in the ranks of the dominant political élites. Indeed, Abu Bakr, the ex-policeman, from more humble origins[52] and with definitely lower expectations than the university students of NJAC and the returning professionals of the NJM, does not really fit the bill as being an example of the state-building middle class élite. In many respects, Bakr is an updated, urban version of Eric Hobsbawn's "social bandit" or "noble robber", described here:

First, the noble robber begins his career of outlawry not by crime, but as the victim of injustice, or through being persecuted by the authorities for some act which they, but not the custom of his people, consider as criminal. Second, he 'rights' wrongs. Third, he 'takes from the rich to give to the poor'. Fourth, he 'never kills but in self-defense or just revenge'. Fifth, if he survives, he returns to his people as an honourable citizen and member of the community. Indeed he never actually leaves the community. Sixth, he is admired, helped and supported by his people. Seventh, he dies invariably and only through treason, since no decent member of the community would help the authorities against him.[53]

The noble (or midnight) robber seeks to redress wrongs as he asserts his manhood in a cruel world, but his drive for state power is blunted by the fact that he is not part of a group which from birth is trained in the knowledge that one day they will rule. At the same time, despite the absence of deep fissures in the ruling élites, the racially divided, plural, fractured nature of Trinidadian society creates the illusion that individual mavericks, if they are sufficiently prepared, might be able to take the power. In this Byzantine world, very different from the layered and crystallized social structures of a Grenada, or further north, a Jamaica, revolutionary carpetbaggers still ply their trade; but when the insurrection has failed, they discard their costumes and seek shelter in the surety of Ash Wednesday.

To retrace our steps then, we can suggest that in 1970 there was a popular movement, but only incipient crisis up above, and no developed programme of insurrectionary tactics. In 1990, a simplified but clear notion of appropriate tactics existed, but there was definitely not a revolutionary situation. In 1979, there was a revolutionary situation and effective insurrectional tactics were adopted. These, together with a window of opportunity – the permissive world context – accounted for the success of the insurrection and the initial consolidation of a revolutionary government. But because of the inevitable way in which power was taken and given the structure of the (Leninist) NJM, a pattern was set which affected the future direction of the revolution.

Marx and Engels' assessment of revolution as an art and Lenin's fine-tuning of this framework – and not Black Power, C. L. R. James' thought or Islam – provided the most feasible blueprint for the seizure of power, as attested to in the success of the Grenadian example. But in its very pattern of clandestinity, hierarchy and centralism, insurrectional, Leninist tactics, lay the basis for a postrevolutionary hierarchical order fraught with negative consequences for the future of the victorious revolutionary movement. The paradox is that Leninism in Grenada may have led to success in 1979, but contributed immeasurably to defeat in 1983.

Conclusion

One of the central problems in understanding revolutions, as in any other social issue, is to arrive at some common agreement on the meaning of the central terms. While one might, with some imagination, seek to find the common thread which joins Trinidad in both 1970 and 1990 and Grenada in 1979, it becomes even more difficult when one ventures further afield. Is there really any common link between a minor mutiny in Trinidad with virtually no casualties and the prolonged and bloody civil war in El Salvador? Can the Grenada revolution, involving less than fifty in the initial overthrow, be discussed in the same breath as the sanguinary *Sendero Luminoso* uprising in Peru? Or are these all separate and discrete events, united only by a common title given to them, with the logical conclusion that any causal theory would inevitably be tautological and ideological?[54] While there are often vast quantitative and historical differences between these events and others too numerous to mention, there seems to be at least one underlying theme. At some point, persons (and in some instances large numbers of them) feel sufficiently aggrieved to abandon their normal obedience to the state and to take up arms against it without the assurance of success, and with the likelihood of drastic consequences if they fail. Volcanic approaches and structural approaches of various kinds can, at best, give only partial explanations of why uprisings and revolutions occur if they do not frontally address this human dimension.

While our Caribbean trio, with their compressed periods of actual uprising and physical confrontation may not provide the best examples, the relevant, and still not yet adequately answered question is why do people revolt? The most favourable ground for answering such a question would seem to lie in an examination of the cases where open-ended insurrections have persisted for years without any likelihood of early success, but yet with significant popular support. Clearly, if a rapid insurrectionary movement appears to be gaining ascendancy, then there is likely to be a bandwagon effect, with uncommitted persons eventually coming over to the side of the revolutionaries. But if there is no immediate victory in sight, why should large numbers of people support the movement with the likelihood of great personal privation and possibly death? Jeff Goodwin, in an important study of the Peruvian, Guatemalan and Salvadorean insurrectionary movements[55] arrives at novel conclusions as he debunks more traditional perspectives.

Goodwin argues that there has been a narrow dichotomy in the study of revolutions between those that have succeeded and those that have failed. There is a third category, he suggests, and these are persistent insurgencies, such as in Peru, Guatemala and El Salvador, which have shown their ability to persist despite severe governmental repression. Goodwin argues that the critical factor which leads people to support the movement is not economic. Even when land reform is initiated, the mainly peasant support remains committed to the cause. Equally, persistence cannot be attributed to some abstract notion of the role of external assistance, as movements such as those in El Salvador and Peru have remained viable without significant foreign assistance and, particularly in the case of El Salvador, with the government in receipt of massive military aid. Not even the initiation of electoral reform by itself, Goodwin suggests, leads to a cessation of support for the insurgents. What seems to be the critical factor is the degree of military repression:

> . . . mass based insurgencies . . . will not be defeated outright if the armed forces of such regimes do not broadly tolerate dissent and peaceful political protest, but instead, indiscriminately repress virtually all presumed regime opponents, armed and unarmed alike. The continuous, massive abuse of human rights, in other words, especially the indiscriminate repression of social sectors presumed to be sympathetic to the rebels, will serve – however unintentionally – to prolong and perhaps even strengthen a mass-based insurgency, *even if* incumbents have introduced competitive elections.[56]

Goodwin's hypothesis has been introduced because it provides stark empirical examples which fit almost seamlessly with Aya's "vicarious problem solving" approach. While Aya's analysis would seem to refer primarily to the actors above, *ie* those who lead the revolution, Goodwin is also suggesting that from below, an equally rational choice is taken. Faced with an arbitrary, repressive and unforgiving state, peasants or urban poor in a zone of confrontation have no option but to fight with the revolutionaries or face death at the hands of the government troops anyway. Such was the position of the mother in the Nicaraguan town of Esteli at the height of the Nicaragua insurrection of 1978-9: ". . . and I told my children that it would be best for them to go into the Frente [FSLN] because, if they didn't, the Guard would kill them anyway – just for being young, y'know."[57]

The converse of this point would also seem to have some validity, and that is that in situations in which the line between the military and the people has not been so sharply defined, in which the rule of law has not totally yielded to arbitrary power, then the likelihood of deep, persistent, popularly supported insurrections will be less. Thus, while groupings of frustrated, potential state builders, or maverick contenders for power may plot revolt as a result of accumulated grievances against the state, they are unlikely to gain the mass support which they require to give themselves legitimacy, unless the people themselves decide from their own agenda of grievances – on which the economic may rank very low – that there is no rational alternative but to act.

If a focus on the state and its location in a system of nation states is a necessary element in the study of revolution, it is nonetheless insufficient to explain why revolutions occur without a more detailed focus on the human actors, their motivations and their motivating ideas. And if a genuine appreciation of the human actors is to be attempted, they cannot be disembodied from the peculiar political trajectory out of which they emerge.

Notes

1   Insurrection is used as in the *Concise Oxford Dictionary* to mean "rising in open resistance to established authority; incipient rebellion". Thus, an uprising may be the first, intermediate, or last act in a revolutionary sequence or, alternatively, it may take place outside of the context of a revolutionary situation.

2   Theda Skocpol, *States and Social Revolutions* (Cambridge: Cambridge University Press, 1979).

3   See Rod Aya, "Theories of revolution reconsidered", *Theory and Society* 8, no. 1 (1979), for a discussion of volcanic approaches to the understanding of revolution. And, see Barrington Moore, *Social Origins of Dictatorship and Democracy* (Harmondsworth: Penguin, 1987) for the classic economy-centred approach to which Skocpol was opposed. Her position can be found in "A critical review of Barrington Moore's *Social Origins of Dictatorship and Democracy*", *Politics and Society* 4, no. 1 (fall 1973).

4   John Dunn, *Modern Revolutions: an Introduction to the Analysis of a Political Phenomenon* (Cambridge: Cambridge University Press, 1989).

5   Skocpol, *States and Social Revolutions*, 23-24. For a recent critical comment on Skocpol's approach in this vein, see D. Laitin and C. Warner, "Structure and irony in social revolutions", *Political Theory* 20, no. 1 (February 1992), 147-51.

6   See Farideh Farhi, "State disintegration and urban-based revolutionary crisis: a comparative analysis of Iran and Nicaragua", *Comparative Political Studies* 21, no. 2 (July 1988); Farideh Farhi, *States and Urban-Based Revolutions: Iran and Nicaragua*, University of Illinois Press, Champagne, 1990; Walter Goldfrank, "Theories of revolution and revolution without theory", *Theory and Society* 7, nos. 1 & 2 (1979); and Rod Aya, *Rethinking Revolutions and Collective Violence: Studies on Concept, Theory, and Method* (Amsterdam: Het Spinhuis, 1990).

7   Aya, *Rethinking Revolutions*, 9.

8   See Goldfrank, "Theories of revolution", 148.

9   Work on the 1970 Black Power revolution is notoriously inadequate. See for example, Ivor Oxaal, *Race and Revolutionary Consciousness* (Cambridge, MA, London: Schenkman, 1971); Lloyd Best, "The February revolution: causes and meaning", *Tapia* 12 (December 1970); Brian Meeks, "The development of the 1970 revolution in Trinidad and Tobago" (MSc thesis, University of the West Indies, Mona, 1977); Susan Craig, "Background to the 1970 confrontation in Trinidad and Tobago", in Susan Craig (ed), *Contemporary Caribbean: a Sociological Reader*. Vol. 2 (Port of Spain, Trinidad: The author, 1982); Selwyn Ryan, *Race and Nationalism in Trinidad and Tobago* (Toronto: University of Toronto Press, 1972); Paul Sutton, "Black Power in Trinidad and Tobago: the crisis of 1970", *Journal of Commonwealth and Comparative Politics* 21, no. 2 (July 1983), 116-31. A recent and important attempt to fill the gap is Selwyn Ryan and Taimoon Stewart (eds), *The Black Power Revolution 1970: a Retrospective* (Trinidad: ISER, 1995).

10 See Eric St. Cyr, "Some recent trends in prices and wages in Trinidad and Tobago" (Port of Spain, 1972). Mimeo.

11 See S. Ramesar, "A socioeconomic profile of the unemployed in Trinidad and Tobago, 1946-1968", in J. Harewood (ed), *Human Resources in the Commonwealth Caribbean* (St Augustine, Trinidad: ISER, 1972).

12 See Roy Thomas, *The Adjustment of Displaced Workers in a Labour Surplus Economy* (Mona, Jamaica: ISER, 1974).

13 See Meeks, "The development of the 1970 revolution", 162-70.

14 See Oxaal, *Race and Revolutionary Consciousness*, 23, for a chronology of the events.

15 Camejo's 1971 study of the business élite in Trinidad and Tobago showed that 78 percent of those interviewed fell into the category 'fair' or 'very fair' while only 3 percent were considered 'black'. See Acton Camejo, "Racial discrimination in employment in the private sector in Trinidad and Tobago: a study of the business élite and the social structure", *Social and Economic Studies* 20, no. 3 (1971).

16 In the mid fifties, Eric Williams had led a classic and effective anti-imperialist initiative to remove the US naval presence at Chaguaramas on the northwestern tip of Trinidad. When the eventual negotiations had been concluded, however, Williams had settled for a renewal of the agreements instead of the original demand of immediate withdrawal. This was the beginning of the decline of his relationship with the left wing of the nationalist movement, whose most celebrated representative was C. L. R. James. See Ryan's *Race and Nationalism*.

17 Ibid., 224-37. See also Lloyd Best, "From Chaguaramas to slavery", *New World Quarterly* 2, no. 1 (1965).

18 Oxaal, *Race and Revolutionary Consciousness*, 24.

19 See Paul Buhle, *C.L.R. James: the Artist as Revolutionary* (London: Verso, 1988); Stuart Hall, "C.L.R. James: a portrait", in P. Henry and P. Buhle (eds), *C. L R. James's Caribbean* (London and Basingstoke: Macmillan, 1992), 3-16; and C. L. R. James, *State Capitalism and World Revolution* (Chicago: Charles H. Kerr, 1986).

20 See Ryan, *Race and Nationalism*, 462.

21 Oxaal, *Race and Revolutionary Consciousness*, 39.

22 See Meeks, "The development of the 1970 revolution", 246-93.

23 Ian Belgrave, interview with Brian Meeks, in B. Meeks, ibid., 272.

24 See John Gaffar La Guerre, *The Politics of Communalism: the Agony of the Left in Trinidad and Tobago, 1930-1955* (Trinidad: Pan Caribbean Publications, 1982). For a literary and insightful account of left wing politics in Trinidad in this period, see Ralph de Boissiere, *Crown Jewel* (London: Picador, 1981).

25 C. L. R. James, "Marxism and the intellectuals: a critique of Raymond Williams' *Culture and Society*", in C. L. R. James (ed), *Spheres of Existence* (London: Alison & Busby Ltd, 1980), 117.

26 C. L. R. James, *The Black Jacobins: Toussaint L'Overture and the San Domingo Revolution* (New York: Vintage Books, 1989), 346.

27 Walter Rodney, prominent Guyanese historian and political activist, was killed by a bomb in Georgetown, Guyana in June 1980. A leader of the opposition Working People's Alliance (WPA), Rodney had purportedly taken personal delivery of an army walkie-talkie from a member of the Guyanese army. The walkie-talkie had been wired

with explosives and was detonated in Rodney's car shortly after it had been handed over. It was strongly felt – though not yet decisively proved in court – that the soldier had been a double agent and the bomb had been placed by the ruling People's National Congress (PNC) government, then led by Forbes Burnham.

28 C. L. R. James, "Walter Rodney and the question of power", in E. Alpers and P-M. Fontaine (eds), *Walter Rodney, Revolutionary and Scholar: a Tribute* (UCLA: Center for Afro-American Studies and African Studies Center, 1982).

29 F. Engels, *Germany: Revolution and Counter-Revolution* (Moscow: International Publishers, 1933), 100.

30 See V. I. Lenin, "Marxism and insurrection", in W. Pomeroy (ed), *Guerrilla Warfare and Marxism* (New York: International Publishers, 1973).

31 See M. G. Smith, "Structure and crisis in Grenada, 1950-1954", in *The Plural Society in the British West Indies* (Berkeley and Los Angeles: University of California Press, 1965), 269.

32 See Archie Singham, *The Hero and the Crowd in a Colonial Polity* (New Haven: Yale University Press, 1968).

33 See Bernard Coard, *The Role of the State in Agriculture* (Guyana: ISER/IDS, May 1978).

34 See George Brizan, *The Nutmeg Industry: Grenada's Black Gold* (St George's, Grenada n.d., n.p.).

35 *Abstract of Statistics, 1979* (St George's, Grenada: Central Statistical Office, 1980).

36 For the leadership's own interesting self-analysis of its members' social background, see "Questions and answers on NJM", *The New Jewel* 2, no. 8 (1974).

37 See "MAP Position Paper", no. 1 (1972).

38 See Brian Meeks, *Social Formation and People's Revolution: a Grenadian Study* (London: Karia, forthcoming).

39 Ibid. See chap. 3: "The revolutionary situation".

40 There are sharply differing views on the reasons for the collapse of the Grenada Revolution. The dominant view, roughly stated, is that an ultra-left clique conspired and was successful in overthrowing the more moderate and popular leadership of Prime Minister Maurice Bishop. See for example, Gordon Lewis, *Grenada: the Jewel Despoiled* (Baltimore and London: Johns Hopkins University Press, 1987), and Manning Marable, *African and Caribbean Politics: from Kwame Nkrumah to Maurice Bishop* (London: Verso, 1987). My own view is that the very Leninist nature of the party increasingly isolated it from the people, and that the causes of collapse are to be sought firstly in the nature of vanguardist politics and not in conspiracy. See Meeks, *Social Formation*; and Meeks, *Caribbean Revolutions and Revolutionary Theory: an Assessment of Cuba, Nicaragua and Grenada* (London and Basingstoke: Macmillan, 1993).

41 See Selwyn Ryan, *The Muslimeen Grab for Power: Race, Religion and Revolution in Trinidad and Tobago* (Port of Spain: Inprint Caribbean Ltd, 1991).

42 Ibid., 32-33.

43 For a detailed account of the legal and other issues surrounding the contested land at Mucurapo Road, see Ryan, ibid., chap. 3: "The trigger pulled".

44 See David Lehmann, *Democracy and Development in Latin America: Economics, Politics and Religion in the Post War Period* (Cambridge: Polity Press, 1990).

45 Abu Bakr, "Conversations with the Imam", interview by Keith Smith, in *Daily Express, Trinidad under Siege: the Muslimeen Uprising* (Port of Spain: Trinidad Express Newspapers Limited, 1990).

46 See Ryan, *Muslimeen Grab for Power*, 74. From as early as 1985, Bakr had warned in an interview with reporter Keith Smith that any attempt to demolish the mosque would be the beginning of serious conflict. In Bakr's words: "That will be the trigger. That would be it. No more talk. No more dialogue" (Abu Bakr, "Is Abu Bakr fighting a Holy War?", interview by Keith Smith, in *Daily Express*, 13*)*.

47 Estimates of damage as a result of looting and fires varied between TT$300 million and TT$500 million. According to *Daily Express* reporter Marlon Miller:

> Radios and amplifiers were a dime a dozen, there was every brand of liquor available, corn oil, shoes and clothes. Plastic hangers were strewn all over the road along with old, discarded sneakers. Even the vagrant at the corner of Charlotte Street and Independence Square put on a new tie and tried on a different pair of pants. And there were the fires. The first one was at the bottom of Charlotte Street just after eight o'clock and it lit up the night sky (*Daily Express, Trinidad under Seige*, 49).

48 For a useful chronology of the coup attempt and siege, see "Special report on the six-day siege", *Sunday Guardian (*2 September 1990), 22-23.

49 Is there a common lesson to be drawn here about the culture of Trinidadian politics? Why on both occasions do Trinidadian insurrectionists feel that after carrying out the most grave action against the state – its attempted overthrow, including in the 1990 case, some loss of life – they should be given amnesty? Perhaps a not facetious link might be drawn between the masquerade of Carnival Monday and Tuesday and the return to reality on Ash Wednesday. After Carnival, the mask is removed and all is forgiven. The analogy is straightforward.

50 Errol Hill, *The Trinidad Carnival: Mandate for a National Theatre* (Austin and London: University of Texas Press, 1972), 91.

51 For a discussion of the role of 'trajectories' in an understanding of current 'Third World' states, see Jean-François Bayart, "Finishing with the idea of the Third World: the concept of the political trajectory", in James Manor (ed), *Rethinking Third World Politics* (London and New York: Longman, 1991), 51-71.

52 Born in 1941, Lennox Phillips was the eighth of Ma Carmelita Phillips' fifteen children. He grew up in Rich Plain Diego Martin, a mixed community of poor and middle class families. At eighteen, he joined the police force where he stayed for nine years after which he migrated to Canada. There, he became a Muslim and studied for a time towards an engineering degree. Bakr can only with the greatest flexibility be considered a member of the state building middle. See "Special report", 9

53 Eric Hobsbawm, *Bandits* (New York: Pantheon Books, 1981).

54 See Stan Taylor, *Social Science and Revolutions* (London: Macmillan, 1984).

55 See Jeff Goodwin, "A theory of persistent insurgency: El Salvador, Guatemala and Peru in comparative perspective". Paper presented at the 17th International Congress of the Latin American Studies Association (LASA) (Los Angeles, California, 24-27 September 1992).

56 Goodwin, ibid., 31.

57 See "Testimony of a mother from Estelí", quoted in Carlos Vilas, *The Sandinista Revolution* (New York: Monthly Review Press, 1986), 122.

Chapter Six

The Imam,
the Return of Napoleon
and the End of History

At a certain point in their historical lives, social classes become
detached from their traditional parties. In other words, the traditional parties
in that particular organizational form, with the particular men who constitute,
represent, and lead them, are no longer recognized by their class (or fraction
of a class) as its expression. When such crises occur, the immediate situation
becomes delicate and dangerous, because the field is open for violent solutions,
for the activities of unknown forces, represented by charismatic 'men of destiny'.

Antonio Gramsci

My dearly beloved brothers and sisters [the poor and oppressed] of Trinidad
and Tobago, once more my heart cries out and bleeds for you from my cold,
dark and desolate cell at the Royal Jail, Frederick Street . . . I am filled with so
much sorrow and grief as I hear no voices and echoes from your silent pain of
suffering . . . Who is there now to raise a voice for you and the hungry babies, as
you are fed with empty promises by so many political prostitutes . . . Never again
will our people be unwilling or become invisible and indignant because they are
not served with true leadership, love and sacrifice or with the promptness and
fullness their great poverty and neglect demand . . .

Yasin Abu Bakr

This is the hill tall above the city where Taffy, a man who say he is Christ, put
himself up on a cross one burning midday and say to his followers: 'Crucify me!
Let me die for my people. Stone me with stones as you stone Jesus, I will love
you still!' And when they start to stone him in truth he get vex and start to cuss:
'Get me down! Get me down!' he say. 'Let every sinnerman bear his own
blasted burden; who is I to die for people who can't have sense enough to
know that they can't pelt a man with big stones when so much little pebbles
lying on the ground!'

Earl Lovelace

From the early hours of Wednesday, July 1, 1992 a large crowd had gathered outside the state prison on Frederick Street in Port of Spain. The excitement built steadily as 113 men, members of the Jamaat al Muslimeen had, over the previous two hours, walked to their freedom. But nothing could have anticipated the tumultuous uproar which greeted the appearance of the last of them. As the Imam, Yassin Abu Bakr, strode forth in his immaculate white garb, women howled, fists punched the air and a cry of "Allah U Akbar" was shouted by all. Responding later to questions from the press at the Muslimeen headquarters on Mucurapo Road, Bakr indicated that he had no regrets, and that as Muslims, they were free men and had to take the lead to deliver the people: "The people don't know how to use a gun. All free men have guns and land. There must be a vanguard. Somebody must take the lead."[1]

What he was referring to, of course, was the attempted overthrow of the state of Trinidad and Tobago in 1990, the high point of a bizarre sequence of events which, depending on the approach taken to history, could have begun in 1985, 1970, 1937 or even earlier.

July 27, 1990 was a big day in Port of Spain. It was a Friday, the end of the month, and pay day in the capital city. It was also the day on which a crucial match was to be played between the Trinidad and Tobago and Jamaica football teams to help decide the Caribbean champions. A capacity crowd had gathered at the National Stadium in the southwest of the city to watch the feature. As it was about to begin, spectators in the topmost seats of the bleachers noticed thick, black clouds billowing from a fire somewhere towards the centre of the city. While those in the stadium pondered the significance of the smoke. Their friends and relatives at home watching television were soon to be confronted with a more dramatic and startling reality. Regular programming was abruptly interrupted, and the director of news at the lone television station, Trinidad and Tobago Television (TTT), suddenly appeared live with the leader of the Jamaat al Muslimeen, Yasin Abu Bakr. Easily recognizable by most Trinidadians in his flowing white outfit and black fez, Bakr announced that the government had been overthrown, that even as he spoke, Prime Minister A. N. R. Robinson and his cabinet had been arrested and would be put on trial, and that the army – or at least a part of it – was behind the overthrow.[2]

Earlier that afternoon, over one hundred members of the Jamaat had left from their base on Mucurapo Road and from other unascertained points on their mission to take over the government of Trinidad and Tobago. One small group attacked the police headquarters on St Vincent Street, shot the sentry on duty and detonated a bomb which eventually burnt the century-old building to the ground – the source of the smoke seen from the stadium. Another group, heading further down St Vincent Street, set fire to the studios of the National Broadcasting Service (NBS) and retreated. Workers at the site subsequently doused the flames and the

NBS remained on air for the duration of the crises. Then, a larger group of some fifty men led by the Wazir for Education of the Jamaat, Bilaal Abdullah, invaded the Red House, seat of the country's parliament, and took the Prime Minister hostage, along with members of his cabinet, government and opposition MPs and others – some seventeen in all. A similar scene was enacted on Maraval Road at the studios of TTT, but with Abu Bakr himself in charge.

Over the next few hours he was to appear repeatedly on the air, railing against the corruption of the government, declaring himself the leader of the revolution, announcing by decree the abolition of the highly unpopular value added tax (VAT), indicating that new elections would be held in ninety days and calling on the people not to engage in looting. But while there were no defections from the military in support of Bakr, and while no popular uprising accompanied his announcements, almost on cue, his 'no looting' appeal was responded to with an orgy of looting in downtown Port of Spain and along the urban east-west corridor of northern Trinidad. Few retail establishments were spared as the disgruntled urban poor sought to reclaim in stolen goods what they had lost over the previous months and years in recession and IMF inspired structural adjustment.[3]

As events unfolded on the first morning following the action, it was apparent that what had begun as an attempt to overthrow the government, had, by force of events, been transformed into a hostage situation. The people had risen, but in order to satisfy narrow economic ends and not in support of the Muslimeen; the army and police had remained loyal to the regime; and, critically, not only was there a rump group of ministers on the outside to form a mini-cabinet, but the acting president – the head of state – was free and thus, constitutionally, the government remained intact.[4] From this moment on, with large contingents of well armed soldiers and police surrounding the Red House and TTT, the real issue was whether the Muslimeen would surrender, and, if so, what would be their terms, and at what human cost.

Despite serious divisions between the prime minister and other captives on one hand and some of those who remained on the outside, an amnesty was eventually agreed on and signed by acting President Carter. Dated July 28, 1990, it said:

> I, Joseph Emmanuel Carter as required of me by the document Major points of Agreement hereby grant an amnesty to all those involved in acts of insurrection commencing approximately 5.50 p.m. on Friday 27th July 1990 and ending upon the safe return of all members of parliament held captive on 27th July 1990. This amnesty is granted for the purpose of avoiding physical injury to the members of parliament referred to above and is therefore subject to the complete fulfillment of the obligation safely to return them.[5]

Almost two years later, on July 1, 1992, after charges including treason, murder, arson and unlawful imprisonment had been filed against the 114 insurrectionists; after the issue had been taken through the Trinidad and Tobago legal system and then on to the Privy Council in Great Britain, Justice Clebert Brooks ultimately ruled that the amnesty had been valid; that it had not been obtained under duress; and that, therefore, the applicants should be released immediately with costs against the state.[6]

Since the 1990 insurrection attempt, numerous statements of varying quality and length[7] have appeared in an attempt to chronicle the events or to grasp their significance or both in the wider context of Caribbean politics. Most have recognized the connection between the 1990 events and the 1970 'Black Power revolution': Between February and April 1970, tens of thousands of urban, overwhelmingly black Trinidadians, led by the National Joint Action Committee (NJAC), marched and demonstrated throughout the country. They were demanding 'Black Power' – a slogan which encompassed national ownership of the economy, unity between Afro and Indo-Trinidadians, and an assertion of the role of black people in all areas of the country's life.[8]

On 13 April, the deputy leader of the ruling People's National Movement (PNM), Arthur Napoleon Raymond (A. N. R.) Robinson, urging a conciliatory line between the government and the demonstrators, but fearing that a hard line position was winning the day, resigned in protest from the government. On April 22, a state of emergency was declared and, in response, a part of the army, led by young officers, rebelled, purportedly in support of their 'black brothers' in Port of Spain. However, on the way from their base at Chaguaramas on the Western tip of the island to the capital, they were confronted by loyal army units, refused to engage them, and, after some moments of hesitation, negotiations were initiated. A verbal agreement was established, including amnesty for those who had rebelled and their right to retain arms, but as soon as the rebels had put down their weapons they were arrested and charged with mutiny and treason – although, it is important to note, some years later they were freed as the result of a general pardon. The striking parallels between the two events – twenty years apart – led Selwyn Ryan to muse as to whether 1990 simply represented the latest phase of an "unfinished revolution".[9]

Pantin's Economy-Centred Approach

Dennis Pantin, in a commentary that was one of the most penetrating, has argued that the root cause of the 1990 crisis lay in "the continued failure to transform the rentier economy, and hence state".[10] He argues that there were three main elements in the political crisis:

The first was the Muslimeen uprising which led to the seizure of the mainly governmental parliamentarians present at the sitting of Parliament, as well as of journalists and support staff in the country's sole television station. The second element was widespread looting, and the third [was] an even more widespread expressed lack of sympathy for, if not wished demise of certainly the governmental hostages.[11]

Pantin asks whether these three elements were caused, as some pundits were suggesting, by the fall out from the 1988 IMF standby agreement, under which Trinidad had undertaken a programme of structural adjustment to its economy.[12] In relation to the actual Muslimeen insurrection attempt, he suggests that "the IMF agreements were coincidental to an action that would have been attempted once the political conditions, whatever their causes, were considered to be opportune".[13]

With regard to the looting, he convincingly posits that this would have occurred in any context where law and order had broken down, and was, therefore, neither unique to Trinidad nor to the specific event. However, with regard to the sustained lack of sympathy for the government where, in polls conducted later, as much as 73 percent of the people expressed negative attitudes towards the prime minister,[14] he suggested that the IMF agreements only formed part of a wider explanatory picture. Rentier states gain political support by extracting rent from traditional exports such as oil. They use this to retain power through the fostering of patron-client relationships with the dependent population. When rents are high, the system functions in its hierarchical manner, but when rents fall, the state is unable to distribute scarce benefits, support falls and crisis results. Thus:

> The Trinidad and Tobago experience shows that in this century there has been at least one unequivocal slump period in the 1930s. There also was a social upheaval in 1970 marked by a combination of worsening economic conditions and hence, shrinking rent, and disappointment with the failure of the PNM to deliver on its promised decolonization of the society following political independence in 1962. In each of these two above-cited historical examples the attempt to impose an overly inequitable burden on the most vulnerable breached the society's pain threshold leading to the so-called 1937 riots and the 1970 Black Power or 'February' revolution.
>
> The 1990 political crisis also coincides with a substantially reduced rent and efforts to shrink the shares going to the most vulnerable groups since as early as 1982.[15]

Pantin's analysis, in examining the structure of the Trinidad economy, the character of its insertion into the global system and the particular moment of international and local recession, points to an important, indeed vital element in understanding the 1990 crisis. But there are also at least two serious weaknesses in this approach. First, it fails to focus on the state as an object of analysis in its own right – indeed, as a central factor in determining the origins and course of the crisis; and second, it fails to examine the character and motivations of the insurrectionists. For, after all, it is Abu Bakr and his men who seized a particular moment, and without their intervention that moment might well have passed.

The weakness in an economy-centred approach is most evident in his argument that the inequitable economic burden cracked the society's 'pain threshold'. The stress placed by Pantin is on the economic variable,[16] but the hidden object of analysis is this concept of the pain threshold. The notion that a society has a pain threshold implies something quantifiable, or at least identifiable; suggests that it may vary from society to society; but more critically, implies that the most important thing may not be the degree of frustration and dissatisfaction which is brewing *per se*, but rather whether it is sufficient to breach the pain threshold 'dyke'. The implication, in other words, is that a society could hypothetically undergo severe structural adjustment, with high levels of unemployment, 'stagflation', etc., but if its pain threshold is high enough, then it will remain stable. Such an approach – which is never Pantin's focus – might explain why both Jamaica and Guyana which have undertaken severe structural adjustment measures over the past two decades have not experienced profound and overt threats to the survival of the state; and why Grenada, in both 1974 and 1979, without the severe economic pressures associated with any of the above three, experienced revolutionary upheaval in 1974 and the seizure of power by a revolutionary party in 1979.

The weakness in Pantin's analysis is that in tracing the impact of cyclical crises on the society, he leaves out a critical aspect of the picture, *ie* the particular character of the Trinidad and Tobago state as a peculiar state form with its own history, political culture and 'trajectory'.[17] Following Bayart, we can suggest that to understand a society's trajectory is to grasp the peculiarities of its history, its relationship with the colonial power and the subsequent colonial rupture and of its current conjuncture, without falling prey to evolutionary or teleological approaches. It is possible, Bayart argues, both to accept the heterogeneity of societies and at the same time engage in comparative analysis to better understand their individual peculiarities. Structuralist or economistic accounts are inadequate, because in the end ". . . the social foundations of the state cannot be analysed without simultaneously taking the cultural construction of politics into account".[18]

Re-imagining the Caribbean State

There have been numerous attempts to define and understand the character of the West Indian state. M. G. Smith's plural approach saw the state as existing above society, as dominant, but also as the mediator between antagonistic ethnic groups who shared little in common.[19] C. Y. Thomas has more recently mooted the notion of the 'authoritarian state' which rules from above with little genuinely democratic content as symptomatic of peripheral states and with relevance to the Caribbean.[20] Carl Stone has described the Jamaican political system as based on clientelistic relations where the patrons dominate, but in which the clients, not infrequently, get their way,[21] while Obika Gray has contradicted this by describing Jamaican politics with the more orthodox notion of authoritarian democracy.[22] With due respect to the relative value of these different approaches, a far more useful way to address the problem, particularly from the point of view of understanding insurrections and revolutionary events, might be a comparative approach, with the focus of analysis being the *strength* of the particular state.

Strength of state is not here used in the Weberian[23] sense to mean the extent or complexity of bureaucratic organization, though this may be a contributory factor. Instead we are referring to the extent to which a state is resilient in the face of threats to its continued authority and dominance. Dominance is here used as a modified version of the Gramscian notion of hegemony, or the ability of the state, and the alliance of social groups who normally dominate in it, to exercise effective intellectual, moral and political leadership.[24] A resilient state is one which is able to absorb, incorporate, head off in advance, or, if necessary, crush effectively significant threats to its survival, integrity and coherence. A fragile state is one in which the nature of its domination is such that it is often unable to respond adequately to tests to its survival. As a direct result of this weakness – a fact well known to those who reside within its boundaries – tests to its integrity occur more frequently.

With this in mind, we might suggest three (not all inclusive) state forms which have evolved in the contemporary Caribbean: the strong state, of which Jamaica is the model; the fragile state, of which the outstanding example is Trinidad and Tobago; and the fractured state, best illustrated in the case of Grenada from the pre-independence period of the early sixties until the 1979 revolution. The trend of thought which led to the characterization of the Trinidadian state as fragile, comes in the form of an anecdote.

During the 1990 crisis and subsequently in many discussions of the issue in and out of Jamaica, there has been one recurrent conclusion, *ie* that "it could not have happened in Jamaica". My interpretation of the meaning of this suggests three interdependent interpretations:

- Had the Muslimeen been Jamaicans, they would not have contemplated overthrow, because they would have known in advance that the consequences for failure would be dire.
- Had they, despite this knowledge, tried, no one would have emerged alive, because the military option rather than the soft solution, would have been taken.
- Had the military option not been the chosen path, then the amnesty would never have been adhered to.

Of course, there is no way of ascertaining what might have happened in a hypothetical seizure of parliament in Jamaica, although the ruthlessness of sections of the Jamaican police force is well documented, but such a strong feeling is worth further examination. The approach to understanding the fragility of the Trinidadian state might instead lie in a comparative assessment of the relative responses to the events of 1970 and 1990.

The Fragile State

In the weeks before the declaration of the State of Emergency in 1970, while massive, increasingly anti-government demonstrations took place on a daily basis and some buildings in the capital were burnt, there was prevarication and division on the right course of action within the ruling PNM government. Thus, while A. N. R. Robinson was calling for conciliation, Karl Hudson-Phillips was calling for a firm response and Prime Minister Williams wavered between the two.[25] This indecisiveness once again appears as the central element in 1984/5 when the issue of the Muslimeen occupation of the land at No. 1 Mucurapo Road came to national attention. The issue had been a contentious one, going back to 1969 when the Williams government had granted a piece of land to the Islamic Missionaries Guild (IMG) in the swampy Mucurapo area to build a cultural/religious centre. The government initially denied any connection between the IMG and the Jamaat al Muslimeen who had later occupied the land and sought in January 1985 to demolish buildings, including an unfinished mosque, which it was argued were being illegally built by squatters. When, however, police arrived to carry out the order, they were obstructed from doing so by a large and hostile crowd and were forced to retreat.

In 1986, A. N. R. Robinson and his National Alliance for Reconstruction won the general election with a resounding mandate. Decisively ending twenty-eight years of PNM domination, the NAR received 65.8 percent of the votes and 33 seats, leaving the PNM with 31 percent of the votes and a rump parliamentary group of three.[26] With his multiracial coalition, conciliatory 'One Love' slogan and a general mood of euphoria throughout the country, Robinson no doubt felt that he had been vindicated after his resignation in 1970 and almost two decades out of office. Napoleon, as it were, had returned in triumph from exile in the political wilderness. For Bakr and the Jamaat, the NAR victory also signalled hope. They had supported some of Robinson's candidates and the NAR, in turn, had advocated in its manifesto a moratorium for all squatters on government lands during which no building would be destroyed, to facilitate the regularization of ownership.[27] Discussions surrounding the land at Mucurapo were initiated between the Islamic Missionaries Guild and the new Minister of Local Government Brinsley Samaroo. These stretched on through 1988, and despite apparent breakthroughs no final agreement was ever reached. From then until April 1990 when soldiers occupied a part of the land without, however, hindering the business of the Jamaat, the issue remained unresolved.

Bakr had confronted the Trinidadian state and, by remaining on the land with all his organization's buildings intact, appeared to have won. It is little wonder that in the years following the 1985 standoff, Bakr, in numerous public meetings not only criticized the government, but made numerous public threats against individual ministers. In April 1986 for example, in response to continued, if ineffective harassment from the police and the City Council, Bakr said: "We will not fight them when they surround the mosque, we will take them in their sleep."[28] The response of the *Trinidad Guardian*, always the voice of the conservative establishment, is noteworthy. In response to Bakr's threats, the editorial of April 22, 1986 warned that the toleration of the settlement at Mucurapo in breach of the law had legitimized a pole of lawlessness in the society, and that Bakr was now an untouchable in his own kingdom.[29] The response of then Minister of National Security John Donaldson to the earlier failure to evict the Muslimeen is also noteworthy. When criticized for treating Bakr with kid gloves, Donaldson responded that he was not seeking to protect Bakr but to avoid bloodshed. The police, he noted, were not prepared for what they encountered and acted wisely. He also noted that a visit by the pope was only a few weeks away and it was deemed important to avoid any confrontation with a religious group that might give rise to embarrassment.[30]

We can once again point to a specific political culture, manifest in the behaviour exhibited in the resolution of both crises. Recall that in 1970, rather than confronting loyal members of the military and fighting it out to the bitter end, the rebels sought almost immediately to negotiate, and were willing to lay down their arms on the mere verbal agreement of amnesty. As we have mentioned, this amnesty was almost immediately ignored and the men were charged with mutiny and treason. In 1990, while there were sharp exchanges of gunfire between the soldiers and the insurrectionists, and while many commented on the discipline and commitment of the Muslimeen,[31] what had initially been described by Bakr as 'overthrow' was later downgraded, in his own words, to "a little family squabble we're trying to patch up".[32] An amnesty was again the critical demand; however, on this occasion not only was it written, but also signed by the head of state. While the government sought to travel the old route of arguing that agreements could be breached once they are made under duress, in the end the strength of the evidence and the intervention of the Privy Council held sway, and Bakr and his comrades-in-arms were freed.

If these two events are taken separately, then specific arguments might be advanced as to why 1970 evolved as it did, or why the amnesty, for example, was adhered to in 1992. However, when we approach them together, we are looking instead at a broader picture – the specific crisis response of a particular type of state on a particular trajectory. Many of the overtly cultural features have been well documented. Thus, in the late nineteenth century, when a pattern of hierarchy based on colour and class had been established in Jamaica for well over a century, Trinidad was still at the frontier. Gordon Rohlehr aptly describes it:

> . . . wildcat immigration into a country of small towns, large plantations, virgin forests, extensive swamps and wildernesses of sodden mudtracks; its result in unemployment, urban overcrowding, street gangs and the desire to seek revenge on the privileged, both verbally by scandalizing their women in song, and visually, by attacking with open obscenity their sexual prudery and hypocrisy.[33]

Gordon Lewis, in his inimitable way, also understood the significance of Trinidad entering the anglophone sphere relatively late, in 1802:

> It meant the survival of a certain Franco-Spanish cultural imprint, not least of all the tradition, in the form of the Cabildo, of a local government system . . . The comparative shortness, again, of the slavery period meant that the Trinidadian Negro, unlike his Barbadian or Kittitian brothers, escaped the debilitating effect of centuries of bond slavery, which perhaps explains today his style of raucous ebulliency as compared to the social deference of those others. The general Trinidadian eudaemonism – invariably the first impression of visitors – certainly lends itself to some such interpretation.[34]

When these genetic features are placed in the context of a society which, if not plural in the strict sense, is nonetheless sharply fractured along lines of tribal loyalty[35] – Indians and Blacks, North and South, Tobagonians and Trinidadians – then the outlines of an alternative approach to the character of the Trinidadian state becomes somewhat clearer.

The critical feature which explains the notion of fragility is the indecisiveness of the Trinidadian state. Indecisiveness emerges from a society in which the ruling party depends for its electoral survival on the loyalty given to it by an alliance of ethnic groups.[36] When members of the core group protest, even violently, against the government, care has to be taken with how they are handled.

There is no deep-seated belief in the state *qua* state of either those in power or of the people in general. Hegemony is incomplete. This reality 'stays' the hand of the state in moments of crisis, for it fears that if its core ethnic group is isolated, then the basis for remaining in power will ultimately be undermined. Equally, contenders for power, or disgruntled citizens, particularly if they come from the same ethnic group as those in charge of the state, feel that if they bid for power, they have an outside chance of succeeding. The fragility and tenuousness of the alliances at the top, the porousness and lack of closure – the absence, in other words, of hegemony in its sense of intellectual, moral and political leadership – enhances the feeling that success is possible, and suggests to them that failure may not lead to the ultimate penalty.

Aya has argued that in revolutionary situations, insurgents seek to satisfy some want or aspiration and "search till they find a course of action whose outcome's pay off (value)" meets or exceeds their "aspiration level".[37] In this sense, they do not maximize their objectives, but they 'satisfice', or pick the best available option of which they are aware. Applied to armed revolutionaries, such a rational choice approach might conclude that contenders for power do not arbitrarily risk their lives in military activity, unless (a) the regime is so patently weak that the chances of winning are good; (b) there is the possibility in the specific geography of the country for tactical retreat into, for example, a guerrilla hinterland after the failed uprising; (c) the likelihood of the state forgiving and forgetting is a real possibility and (d) there is a fourth option outside the realm of rational choice, in which the insurgents disregard logic, are fanatical and willing to die for a higher cause.

While the fourth option might be considered a real possibility given the apparent Islamic fanaticism of Bakr and his followers, the ultimate decision to put themselves at the mercy of the Trinidadian state rather than fight to the finish suggests a far from fanatical calculation. In the end, Bakr and his deputy Abdullah recognized that they could not win. There was, however, an instinctive feeling that the amnesty might hold, for the Trinidadian state had evinced a tendency to accommodate rebellion of even the treasonous kind, particularly in instances when the rebels derived from the dominant ethnic element.

We can digress briefly in order to sketch two other kinds of Caribbean state. In the case of Jamaica, the postindependence political scene has been characterized by sharp political skirmishes between the People's National Party and the Jamaica Labour Party. This came to a head in 1980 when over 800 persons were killed in the run-up to the general election.[38] Yet, after each contentious exercise, the losing party concedes and, despite occasional boycotts, eventually assumes its position as loyal opposition. Insurgent attempts to shift this two-party monopoly, such as the nascent Black Power movement of the late sixties, are either co-opted into the dominant party system or, as with the case of the Marxist Workers Party of Jamaica (WPJ), kept out in the cold by force of tradition and instrumentalist action until, demoralized and faced with a new international situation, they implode.[39] On the rare occasion of a more overt threat to this state, the action – as with the arrest, trial and execution of Ronald Henry and his co-putschists in 1960[40] – is swift and decisive. The end result is a solid, hegemonic bloc, contentious on the outside, but accommodative within, born out of a society rigidly delineated along lines of class and colour, and based on the assumed and largely accepted right and ability of the educated élites to rule. Counter-hegemonic forces are constantly at work, and never more so than in today's Jamaica, but the established and flexible system of élite hegemony is far from moribund.

The Grenadian case is a third example in which Eric Gairy, representing a newly insurgent black element, gained dominance in the state but was never able to establish a truly hegemonic hold over the state and society. Such a situation was fraught with the potential for crisis. From 1951, when the British government called on Gairy to mediate and rejected the armed force of the planters in order to end the islandwide disturbances,[41] and even more so in the late sixties and early seventies as Gairy tightened his grip, it was clear that there was no consensus as to how the state should be constituted and governed. The likelihood for aggrieved, potential revolutionaries entering into this fissure and seizing power is great, if other conditions facilitating revolution exist.[42]

From this triangulation, the Trinidadian state stands in the middle. It cannot, certainly, be described as a consolidated hegemonic bloc as is the case with Jamaica. It is shot through with communal loyalties which fracture that possibility and create instead a Byzantine market place, where bargaining and jostling are the order of the day. But it is not a fractured state in the Grenadian sense, in which the fissures are so great, that reconciliation and hegemony are almost impossible.

The Imam

Where in all of this can we fit the Imam and his followers? To understand Bakr, we need to remember that his social background is very different from that of most of the recent left wing Caribbean politicians who preceded him. Maurice Bishop's father was a businessman and he went on to study law at the Inns of Court in London. Trevor Munroe's father was the Jamaican Director of Public Prosecutions and he, sometime leader of the WPJ, was a Rhodes Scholar. Bakr's father was a soldier. He was the eighth of Ma Carmelita Phillips' fifteen children and grew up in humble circumstances in Richplain Road, Diego Martin, on the western outskirts of Port of Spain. After nine years in the police service, he opted out on medical grounds and moved to Canada where he became a Muslim.[43] Bakr is the product of Trinidadian frontier society in which the maverick contender, the man who is not a Rhodes scholar, who has never been to university, perceives that he has an equal right to be taken seriously and to contend for state power.

Bakr emerges at the end of a long narrative of failures. It is the failure of the Rhodes scholars and the university graduates – of 1970 – and of NJAC; the failure of the PNM to capitalize on the oil boom and of the 'one love' strategy of Robinson's NAR to bring the society together. It is all of these things and the falling living standards, growing anomie, increasing communalism and disillusionment which helped to bring the Muslimeen to the fore. Indeed, even as the Jamaat was a member of the Summit of People's Organizations (SOPO),[44] as Lloyd Best suggests,[45] the Muslimeen action confirms the failure of SOPO, MOTION (Movement for Social Transformation) and other elements of the traditional left to move beyond a narrow, statist notion of politics.

Bakr is Janus-faced. He represents simultaneously the future and the past. His organization, in its genuine if controversial attempts to solve the drug problem by direct action against the pushers and by rehabilitation programmes, represents an Anglo-Caribbean variant of the Latin American *basismo*[46] tradition. In an interview with Keith Smith in 1985, it is evident that Bakr was conscious of the novelty in his approach:

> As portrayed by Abu Bakr, these black Trinidadians were different from the ordinary cut of Trinidadians of African ancestry in that 'we have an operation here in which we cut out "dependecitis"' – and he cited a number of examples to prove the point: We have had a school here for years which we run without any help from the government, without asking them for a black cent and we have managed to go in places at the level of the convents and colleges. We have built a mosque here by ourselves without getting a nail from anybody. We have an organization here that operates completely independent from any other organization and these things are not the norm for African people and such independence threatens those people who are used to having us depend on them.[47]

It is a new and important phenomenon, of the poor helping the poor, without dependence on patronage and the state. But here lies the paradox: for while Bakr sought (and seeks) to break the statist bond, to redefine the relationship between civil society and the state, he does so with medieval attitudes on the question of women's rights;[48] a highly authoritarian and disciplinarian structure; a fundamentalist and prophetic sense of destiny and leadership; and an implicit distrust for democracy, evident in his praxis of 'direct action'.[49]

Bakr is not simply, as Searle posits, a "backward-looking alternative",[50] a throwback to the past. He is the leader of the first genuinely postmodernist political organization to emerge in the Caribbean, with all the implications for ". . . irony, artifice, randomness, anarchy, fragmentation, pastiche and allegory"[51] inherent in that term.

In the summer of 1989, American philosopher Francis Fukuyama published his prophetic and now well-ploughed article "The End of History?"[52] In it, and subsequently in his book of a similar title,[53] he argued that the imminent collapse of the Soviet system signalled the triumph of liberalism and the Western idea, and that the central issue in the dialectical unravelling of modern history has been the issue of self-recognition which had now triumphed. If Bakr's abortive insurrection of 1990 tells us anything, it is that below a line extending from Washington, through London and Paris and on via Berlin and Moscow to Tokyo, history is continuing at breakneck speed. Certainly, the traditional narrative of the left has been exhausted; but so too has a particular notion of Western democracy in its Third World export variation. However, in the absence of grand narratives, prophecy asserts itself.

Bakr may be quirky and considered anachronistic, but he is now free, and given the peculiar and fragile nature of Trinidadian society and its state, and the warm reception he received on his release last summer, one thing appears to be evident, and that is that in the fractured marketplace of the Trinidadian drama his role is not yet over. Ole mas has ended. Las' lap is yet to come.

Notes

1 *Daily Express* (July 2, 1992), 6.

2 See Raoul Pantin, "The days of wrath: an eyewitness account of the capture of Television House (TTT)", in *Trinidad Under Siege – the Muslimeen Uprising: 6 Days of Terror* (Port of Spain: Daily Express Newspapers Ltd, 1990), 30-37.

3 Estimates of damage ranged from TT$300 million to $500 million, primarily in the retail sector. See, for example, David Maynard, "The lunacy of looting", *Daily Express* (August 1,1990). Not all commentators considered the looters as little more than lunatics. An unidentified writer in *Motion*, the paper of the tiny leftist Movement for Social Transformation, saw the whole event as the expression of the still unfocused social anger of the dispossessed, whose vision would be less clouded the next time around. See "I the looter", *Motion* (October 1990).

4 The President, Noor Hassanali had been out of the country and was not able to return until later, when critical decisions had already been taken by acting President Carter. On the constitutional question, see Hamid Ghany, "The Constitution prevailed", *Caricom Perspective* 49 (July-December 1990).

5 *Exhibit "B.A.1" in the affidavit of Richard Bradshaw, Carlton Alexander, Edward Bosland and Dominic Bethelmy, 9 October 1990.* Hostility to any compromise agreement was particularly severe from the police, who had suffered the loss of a number of colleagues and the destruction of their headquarters. Repeated ceasefires appear to have been breached by renegade policemen, many of whom were calling over the police radio for the elimination of both the parliamentarians and the Muslimeen. See Sherrie Ann DeLeon, "Coup – Day 2 – Radio Log", *TNT Mirror* (August 17,1990).

6   See "The amnesty ruling: Carter had many choices", *Trinidad Guardian* (2 July 1992).

7   Among the many, the most comprehensive is: Selwyn Ryan, *The Muslimeen Grab for Power: Race, Religion and Revolution in Trinidad and Tobago* (Port of Spain: Inprint Caribbean Ltd, 1991). Others include: Neville Duncan, "The Muslimeen revolt", *Caricom Perspective* 49 (July-December 1990); Dennis Pantin, "IMF/World Bank agreements and the July 27, 1990 political crisis in Trinidad and Tobago: cause or coincidence?" (Draft paper for *Cimarron*); and Vitruvius E.T. Furlonge-Kelly, *The Silent Victory* (Port of Spain: Golden Eagle Enterprises, 1991).

8   See Raoul Pantin, *Black Power Day* (Port of Spain: Hatuey Productions, 1990); Brian Meeks, "The development of the 1970 revolution in Trinidad and Tobago" (MSc thesis, UWI, Mona, 1976); Ivor Oxaal, *Race and Revolutionary Consciousness* (Cambridge, London: Schenkman, 1971); Selwyn Ryan, *Race and Nationalism in Trinidad and Tobago* (Toronto: University of Toronto Press, 1972); and Susan Craig, "Background to the 1970 confrontation in Trinidad and Tobago", in Susan Craig (ed), *Contemporary Caribbean: a Sociological Reader.* Vol. 2 (Port of Spain: The author, 1982).

9   See Ryan, *Muslimeen Grab for Power*, 335.

10 Pantin, "Political crisis", 4.

11 Ibid., 4-5.

12 Among the main elements of the Trinidad programme were the introduction of a regressive 15% value added tax; a 10% cut in public sector wages; a suspension of both cost of living allowances (COLA) granted to public sector employees and merit increases; and what was considered by many unions as an unrealistic 6% wage increase offered to their workers by the Industrial Court in the face of much higher levels of inflation.

13 Pantin, "Political crisis", 5.

14 See Ryan, *Muslimeen Grab for Power*, 227. In a survey conducted in June 1991, Ryan found that as a result of the events of a year earlier, only 9% of the sample were more sympathetic to Robinson while 32% were less sympathetic and a further 41% remained negative towards him. An almost exact percentage expressed negative attitudes towards his party, the National Alliance for Reconstruction (NAR).

15 Pantin, "Political crisis", 14.

16 Pantin's analysis is very close to what Aya describes as the volcanic approach to understanding revolutions. This, broadly speaking, encompasses a number of thinkers who see revolutions as originating out of the build up of frustration in the minds of men, resulting ultimately in a volcanic explosion of violence. Such an approach, he argues, is inadequate, because it disregards the independent role of the state, and makes an unwarranted assumption that frustration is necessarily and automatically channelled into aggression. See Rod Aya, *Rethinking Revolutions and Collective Violence: Studies on Concept, Theory and Method* (Amsterdam: Het Spinhuis, 1990); and "Theories of revolution reconsidered", *Theory and Society* 8, no. 1 (1979).

17 See Jean-François Bayart, "Finishing with the idea of the Third World: the concept of the political trajectory", in James Manor (ed), *Rethinking Third World Politics* (London and New York: Longman, 1991).

18 Ibid., 59.

19 See M. G. Smith, *The Plural Society in the British West Indies* (Kingston: Sangster's, 1974), especially chap. 7, "The plural framework of Jamaican society".

20 See C. Y. Thomas, *The Rise of the Authoritarian State in Peripheral Societies* (New York: Monthly Review, 1986).

21 See Carl Stone, *Democracy and Clientelism in Jamaica* (New Brunswick and London: Transaction Books, 1980).

22 See Obika Gray, *Radicalism and Social Change in Jamaica, 1960-1972* (Knoxville: University of Tennessee Press, 1991).

23 See, for example, Max Weber, *Economy and Society.* 2 vols. (New York: Bedminster Press, 1978), and Anthony Giddens, *Capitalism and Modern Social Theory: an Analysis of the Writings of Marx, Durkheim and Weber* (1971; reprint, Cambridge: Cambridge University Press, 1990).

24 See Antonio Gramsci, *Selections from the Prison Notebooks* (London: Lawrence and Wishart, 1986), 55-60.

25 See Ryan, *Muslimeen Grab for Power*, 335.

26 Selwyn Ryan, *The Disillusioned Electorate: the Politics of Succession in Trinidad and Tobago* (Port of Spain: Inprint Caribbean Ltd, 1989), 85.

27 See Ryan, *Muslimeen Grab for Power*, 67.

28 See "Saga began Jan. 1969", *Special Report, Sunday Guardian* (2 September 1990).

29 See *Special Report, Sunday Guardian* (2 September 1990), 61.

30 Ryan, *Muslimeen Grab for Power,* 62.

31 See Pantin, "The days of wrath", 36.

32 Raoul Pantin, "Among the believers: Emancipation Day", *Daily Express* (14 August 1990).

33 Gordon Rohlehr, *Calypso and Society in Pre-Independence Trinidad* (Trinidad: The author, 1990), 19.

34 Gordon Lewis, *The Growth of the Modern West Indies* (London: McGibbon and Kee, 1968), 197.

35 In LaGuerre's *The Politics of Communalism: the Agony of the Left in Trinidad and Tobago, 1930-1955* (Trinidad: Pan Caribbean Publications, 1982), he discusses the role of race and ethnicity as critical factors in the fracturing of the Trinidadian left in the pre-independence era.

36 I agree with Premdas' description of Trinidad as a case of a "bifurcated" as opposed to an "intensely segmented" multi-ethnic society. But precisely because it is not a case of extreme separation, I think that his proposal of some form of consociational democracy will tend to crystallize and institutionalize ethnic divisions rather than solve the problem. See Ralph Premdas, "Ethnic conflict in Trinidad and Tobago: domination and reconciliation", in Kevin Yelvington (ed), *Trinidad Ethnicity* (London and Basingstoke: Macmillan, 1993).

37 Aya, *Rethinking Revolutions*, 97.

38 See, for example, Michael Manley, *Jamaica: Struggle in the Periphery* (London: Writers and Readers, 1982); Michael Kaufman, *Jamaica Under Manley: Dilemmas of Socialism and Democracy* (London: Zed, 1985); Evelyne H. Stephens and John D. Stephens, *Democratic Socialism in Jamaica* (London and Basingstoke: Macmillan, 1986).

39 The debate on the reasons for the demise of the WPJ is only just beginning. Rupert Lewis, a former member of the Central Committee of the party has launched an early volley in suggesting that among the primary causes were: the defeat of the Manley

regime in 1980; the invasion of Grenada and the rise of Reaganism; the defeat of WPJ candidates in the 1986 local government elections; the collapse of communism in Eastern Europe; the political misreading of the changes taking place in the world by the WPJ leadership; and the blocking of democratic debate within the party by its leader, Trevor Munroe. Missing from this otherwise accurate listing is a sense of how the state operated in the background to erode the legitimacy of the party over time. See Rupert Lewis, "Which way for the Jamaican Left"? *Third World Viewpoint* 1, no. 1 (May 1993). See, for a more recent comment, Horace Campbell, "Progressive politics and the Jamaican society at home and abroad", *Social and Economic Studies* 43, no. 3 (September 1994).

40 See Gray, *Radicalism and Social Change*, 51. The Ronald Henry incident has been under-researched and is perhaps fertile ground for the further study of Caribbean insurrections and the nature of the Jamaican state.

41 See Brian Meeks, *Social Formation and People's Revolution: a Grenadian Study* (London: Karia, forthcoming).

42 See Brian Meeks, *Caribbean Revolutions and Revolutionary Theory: an Assessment of Cuba, Nicaragua and Grenada* (London: Macmillan, 1993), and David Lewis, *Reform and Revolution in Grenada: 1950-1981* (Havana: Casa de las Americas, 1984).

43 See "A man obsessed", *Special Report*, *Sunday Guardian* (2 September 1990).

44 SOPO was formed on 8 February 1990 on the initiative of the Joint Trade Union Movement and was an attempt to bring together a united front of all groups in opposition to the structural adjustment policies of the NAR government. See Summit of People's Organizations (SOPO), "Public statement on National People's Assembly, 1990:05:07" (Port of Spain, Trinidad: SOPO).

45 Lloyd Best, "From Eric Williams to Abu Bakr", *Trinidad and Tobago Review* 12, nos. 11 & 12 (September 1990).

46 See David Lehmann, *Democracy and Development in Latin America: Economics, Politics and Religion in the Postwar Period* (Cambridge: Polity, 1990).

47 Abu Bakr, "Conversations with the Imam", interview by Keith Smith, *Daily Express* (1 August 1990).

48 See Suzanne Lopez, "My week at the Jamaat Al Muslimeen", *Daily Express* (1 August 1990).

49 Bakr's distrust for the slow, incrementalist approach to organization adopted by SOPO and other left wing organizations was evident in his sympathy for the Castroite approach to seizing power in an interview I conducted with him at the prison in 1991. The notion of a small vanguard leading the yet-to-be conscious masses is an oft-repeated theme. In Smith's 1985 interview, he openly called for the overthrow of the iniquitous Trinidadian system of government. When Smith "pooh-poohed" his intentions, he responded: "History will show that all the prophets defeated whole armies." See Abu Bakr, "Is Abu Bakr fighting a Holy War?", interview by Keith Smith, *Daily Express* (1 August 1990).

50 Chris Searle, "The Muslimeen insurrection in Trinidad", *Race and Class* 33, no. 2 (October-December 1991).

51 Michael Ryan, "Postmodern politics", *Theory, Culture and Society* 5, nos. 2-3 (1988).

52 Francis Fukuyama, "The end of history?", *The National Interest* (summer 1989).

53 Francis Fukuyama, *The End of History and the Last Man* (New York: Avon Books, 1993).

For three useful criticisms of Fukuyama's thesis, see Fred Halliday, "An encounter with Fukuyama", Michael Rustin, "No exit from capitalism?", and Ralph Miliband, "Fukuyama and the socialist alternative", all in *New Left Review*, no. 193 (May/June 1992).

Chapter Seven

Re-Reading *The Black Jacobins*: James, the Dialectic and the Revolutionary Conjuncture

It is no mystery, we making history

Linton Kwesi Johnson

The transformation of slaves, trembling in hundreds before a single white man, into a powerful people able to organize themselves and defeat the most powerful European nations of their day, is one of the great epics of revolutionary struggle and achievement.

C. L. R. James

If *Beyond a Boundary*[1] is C L R James' classic cultural study, *Notes on Dialectics*[2] his crowning philosophical work, then *The Black Jacobins*[3] is unquestionably his most important historical effort and, arguably, the single most important historical study by any writer in the anglophone Caribbean. Yet, despite a general revival in interest in James' *œuvre* since his death, critical examination[4] of *Black Jacobins* has been sparse and largely unsatisfying.

Black Jacobins first appeared propitiously in 1938 – the year of the Jamaican labour riots, one year after the oilfield workers' uprising in James' own Trinidad and Tobago, four years after the Italian invasion of Abyssinia, and on the verge of the Second World War. Published on the heels of his 1937 critique of the Communist International, *World Revolution*, and in the wake of the launching of the International African Service Bureau[5] in which he played a pivotal role, *Black Jacobins* was, in a sense, the necessary extension of his political activities. James had at least five objectives in mind. First, the successful Haitian revolutionary struggle was to be used as a tool to teach a new generation of anticolonialists, particularly on the African continent, that it was possible for black people to free themselves. Secondly, James hoped to expose what he saw as the machinations of the colonial/imperial powers as a means of providing the anticolonial movement with a guide and a warning as to what to look out for and avoid in the imminent struggles. Thirdly, while using a West Indian study to draw lessons for the African continent, he also sought to highlight the peculiar role of the West Indies in world history and to identify the unique contribution of a certain 'WestIndianness'[6] in the making of the Haitian revolution. Fourthly, he sought to explore the characteristics and dynamics of revolution, *sui generis*, as a nodal moment in the historical process. Fifthly, he sought to demonstrate the usefulness and effectiveness of a certain interpretation of Marxist methodology in the analysis and understanding of history.

If the book was not, perhaps, as widely read among the leaders and followers of the political movements he hoped to inspire, it nevertheless, did, and continues to, inspire many with its heroic portrayal of the San Domingo[7] blacks. It is fairly accurate to suggest that *Black Jacobins* has served as an important part of that broad array of texts and theories, myths and cultural artifacts which together constitute the 'imagined community'[8] of modern West Indian and, beyond it, Pan African nationalism. Further, from the perspective of its times, it suggested the possibility of an independent future, even as it sought to understand the twists and turns of the tortured past.

The aspect of the study, however, on which least focus has been directed, lies at its very heart. James' methodology, which in form and stated intent is clearly Marxist, nevertheless follows its own peculiar trajectory. What is the Jamesian method? How does it differ from other contemporary Marxist schools? How does this affect his conclusions? And how can we better understand his overall intellectual direction from this? This essay hopes to begin to answer, though it makes no pretensions in its ability to exhaust, these questions.

If one looks at the critical debate in and around the Marxist tradition in the mid to late twentieth century, a surprisingly large part of it is devoted not only to the 'correct' interpretation of this or that historical event or period, but more specifically to the methodology used to interpret history. The debates between E. P. Thompson and Perry Anderson[9] generated by Thompson's path breaking use of social history;[10] the acerbic critique of Althusser's 'structural Marxism' by Thompson;[11] the development and use of the notion of 'hegemony' by Gramsci[12] and subsequent Gramscians have all been to some extent methodological responses to lacunae detected in 'classical' Marxism. Developing from this impulse, other writers have broken from the Marxist canon and proceeded to elaborate frameworks of interpretation with only tentative connections to the core conclusions of historical materialism. Thus, the rise of much of the modern school of Historical Sociology;[13] Theda Skocpol's[14] attempt to "bring the state back in" as a central tool of analysis; agency-focused approaches such as "rational choice Marxism";[15] and even more eclectic and ambitious attempts to re-invent the tools for interpretation such as Mann's,[16] Runciman's[17] and Unger's[18] promethean studies can all be seen as part of an uncompleted project. Alongside these, there have been important attempts to defend the Marxist tradition: To a certain extent, Robert Brenner's[19] work can be seen as a counter to Skocpol and an assertion of the importance of the productive forces in historical determination; Cohen's[20] study sought to reinterpret Marxist analysis in the context of postRawlsian liberal philosophy; and Callinicos, perhaps the most ambitious of all, has struggled in his work[21] to find a middle road between crass determinism and human goal-oriented inventiveness.

The central issue has been the relative importance to be placed in historical determination on subterranean economic or productive forces, or on 'superstructural' elements, including race, religion, political factors and, most critically, human agency. Indeed, the wider debate has been given permanent fuel by Marx and Engels themselves, with their glaring silences on questions of the state, politics and historical analysis – the famous absence of Marx's theory of politics.[22] Thus, within the Marxian *œuvre*, we can easily shift between the relatively deterministic notions of *The Communist Manifesto* and *Capital* to the far more sophisticated and nuanced *Eighteenth Brumaire of Louis Bonaparte*,[23] where the role of the superstructure, of ideas and of men (if only in peculiar circumstances) attains a degree of independence hardly imaginable in other readings. Indeed, Engels, often considered the more 'scientific' and deterministic of the two, produced a model of faceless determinism in *The Part Played by Labour in the Transition from Ape to Man*.[24] But there is also the *Letter to Bloch*,[25] in which uncertainty, tentativeness and human intervention play far more critical roles.

Borrowing liberally from Levin,[26] it is possible to suggest at least three distinct approaches to the relationship between base and superstructure in Marx and Engels. In the first, appropriate to *The Communist Manifesto*, politics is strictly subordinate to economics. In the second, characteristic of *The Eighteenth Brumaire*, politics is autonomous from the base in unique historical circumstances. In the third, probably more typical of the younger postHegelian Marx, politics is always relatively autonomous from the productive base. These issues are never really resolved and as good an attempt as any is provided by Callinicos and Anderson[27] who, separately, suggest that the extent of human intervention varies depending on the particular epoch. Thus, over the last two hundred years, the pendulum has swung in favour of agency and away from determination by the productive base.

If the collapse of the Berlin Wall signalled the end of a certain model of 'socialism' it also signalled an explosion in the debate on the relevance of Marxist analysis.[28] Indeed, an earlier split from Marxism occurred in the seventies and eighties with the expansion of the feminist debate and the development of various postmodernist schools including Foucault's[29] dissection of the sources of power and Lyotard's rejection of 'grand narratives'.[30] Since then, the reemergence of the Hegelian[31] version of the dialectic and, far more critically, the dramatic assertion of neoliberalism as a dominant ideological form in the 1980s have further served to bring into focus the relevance and usefulness of Marxist analysis and what one can consider as a central weakness in the historical materialist argument.

Essentially, the debate goes something like this: If history is made by inexorable forces, but yet is presumably in the direction of human improvement and flourishing, then what kind of human flourishing can be considered acceptable which subordinates human goals and human will to abstract material forces? The classic neo-liberal argument, developed by F. A. Hayek[32] and put succinctly by Robert Nozick,[33] despite its unsavoury baggage of entrenched inequality, remains largely unanswered in its central tenet that 'freedom upsets patterns'. There can be little freedom for experimentation in a teleological model, and if there is freedom there can be no *telos*. Equally, if there is a *telos*, then it must take precedence over the will of individuals or even the stated will of 'the people', which may simply be an expression of 'false consciousness'. The ultimate and almost inescapable conclusion, then, is that any democratic notion of popular will, as Levin suggests, is incompatible with a teleological outlook:

> . . . we noted that scientific socialism was identified as the 'real will' of the proletariat, which they were destined somehow to achieve in time. Until then the party was the carrier of working class interests. Thus, although the liberal ideal of a participatory citizenry is accepted, and in some ways extended, it is rendered nugatory by taking as predetermined the appropriate aims of the participants. This elitist presupposition lies at the core of Marxism's inability to transcend liberal democracy in practice.[34]

This is the central field of combat. The issue of determination by agency or by productive forces, or more broadly put, the relationship between the two, is not to be restricted to some arcane debate between historians or political scientists, but extends into the very core notions of democracy and the relevance of Marxism as a tool not just for analysis, but for human emancipation. It is, as has been suggested, a central, but hidden issue with which James, in writing *The Black Jacobins*, was concerned.

The main hypothesis can be stated at the outset. James, in his study, adheres formally to a Marxian position, but his honest reading of the St Domingue revolution, his own sensitivity to the colonial and, critically, racial questions, carry him to the verge of severance with the Marxist canon. In the end James remains a Marxist, but in order to so do, he elevates the individual and agency to levels unprecedented in classical Marxism. In order to substantiate this conclusion, we need to retrace the sequence of James' history from the plantations of St

Domingue to the final expulsion of the French and declaration of Haitian independence in 1803.

The Sequence

James' style is compelling. Writing in vivid sweeps from Paris to St Domingue, to London and back to Paris again, he effectively captures the rhythms of wind and sail of late eighteenth century technology, in a convincing explanation of the causes of the revolt.[35] The first two chapters trace the origins of French control over the western third of Hispaniola and then describe the economic system with its contending social forces. James sketches, in compact fashion, the character of slavery, its innate brutality and repressiveness and the inevitably deep resentments this engendered in the slave population. On the surface, there was an overt fatalism and a feigned stupidity, but beneath it lurked darker forms of resistance, manifest in the regular use of poison against the white owners and the not infrequent occurrence of rebellion.

In his chapter on "The Owners", James details the schisms and alliances which existed between the classes 'above' at the height of the colony's prosperity. Big whites were opposed to the French colonial state which, through the *Exclusive*, controlled trade and thus restricted the options available to them to make profits. Small whites were opposed to the big whites who lauded it over them and to whom they were often indebted, while both were opposed to the mulattoes who, industrious and legally able to inherit land from their white parents, had grown wealthy. Small whites, in particular, hated mulattoes because 'whiteness' alone gave them status in the society and the existence of wealthy mulattoes contradicted this tenuous position. In turn, mulattoes despised the small free black population and both despised the slaves who, naturally, reciprocated this hostility.

It was sugar and the slave trade on which the entire economy of St Domingue was built that made France prosperous and, in turn, provided the economic basis for the French Revolution:

> The fortunes created at Bordeaux, at Nantes, by the slave trade, gave to the bourgeoisie that pride which needed liberty and contributed to human emancipation.[36]

In turn, the French were faced with intense competition from the British. After American independence, the British saw the benefits to be derived from free trade and became pro-abolitionists, pressuring the French. When, later, the fall of St Domingue seemed imminent, abolition was conveniently dropped from the British agenda as they sought to gain control of the foundering colony.

While St Domingue was increasingly prosperous, that prosperity, rather than calming the waters, was exacerbating the social tensions which wracked the society. James suggests at least four factors at play which hastened the possibility of crisis. First, the increase in slave labour to work the expanding estates meant that there was greater discontent, for creole slaves tended to be more docile than African born; secondly, the need to find food to feed the expanding population meant greater opposition to the *Exclusive* which restricted trading to French vessels and in effect rationed supplies; thirdly, with greater profits more planters became absentee owners, neglecting the day to day management of their estates; and fourthly, as a distinct factor, returning mulattoes from the Seven Years War were more willing to fight for equality for themselves, but were met with great hostility – further deepening tensions.

1788-1789 The Revolution Begins

In France itself, the bad winter of 1788 had encouraged the powerful maritime bourgeoisie and its allies to make their bid for power. The French Revolution had begun. In St Domingue, the big whites, following closely the events in France, sought to use the revolution to consolidate its own power at home. James is very clear that despite longstanding grievances of the deepest kind held by the slaves, it is the crisis among the French ruling classes with the necessary lateral fissures into St Domingue which initiates the process, after which, a complex series of events occur which push it from a controlled rebellion at the top to a full scale, and ultimately successful, revolt of the slaves. The critical stages can only be captured in the broadest brush strokes.

In the early stages of the revolt, three white fractions emerge in the colony. They are the royalist bureaucracy which is counterrevolutionary; the Assembly of St Marc or the 'patriots' which is dominated by small whites; and the Assembly of the North based in Cap François (Le Cap) which is dominated by big whites. All fractions despise the mulattoes, but both the royalists and the big whites appreciate their numerical importance in any frontal struggle. In France, the new Constituent Assembly was itself split between the pro-planter lobby which was against any change in the status quo in St Domingue and the humanitarians on the left who supported mulatto rights but were in this early phase in a minority. The failure of the Constituent Assembly to grant mulattoes equal rights in this period led to a mulatto revolt which, however, was poorly timed and its leaders, Ogé and Chavannes, brutally tortured and executed.

1791 The Blacks Revolt

The subsequent stalemate in the colony is broken by the intervention of the Parisian masses and, with it, the lurching of the revolution to the left. Louis XVI's attempt to leave the country in April and the role of the people in intercepting him strengthened the hand of the left faction and engendered a debate on mulatto rights out of which limited advances are made. In May, the franchise is given to every mulatto who can prove that both parents were free, but even this limited advance is never implemented. A further swing back to the right in September leads to a rescinding of the mulatto bill. But even as these violent conflicts between white and mulatto and white and white are being played out, the hitherto sleeping slave population is beginning to awake:

> Their [the whites'] quick resort to arms, their lynching, murder and mutilation of mulattoes and political enemies were showing the slaves how liberty and equality were won or lost.[37]

In July of 1791, widespread revolt occurs on the North Plain, the most 'proletarian'[38] part of St Domingue. Led by Boukman, the insurrection is largely 'Luddite'[39] in its destructiveness and lacks clear decisive leadership:

> Masses roused to the revolutionary pitch need above all a clear and vigorous direction.but the first coup had failed and Jean François and Biassou, though they could keep order, had not the faintest idea what to do next.[40]

In this gap, Toussaint Breda, later to rename himself L'Ouverture, emerges. Toussaint, son of an African chieftain and steward of the animals on his master's estate – a rare position for a black slave – emerges as a leader only reluctantly. He is already in his forties – an old man by contemporary standards – and his primary interests at first appear to be to protect his master's family and his own. But when he does enter the fray, it is increasingly evident that as a leader he has no rivals. Two other factors enhance the black revolt. First, the indiscriminate persecution of all blacks – revolutionary or passive – forces thousands of bystanders into active involvement; and, critically, the mulattoes, with their own agenda of grievances, revolt once again in the West:

> In the advanced North the slaves were leading the mulattoes, in the backward West, the mulattoes were leading the slaves . . .[41]

1792 The Tactical Alliance with the Spanish

At the end of 1791, three commissioners arrive with troops from France to reestablish order. At first, the rebel leaders, among them Toussaint, seek to cut a deal for freedom for the four hundred leading blacks, but the uncompromising planters are insistent that all their former property must submit. It is only at this point that Toussaint clearly grasps that it must be ". . . freedom for all, held at their own strength,"[42] and begins to train an army.

Meanwhile, in France, now under the greater sway of the left, full mulatto rights are granted on March 24 , but nothing yet is said about the slaves. In July, six thousand men under Commissioners Sonthonax, Polverel and Ailhoud sail from France to announce the granting of mulatto rights, but also to quell the slave revolt. The expedition is split between the commissioners who are revolutionaries and the officers who are royalists and while they are at sea Louis is finally overthrown. France, faced with invasion from Austria and a growing revolutionary fervour, moves decisively to the left. The Convention is established and the Jacobins increase in influence although the Girondins hold power.

In St Domingue, the divisions between royalists and revolutionaries give the slave rebels needed breathing space, but the rebellion is at a low point. Faced with starvation, desertions, and relentless pursuit from the French soldiers, the blacks are at the point of collapse when, in early 1793, Britain and Spain declare war on France and the French troops are called away from the interior to defend the vulnerable coast. However, faced with a French army still intent on restoring slavery, Toussaint and the other rebels opt for an alliance with the neighbouring Spanish from Santo Domingo. Among the whites of the French colony, divisions are still deep. When Governor Galboud arrives from France, the white planters support him in opposition to the revolutionary Commissioner Sonthonax who, in turn, calls for the arming of the slaves in and around Le Cap and looses them on the planters. Le Cap is partially destroyed but this act, James argues, signals the end of white domination in St Domingue.

By August 1793, faced with defecting slaves, newly armed and restive blacks, and a Spanish supported insurrection in the hills, Sonthonax, with few options, announces the abolition of slavery, but is met with little response. The blacks in alliance with the Spanish refuse to rally to him as they know his action is not supported with legislation from France. Under the Spanish flag, Toussaint asserts his military prowess. By 1794, he is in charge of the entire northern swathe of the colony. But, even as he consolidates his new victories, the British, who have been carefully watching the weakening position of the French in the richest prize in the Antilles, decide to invade.

1794 The War with the British

The British land in September 1793 and by early 1794 are in charge of most of the western territory and much of the South, except the area held by the mulatto general Rigaud and the redoubt of Môle St Nicholas in the North. In July they capture Port au Prince and all indications are that they are bent on restoring slavery. Toussaint with his forces in the North, grimly observes these developments. Once again in France the revolution changes pace. The Girondin period is over. The Commune gives way to the évêché and Robespierre and the Mountain are in charge. Under constant pressure from the revolutionary masses, slavery is officially abolished on February 4, 1794. This dramatically changed situation creates the basis for an alliance between the revolutionary French and Toussaint's forces which leads to immediate victories in the North. There is now a new correlation of forces. Toussaint is in control of the North, but three years of war has left the North Plain devastated; in the West, the British, strongly supported by the white planters, are dominant; while in the South, Rigaud (with his mulatto army) is in charge.

1795-1796 Toussaint's Prestige Rises: the Mulattoes Revolt

Throughout 1795 Toussaint's prestige as a general and a leader grows in the North. He proves to be incorruptible, wise, humane and untainted by bitterness. Despite his great popularity among the former slaves, he remains loyal to the governor, Laveaux:

> War, politics, agriculture, international relations, long range problems of administration, minor details, he dealt with them as they came, took decisions and gave advice to Laveaux, but, characteristic of his tact, always as a subordinate.[43]

By 1796, James notes, Toussaint stood first in the councils of the governor. But even as Toussaint is consolidating his position, the mulattoes, jealous of their loss of influence in the councils of the governor, are seeking to reassert themselves through revolt. In March 1796 Laveaux is arrested by mulatto conspirators in Le Cap, but with the black masses of the town solidly against them and Toussaint's timely intervention with troops, the nascent mulatto revolt is put down. When a new group of commissioners arrive in May with Sonthonax at its head, they have a specific brief to control the mulattoes. With all this, Toussaint's influence rises immeasurably.

The Alliance With the Mulattoes

Sonthonax engages Rigaud, the mulatto leader in the South, in order to reassert French hegemony over the island. But even as the mulattoes battle with the French and as Sonthonax is increasingly reliant on Toussaint, the latter is in the process of developing a close relationship with Rigaud. By 1797, James suggests that due to skillful diplomacy and a never-failing focus on his main objective of freedom for the blacks, Toussaint is the most influential man on the entire island.

Then, in August 1797 a bombshell occurs. Toussaint demands that Sonthonax, the most consistent friend of the blacks, leave the island. He claims that the commissioner had proposed a plan for the elimination of all whites on the island to which he, Toussaint, was firmly opposed, but James suggests another reason.

Toussaint appreciated the changing winds in Paris and, fearful that freedom might be threatened decided to throw Sonthonax to the wolves at once. His remarkable letter to the Directory in Paris outlined for the first time his willingness to oppose France frontally if freedom were to be threatened:

> But if, to re-establish slavery in San Domingo, this was done, then I declare to you it would be to attempt the impossible.We have known how to face dangers to obtain our liberty, we shall know how to brave death to maintain it.[44]

Even as these uncertainties loom, the largely black armies of the north and mulatto armies of the South are in the process of driving the British from the colony. Then, as the British are on the verge of capitulation, General Hédouville arrives from France with the specific instruction to drive a wedge between Rigaud and Toussaint. Promising Rigaud the world, he is successful in splitting him away from Toussaint, changing in effect the course of the revolution and of subsequent Haitian history, strengthening the basis for the deep, fratricidal divisions between blacks and mulattoes. Hédouville continues his divisive policy by negotiating behind Toussaint's back with the retreating British and appointing white generals in place of blacks in the army. The final straw occurs when Hédouville attempts to arrest Moïse, the most popular of Toussaint's black generals. Toussaint orders Dessalines to march on Le Cap, arrest Hédouville and reinstate Moïse. He states ominously:

> . . . remember that there is only one Toussaint L'Ouverture in San Domingo and that at his name everybody must tremble.[45]

Toussaint, in effect, has seized the power and follows this up with decisive victories against Rigaud's armies in the South. He remains formally under France, but it is a France of a different colour, for Napoleon is now in charge. The major break with the French eventually comes over Spanish Santo Domingo. Commissioner Roume has been given strict instructions not to take over the Spanish colony but Toussaint, fearful of a potentially weak link in his rear, opposes Roume and on January 21, 1800 routs the Spanish and is in effect ruler of the entire island.

1800-1801 Toussaint in Power

In the only period in which Toussaint ruled effectively, James outlines his tremendous abilities and noteworthy achievements. He is able to gain the confidence of the whites and get agriculture and commerce started again. His regime is despotic, but it is based on wage labour and beatings are forbidden. However, there is one mortal weakness. In cultivating the support of the whites, who, in spite of their temporary loyalty to him, will never give full support to a black man, he assumes the automatic loyalty of the blacks and takes them for granted. This political failure is to prove fatal for Toussaint and almost so for the entire revolution in the following months, for Napoleon and the French bourgeoisie are preparing to restore slavery.

1802-1804 The War of Independence

Napoleon, according to James, hated black people. In 1801 he sought to form an alliance with Russia's Czar Paul to defeat the British in India, but the British trumped him by assassinating the Czar. From then, Napoleon prepared for a full scale invasion of St Domingue. Sailing on December 14, 1802, Napoleon's army headed by his brother-in-law LeClerc with some 20,000 troops, is the largest ever to set sail from France. But even as Napoleon is preparing, Toussaint is undermining himself. On the critical North Plain – the birthplace of the revolution – the blacks rise up in opposition to Toussaint's harsh labour policies and his apparent favour towards the whites. Moïse, Toussaint's adopted nephew and militant populist of the revolution, is implicated in the uprising, arrested and executed. Toussaint, James contends, like Robespierre before him, destroys his own left wing and by so doing seals his doom.

LeClerc is given clear, but secret orders. He is to promise the black generals everything before landing. However, once the French army is in place, they are to be arrested and shipped back to France. When they are out of the way, the colony is to be governed by 'special laws' as a prelude to the restoration of slavery. He is able to land and make advances due to vacillation on the part of the black leadership. A huge army has come, but these soldiers are still seen as representatives of revolutionary and pro-abolitionist France. Belatedly, there is spirited and organized resistance, particularly from Dessalines in the West and South and Maurepas and Christophe in the North. But, in the end, despite heroic resistance from Dessalines at Crete à Pierrot, first Maurepas, then Christophe, capitulate to LeClerc. In the end, Toussaint calls for negotiations and puts down his arms on the assurance that the black army will remain in place and slavery will not be restored. Thereafter, Toussaint is arrested and deported to France where he dies in prison.[46] News of Toussaint's deportation and, more alarmingly, of the restoration of slavery in Martinique and Guadeloupe, spread rapidly among the black population and spontaneous insurrection begins. Ironically, it is the black generals who have come to terms with LeClerc who are used to repress the localized uprisings:

> The masses were fighting and dying as only revolutionary masses can, the French army was wasting away, despair was slowly choking LeClerc. But still these black and mulatto generals continued to fight for LeClerc against the 'brigands'.[47]

Secretly, however, Dessalines has formed an alliance with the mulatto General Pétion and is planning a war to the end against the French for independence:

> Crude, coarse and stained with crimes, [Dessalines] deserves his place among the heroes of human emancipation. He was a soldier, a magnificent soldier and had no other pretensions. But hatred of those who deserve to be hated and destroyed had sharpened his wits and he played a great part.[48]

On October 11, 1802, Pétion rises in Le Cap and simultaneously Dessalines moves in the West. Three days later, Christophe joins the uprising. In what is perhaps the most moving part of the book, James describes the war for independence as the most vicious and sustained of all the campaigns. Toussaint dies in prison on April 7, 1803. A month later the Haitian flag is unfurled for the first time. On November 16, 1803, victory is assured with the success of the final offensive on Le Cap. Over 60,000 French soldiers had either perished or were to languish in British prisons after the evacuation of Haiti. Shortly before the final offensive, LeClerc, on his death bed, writing to Napoleon, captures the enormity of the French error and, inadvertently, the glory of the achievement of the St Domingue blacks:

> We have in Europe a false idea of the country in which we fight and the men whom we fight against.[49]

On December 31, 1803 Haiti is declared independent. In October 1804, Dessalines is crowned emperor. Then, in 1805, on Dessalines' orders, all whites in Haiti are massacred,[50] strengthening the basis for the newly independent nation's diplomatic isolation for most of the nineteenth century.

The Argument

It has already been suggested that James had at least five objectives in mind when writing *Black Jacobins*, but if we were to abandon this proposal and seek to find a single, overarching concern, then it might be found in the following assertion:

> The transformation of slaves trembling in hundreds before a single white man into a people able to organize themselves and defeat the most powerful European nations of their day, is one of the great epics of revolutionary struggle and achievement.[51]

Despite a confining determinism, it was the struggle of the spirit against overwhelming odds, the uniquely human endeavour of the Haitian blacks which James sought to understand. But what were the motive forces which generated crisis? What relative weight is to be given to the different causative variables? And how do they come together to explain how history is made? James provides his answers to these questions in the very beginning of the book, in the "Preface to the First Edition". He begins his argument by suggesting that the achievement was largely Toussaint's work:

> By a phenomenon often observed, the individual leadership responsible for this unique achievement was almost entirely the work of a single man – Toussaint L'Ouverture.[52]

Then, following this, he appears to correct himself:

> Yet Toussaint did not make the revolution. It was the revolution that made Toussaint and even that is not the whole truth.[53]

This apparent ambiguity is then clarified in an inimitably 'classical' Marxian sense:

> Great men make history, but only such history as it is possible for them to make. Their freedom of achievement is limited by the necessities of their environment. To portray the limits of those necessities and the realisation, complete or partial, of all possibilities, that is the true business of the historian.[54]

Any room for doubt that great men are but products of their environment, is firmly eliminated in the following passage, where he suggests the peculiar modalities of historical determination in that rare moment of revolution:

> In a revolution, when the ceaseless, slow accumulation of centuries bursts into volcanic eruption, the meteoric flames and flights above are a meaningless chaos and lend themselves to infinite caprice and romanticism unless the observer sees them always as projections of the subsoil from which they came. The writer has sought not only to analyze, but to demonstrate in their movement, the economic forces of their age; their moulding of society and politics, of men in the mass and individual men; the powerful reaction of these on their environment at one of those rare moments when society is at a boiling point and therefore fluid.[55]

James, then, formally operates within Marxist parameters. If one were to ask "which Marx?", the answer would have to be Marx at his most creative and flexible in *The Eighteenth Brumaire*. From this perspective, men make history but within the parameters set by the environment. There is room for experimentation and innovation but these are firmly grounded, indeed, 'moulded', by the terms of reference of the subsoil from which individual agents are 'projected'. In the final count, social consciousness is determined by social being; human agency is underwritten by material context.

To what extent is James loyal to this stated ideological stance and methodological position? The simple answer is that he is very loyal, until he begins to discuss the details of leadership, the character of the leaders and the actual sequence of events in the making of the revolution. Once on this field, James is at a loss to find an adequate explanation for how things actually develop and instead proposes a series of cultural and psychological explanations, eventually yielding to the view that in revolutionary situations a different set of principles apply and that agents do have room to act independently and autonomously.

James is at his most convincing when he is on relatively safe ground, for example, when he describes the social and economic pressures which generated crisis at both the international and local levels. Thus, his description of the nature of the three-way competition between French, British and St Domingue planters is both concise and compelling:

> Men make their own history, and the Black Jacobins of San Domingo were to make history which would alter the fate of millions of men and shift the economic currents of three continents. But if they could seize opportunity they could not create it. The slave trade and slavery were woven tight into the economics of the eighteenth century. Three forces, the proprietors of San Domingo, the French bourgeoisie and the British bourgeoisie, throve on the devastation of a continent and the brutal exploitation of millions. As long as these maintained an equilibrium, the infernal traffic would go on, and for that matter would have gone on until the present day. But nothing, however profitable, goes on forever. From the very momentum of their own development, colonial planters, French and British bourgeois, were generating internal stresses and intensifying external rivalries, moving blindly to explosions and conflicts which would shatter the basis of their dominance and create the possibility of emancipation.[56]

This position is faithfully carried over into his important discussion of race and colour in St Domingue. Small whites hated mulattoes; mulattoes hated blacks; blacks resented them all. James reminds us that these are 'superstructural' factors and quotes for the first and only time from *Eighteenth Brumaire* to support his argument:

> Upon the different forms of property, upon the social conditions of existence as foundation, there is built a superstructure of diversified and characteristic sentiments, illusions, habits of thought, and outlooks of life in general. The class as a whole creates and shapes them out of its material foundation and out of the corresponding social relationships. The individual in which they arise, through tradition and education, may fancy them to be the true determinants, the real origin of his activities.[57]

It is later on that the problem arises. For as the struggle unfolds through the alliance with the Spanish, anti-British, anti-mulatto and ultimately anti-French phases, it is evident to all that the existence of an organized army, the possibility of an islandwide alliance including whites and mulattoes and, most of all, the defeat of the Spanish and far more importantly, the British forces, are due to the prodigious efforts and abilities of a single man. How can this individual, his talents and his remarkable intervention into history be accommodated within the boundaries of the materialist explanation which James begins with? The short answer is that he cannot be comfortably accommodated.

James searches to comprehend and understand the character of the man. His father was an African chieftain;[58] he was extremely bright, could read and write and, importantly, had read the Abbé Raynal's stinging condemnation of slavery. He had been given the important job of steward on his master's plantation which had taught him how to command and demand respect. Critically, and in this, Toussaint is contrasted with Dessalines: he had never been whipped and could thus approach relationships with whites without that deep hatred which lived in others like Dessalines:

> An important thing for his future was that his character was quite un-warped. Since his childhood he had probably never been whipped as so many slaves had been whipped.[59]

In summary, he was a natural leader long before the revolution broke out:

> His comparative learning, his success in life, his character and personality gave him an immense prestige among the negroes who knew him and he was a man of some consequence among the slaves long before the revolution.[60]

This is to be contrasted with Dessalines:

> . . . with the marks of the whip below his general's uniform . . . crude, coarse and stained with crimes [with]. . . no other pretensions but hatred of those who deserve to be hated.[61]

In the end, it is a most unmaterialist psychological theory on the formation of the individual which has to be called on to explain Toussaint's character and, out of this, his profound impact on subsequent events. Had Toussaint been 'warped' by the whip, it would seem logical to argue, then he might very well have played a role, but he would never have been able to balance the various interests in the diplomatic manner he did. It was precisely Dessalines' 'warpedness' which prevented him from seeking compromise with the whites after the revolution, with disastrous and bloody consequences for the new nation.

This psychological approach is carried over into a specifically Jamesian and equally nonmaterialist[62] theory to explain the role of intellectuals in revolutionary situations. Toussaint cultivated the whites and even went so far as to execute the well loved Moïse for daring to oppose this policy. Further, when LeClerc landed with his 20,000 soldiers and sailors, Toussaint eventually decided to seek a compromise rather than fight to the death for independence, with the potential implications of decisive break with French culture and economy. James repeatedly returns to this question as to why this remarkable leader, so decisive in the early phases of the struggle, failed to carry through his objectives to the end. It is worthwhile to quote extensively on this:

> Yet Toussaint's errors sprang from the very qualities that made him what he was. It is easy to see today as his generals saw after he was dead, where he had erred. It does not mean that they or any of us would have done better in his place. If Dessallines could see so clearly and simply, it was because the ties that bound this uneducated soldier to French civilization were of the slenderest. He saw what was under his nose so well because he saw no further. Toussaint's failure was the failure of enlightenment, not of darkness.[63]

Once again, searching for explanation, James moves beyond the bounds of his methodological frame. In the first instance, he does this to explain Toussaint's success. Now he does it to explain his failure. His theory of the intellectual, who as a category may be damaging to the immediate progress of the revolution because of 'enlightenment' and greater appreciation of long term consequences, is novel and controversial. Dessalines the 'barbarian' as vehicle for human progress as opposed to Toussaint the enlightened is a uniquely Jamesian but not Marxist[64] category which is developed in *Black Jacobins* and reappears in other works, though with special clarity in his critique of the intellectual Ishmael in *Mariners, Renegades and Castaways*.[65]

Finally, having described at length the pivotal role of one man in the making of history, James, reflecting on the impossibility of grasping the twists and turns of the process without yielding centre stage to its primary agent, makes a critical concession. In his assessment of 'the Black Consul', he in effect reformulates his earlier methodological position:

> The revolution had made him; but it would be a vulgar error to suppose that the creation of a disciplined army, the defeat of the English and the Spaniards, the defeat of Rigaud, the establishment of a strong government all over the island, the growing harmony between the races, the enlightened aims of the administration – it would be a crude error to believe that all these were inevitable. At a certain stage, the middle of 1794, the potentialities in the chaos began to be shaped and soldered by his powerful personality, and thenceforth it is impossible to say where the social forces end and the impress of personality begins. It is sufficient that, but for him, this history would be something entirely different.[66]

From the perspective of method, this is perhaps the most important passage in the entire book. How different this is from his early remarks of a superstructure firmly wedded to the subsoil! James here concedes the primacy of agency and, by implication, opens up many alternative possible trajectories for history to take. It might be somewhat self-indulgent, but necessary, to engage in a simple exercise of 'what ifs'[67] as we trace some of these potential trajectories not taken.

What if Hédouville had not been able to divide Rigaud and Toussaint and instead, the two, united and presenting a common front to Napoleon, had been able to convince him that they were more worthwhile as allies in the imminent battles with Britain? Napoleon would have saved the lives of 60,000 of his best revolutionary soldiers, countless ships, guns and stores, not to mention the morale of his entire army and navy for the crucial encounters to come. What, then, if with these extra resources, Napoleon had not lost at Waterloo? What would nineteenth century Europe and by extension, the rest of the world have looked like with a powerful, revolutionary, albeit now Napoleonic France at its centre?

What if Toussaint had not come to terms with LeClerc, but inspired by the early victories against the French had sought to resist? Would he not have sooner, rather than later, come to Dessalines' conclusion that independence was necessary? Surely if that were the case, then Toussaint's policies towards the whites would have been more conciliatory. Haiti would then have entered the new century not so much as an international pariah, but as a legitimate part of the family of emergent Latin American states. That would not have prevented neocolonialism, but what kind of example would a renascent black Haiti, more of a success than a failure have set for the rest of the West Indies?

Finally, what if Toussaint had been killed in the early days of the revolt, long before the Spanish alliance? This is not, of course, how history went. But it did not go any of these ways because living men made profound decisions which have had lasting implications. James carries us to the ideological abyss in asserting the possibility of agents taking precedence over disembodied social forces, but does not follow through to the evident conclusion. For, if at a critical moment the agent is able to intervene and alter the outcome, then that 'temporary' effect has to some extent affected the entire future trajectory. This new trajectory is, in turn, open by the same logic, to be altered in novel and even more unprecedented directions by future actors. The opening of the Pandora's box of the temporary primacy of agents which James in the last instance does, is a troublesome genie which refuses to go back into the bottle. It is not that productive forces do not play their role in shaping events, but that people adamantly refuse to play the minor parts assigned to them.

Notes

1 C. L. R. James, *Beyond a Boundary* (London: Stanley Paul, 1986).

2 C. L. R. James, *Notes on Dialectics: Hegel, Marx, Lenin* (Westport: Lawrence, Hill and Co., 1980).

3 C. L. R. James, *The Black Jacobins: Toussaint L'Ouverture and the San Domingo Revolution*, (New York: Vintage Books, 1989). Henceforth referred to as BJ.

4 See for one of the earlier and more important comments, George Lamming, *The Pleasures of Exile*, 2d ed (London: Alison & Busby, 1984). Among the more recent commentaries, see Stuart Hall, "CLR James: a portrait", in P. Henry and P. Buhle (eds), *CLR James's Caribbean* (London and Basingstoke: Macmillan Caribbean, 1992), Selwyn R. Cudjoe, "C.L.R. James misbound", *Transition* 58 (1993), and Robin Blackburn, *The Overthrow of Colonial Slavery* (London, New York: Verso, 1988).

5 See Paul Buhle, *C.L.R. James: the Artist as Revolutionary* (London: Verso, 1988).

6 This theme is subliminal throughout the study, but is made explicit in his seminal appendix "From Toussaint L'Ouverture to Fidel Castro", in which he makes his case – often repeated, but seldom with as much force – for a distinct West Indian nation. (See *BJ*, 391ff.)

7 James uses the unusual 'San Domingo' instead of the now more commonly accepted 'St Domingue'. This may have been his attempt to translate the territory's colonial name for the reader unaccustomed to French. This name appears as 'St Domingue' in the rest of the text.

8 See Benedict Anderson, *Imagined Communities: Reflections on the Origins and Spread of Nationalism* (London: Verso, 1991).

9 See Perry Anderson, *Arguments within English Marxism* (London: Verso, 1980).

10 See E. P. Thompson, *The Making of the English Working Class* (Harmondsworth: Penguin, 1980), and *The Poverty of Theory and Other Essays* (New York and London: Monthly Review Press, 1978).

11 Ibid.

12 See Antonio Gramsci, *Selections from Prison Notebooks* (London: Lawrence and Wishart, 1986).

13 For a description and critique, see Dennis Smith, *The Rise of Historical Sociology* (Cambridge: Polity Press, 1991).

14 See Theda Skocpol, *States and Social Revolutions* (Cambridge: Cambridge University Press, 1989).

15 See, for example, Jon Elster, *Making Sense of Marx* (Cambridge: Cambridge University Press, 1985).

16 See Michael Mann, *The Sources of Social Power*. Vol. 1, *A History of Power from the Beginning to 1760* (Cambridge: Cambridge University Press, 1989).

17 See W. G. Runciman, *A Treatise on Social Theory* (Cambridge: Cambridge University Press, 1983).

18 See Roberto Mangabeira Unger, *False Necessity: Anti-Necessitarian Social Theory in the Service of Radical Democracy* (Cambridge: Cambridge University Press, 1987). For useful criticisms of Mann, Runciman and Unger, see Perry Anderson, *A Zone of Engagement* (London: Verso, 1992).

19   See, for example, Robert Brenner, "The social basis of economic development", in J. Roemer, *Analytical Marxism* (Cambridge: Cambridge University Press, 1986).

20   See G. A. Cohen, *Karl Marx's Theory of History: a Defence* (Princeton, NJ: Princeton University Press, 1980).

21   See Alex Callinicos, *Making History: Agency, Structure and Change in Social Theory*, (Cambridge: Polity Press, 1987).

22   See David McLellan, *Marxism after Marx* (London and Basingstoke: Macmillan, 1989).

23   See Lewis S. Feuer (ed), *Marx and Engels: Basic Writings on Politics and Philosophy* (Glasgow: Collins, 1974).

24   See *Karl Marx and Frederick Engels Selected Works in Three Volumes: Volume Three*, (Moscow: Progress Publishers, 1975).

25   See *Marx-Engels: Selected Correspondence* (Moscow: Progress Publications, 1975).

26   See Michael Levin, *Marx, Engels and Liberal Democracy* (London and Basingstoke: Macmillan, 1989).

27   See Callinicos, *Making History*, and Anderson, *Arguments*.

28   See Ralph Miliband and Leo Panitch (eds), *The Retreat of the Intellectuals: Socialist Register 1990* (London: Merlin, 1990); Robin Blackburn (ed), *After the Fall* (London: Verso, 1991); Goran Therborn, "The life and times of socialism", *New Left Review*, no. 194 (July/August 1992); Eric Hobsbawm, "Today's crisis of ideologies", *New Left Review*, no. 192 (March/April 1992); and G.A. Cohen, "The future of a disillusion", *New Left Review*, no. 190 (Nov/Dec 1991).

29   See Michel Foucault's, *The History of Sexuality*, vol. 1 (Harmondsworth: Penguin, 1990) and *The Archaeology of Knowledge* (Great Britain: Routledge, 1990), and Stephen K. White, *Political Theory and Postmodernism* (Cambridge: Cambridge University Press, 1991). Among the better critiques of postmodernism, see Jurgen Habermas, *The Philosophical Discourse of Modernity: Twelve Lectures* (Cambridge: Polity Press, 1987), and Alex Callinicos, *Against Postmodernism* (Cambridge: Polity Press, 1989).

30   See Jean François Lyotard, *The Postmodern Condition: a Report on Knowledge* (Manchester: Manchester University Press, 1991).

31   See Francis Fukuyama, *The End of History and the Last Man* (New York: Avon, 1992); and for critiques, Fred Halliday's, "An encounter with Fukuyama", *New Left Review*, no. 193 (May/June 1992) and Ralph Miliband's, "Fukuyama and the socialist alternative", *New Left Review*, no. 193 (May/June 1992).

32   See F. A. Hayek, *The Constitution of Liberty* (London: Routledge, 1990).

33   See Robert Nozick, *Anarchy, State and Utopia* (Oxford: Basil Blackwell, 1991).

34   Levin, *Liberal Democracy*, 152.

35   An attempt is not being made here to investigate James' study *qua* history. That would be the substance of another paper or far more substantial study. Rather, taking on face value James' own interpretation, we are seeking to uncover the logic in his method. Among the large body of literature on the revolution itself, see David Geggus, *Slavery, War and Revolution: the British Occupation of St Domingue* (Oxford: Oxford University Press, 1982); Carolyn Fick, *The Making of Haiti: the St Domingue Revolution from Below* (Knoxville: University of Tennessee Press, 1990); Thomas Ott, *The Haitian Revolution 1789-1804* (Knoxville: University of Tennessee Press, 1973), Tabiri Hasani Tabasuri, "A theory of revolution and a case study of the Haitian revolution" (PhD diss.,

University of Oklahoma, 1981), Pierre Pluchon, *Histoire des Antilles et de la Guyane* (Toulouse: Privat, 1982), and Blackburn, *Colonial Slavery*.

36 *BJ*, 47.

37 *BJ*, 82.

38 *BJ*, 85-86.

39 *BJ*, 88.

40 *BJ*, 94-95.

41 *BJ*, 102.

42 *BJ*, 167.

43 *BJ*, 160.

44 *BJ*, 197.

45 *BJ*, 220.

46 While no claim is made in the book for a case of treachery in the ranks of the black generals as the reason for Toussaint's arrest, in the play with the same title, James implies that Dessalines had plotted to get Toussaint removed from the scene in order to sieze the leadership and take the country into a despotic independence. See C.L.R. James, "The Black Jacobins" in Anna Grimshaw (ed), *The C. L. R. James Reader* (Oxford, U.K., Cambridge, USA: Basil Blackwell, 1993), 104. For a comment on James' liberal use of artistic license in the play, see Marie-José N'Zengou-Tayo, "Re-imagining history: the Caribbean vision of the Haitian revolution and the early independence days" (Paper presented at the third annual conference of the Haitian Studies Association, Boston, October 1991).

47 *BJ*, 346.

48 *BJ*, 353.

49 *BJ*, 356.

50 Again, it is in the play "The Black Jacobins" not the book, that James makes the claim that Dessalines' decision to massacre the whites was, at least in part, instigated by the British who hoped to drive a permanent wedge between the French and the Haitians. See Grimshaw, *Reader*, 109-10.

51 *BJ*, ix.

52 *BJ*, ix.

53 *BJ*, ix.

54 *BJ*, x.

55 *BJ*, 11-12.

56 *BJ*, 26.

57 Karl Marx, *The Eighteenth Brumaire of Louis Bonaparte* (quoted in *BJ*, 44).

58 Little more is made of this seminal fact. How did Toussaint's recent memory of an aristocratic African past influence his entire demeanour and character? Equally important, how did the African origin of the majority of revolutionary slaves—a point which James notes repeatedly—influence the militancy and obduracy of the movement? Were the slaves solely inspired by the revolutionary fervour of the times, or did they also bring with them a history of organization and rebellion from West Africa? More pointedly, was there a specific concentration of tribal groupings in the Haitian population which had arrived equipped with a propensity for the military arts?

James, while tilling the soil of revolutionary spontaneity, is silent on the possibly deeper rhythms of African continuity. The pioneering character of the work may partially explain this, but there is also a deeper underlying muffler on the cultural dimension. I thank Rupert Lewis and Louis Lindsay for pointing out this silence in an earlier draft of this paper.

59 *BJ*, 92.

60 *BJ*, 93.

61 *BJ*, 301 and 353. A further textual reading is appropriate in order to examine James' culturally specific and often denigratory attitude towards "half-wild Africans", the "debased" French known as Creole (*BJ*, 19), and the inherent docility of the creole in comparison to the African born slave (*BJ*, 7). James operated within a distinct colonial (if also Marxist) tradition which distinguishes between the culture and enlightenment of Europe and the backward darkness of Africa. See for a relevant, if obscure comment, Sylvia Winter, "Beyond the categories of the master conception: the counter doctrine of the Jamesian poesis", in Henry and Buhle, *James' Caribbean*, 63-91.

62 There are two possible ways of addressing the question as to whether James' approach breaks with a 'materialist' interpretation of history. The first would be to construct an abstract and mechanical 'strawman' interpretation of what a materialist approach is and then knock it down. From such an angle, individuals would have to be seen as intervening in history as unambiguous representatives of material interests, and consequently, social classes. Therefore, once no clear nexus can be established between actor and socioeconomic class, then the conclusion must be that the materialist approach is wanting or the historian has insufficiently marshalled the evidence. In the second approach, individuals intervene in history as "strong evaluators" (Callinicos, *Making History*, 121) with significant room to act independently, but in the end their basic political stance is dependent on social position. This second approach is seductive, if only because, as in our example, it helps to explain why most slaves were for the most part against slavery, most whites were for it and most mulattoes vacillated between the other two groups. But if we approach history from the perspective of the end result – what actually happened – as James does, then it becomes apparent that there is something seriously missing in even Callinicos' more nuanced approach. It is evident in our case, for example, that Toussaint's social position was only one of a number of variables, and not necessarily the most important variable influencing his unique intervention. Put crudely, if psychological disposition and contingency can so drastically change the historical trajectory that the outcome is unpredictable and virtually unrecognizable, then it requires an unsupportable "leap of faith" (See Rod Aya, *Rethinking Revolutions*) to continue relying on the materialist determinant as *the* critical variable.

63 *BJ*, 288.

64 On the contrary, it would seem that while Marx (and Engels) retained a healthy skepticism towards intellectuals, most of their work grants special privileges to a section of this stratum, giving them the right to teach and by implication, lead, the working class movement. This is evident in *The Communist Manifesto* where a necessary part of the revolt against capital involves a renegade section of the bourgeois intellectuals going over to the side of the proletariat (see Feuer, *Basic Writings*, 59), and in "The German Ideology" which supports the above notion by

suggesting that the dominant class possesses a virtual monopoly on ideas and implying that a break will require some of those "generators of ideas" coming over to the proletarian side. See "The German Ideology", *Marx and Engels Collected Works*, vol. 5 (London: Lawrence and Wishart, 1975).

65 See C. L. R. James, *Mariners, Renegades and Castaways: the Story of Herman Melville and the World We Live In* (London and New York: Allison & Busby, 1985).

66 *BJ*, 249.

67 I am thankful to Marie-José N'Zengou-Tayo for bringing to my attention another attempt at envisaging what might have happened if Haitian history had gone differently. See Gary Victor, "L'utopie de l'envers du temps", in *Nouvelles Interdites* (Port au Prince: Henri Deschamps, 1989).

Chapter Eight

The political moment in Jamaica: the dimensions of hegemonic dissolution

Me nuh know how we and dem a go work it out . . . For me nuh have no frien' ina high society

Bob Marley

Freeman and slave, patrician and plebeian, lord and serf, guildmaster and journeyman, in a word, oppressor and oppressed, stood in constant opposition to one another, carried on an interrupted, now hidden, now open fight, a fight that each time ended either in the revolutionary reconstruction of society at large, or in the common ruin of the contending classes.

Marx and Engels

In 1993, Percival J. Patterson, the newly elected leader of the People's National Party (PNP), romped home in Jamaica's twelfth general election since universal adult suffrage with a decisive mandate of fifty-two out of a possible sixty seats and some 60 percent of the popular vote. While there were widespread criticisms of corrupt practices,[1] particularly in the troubled urban constituencies, leading to an initial boycotting of parliament by the opposition Jamaica Labour Party (JLP), and while there was a remarkably low turnout at the polls,[2] there was, nevertheless, a widespread feeling that the victory represented something of a renewal in Jamaica's political life. Prime Minister Manley had, after all, retired a year before, ending a four-decade presence of his family in the topmost echelons of the country's politics. P. J. Patterson was, in the shade conscious reality of Jamaica, unambiguously black, and was perceived as representing the younger and far more confident majority of Jamaica's people. He was also, and importantly, from a rural constituency and therefore seen as being relatively untainted by the violence and corrupt practices that tarnished virtually all previous political leaders, based as they traditionally were in the strategic and troubled Kingston metropolitan area.

The Economic

A year later (in 1994 and at the time of writing), the picture could not be more different. There appears to be widespread despondency and disaffection, led by the seemingly endless economic crisis which has afflicted the country for the past twenty years. The Jamaican dollar, which stood at J$5.50 to US$1.00 in 1989 when Edward Seaga's JLP lost power, plummeted to J$29.00 to US$1.00 in late 1991, then stabilized at J$22.50 after a celebrated initiative by elements in the private sector. In mid 1993, following deflationary budget cuts, it again began to tumble, and has settled at a temporary plateau of some J$33.00 to US$1.00. While Jamaica has been lucky to avoid hyperinflation of the Latin American variety, its rates of inflation have been consistently high. The relatively low figure of 14.9 percent in 1992 was transformed the following year, as the free fall of the dollar contributed to a rate of 40.6 percent,[3] far above the targeted figure of some 11 percent. The popular opinion is that the real rate, insufficiently captured in the basket of goods used by the statisticians, is much higher than this.

Since its return to power in 1989, the nominally democratic socialist People's National Party government has followed textbook neoliberal policies,[4] including an accelerated divestment of nationally owned assets, relaxed import duties, a liberalized foreign exchange regime, high interest rates and tight fiscal policies. This has been largely predicated on the current World Bank and International Monetary Fund (IMF) policies which assume that if Jamaica (and other similar developing economies) can only get the liberalization equation 'right', it can achieve sustained growth and travel the path to success of the South-East Asian newly industrializing countries (NICs).[5] One of the problems, however, is that this at best problematic policy has been followed inconsistently. In 1992, in the months preceding the general election, duties were dramatically lowered on imported automobiles; tax rates were lowered and liberal wage increases granted to elements in the public sector. This typical vote-buying tactic contributed, in effect, to a wave of money printing and laid the basis for the subsequent round of devaluation and inflation which is still feeding through the system today.

It is perhaps too early to say that the government, based on its own criteria, has failed, but at best, the results are disappointing. While there are increasingly large reserves of foreign exchange held in local private accounts, the actual flows into the official banking system were reduced by 50 percent in the last half of 1993, though they are now on the increase again. Largely due to a high and subsequently deflationary interest rate policy, the new Minister of Finance Omar

Davies has been able to preside over the first positive net international reserves position for the country in two decades.[6]

What is evident, however, is that if one focuses on the statistics which would point towards future growth, the picture is not encouraging. Jamaica, particularly in the wake of the long North American recession, has not been an attractive target for foreign investment and there has been no massive inflow of new capital. Despite the positive performance of some nontraditional exports such as garment assembly which itself is now threatened by the new North American Free Trade Area (NAFTA), the downturn in bauxite/alumina exports with the saturation of the world aluminum market has meant that export growth has been sluggish. Imports, on the other hand, have skyrocketed – encouraged by the reduction in automobile duties and spurred on by an abysmal public transport system. In 1993, the balance of visible trade moved from the already bad figure of -US$872.8 million to -US$1,120.7 million.[7] The saving grace to the frightening and mushrooming negative balance of trade picture has been tourism which, quite remarkably, has grown consistently through the recession and increased its earnings from some US$794.2 million in 1992 to US$902.1 million in 1993.[8] Alongside this, the inherently difficult-to-estimate informal economy – legal, semilegal and illegal – has provided a steady flow of resources[9] to sections of the population which might otherwise have been further impoverished.

Nevertheless, it is fair to say that poverty is widespread in Jamaica. Consistently high interest rates[10] – the policy instituted to mop up excess liquidity and under-mine the black market in foreign exchange – have served to increase the disparity between rich and poor, already one of the most notoriously wide in the region. Between 1986 and 1991, the lowest paid 40 percent in Jamaica received, on average, 15.9 percent of the national income, compared with a figure of 19 percent in Barbados, to use a nearby example. For the same period, the UNDP found that 80 percent of rural Jamaicans lived below the poverty line, compared with 39 percent in Trinidad and Tobago, 70 percent in the Dominican Republic, 50 percent in St Lucia and 25 percent in Grenada.[11] The incongruity of the 'Two Jamaicas' is evident to even the most casual observer. The lifestyles of the wealthy in the salubrious communities of Cherry Gardens and Norbrook, and along the North Coast, with their Mercedes Benzs, BMWs and shopping junkets to Miami, rival anything to be found in the USA along, of course, with perfect weather. Descriptions of parties like the following held by an American entertainment executive are common items on the social pages of the daily newspapers:

> The rich and the famous have been flocking to the elegant Round Hill Hotel, Hanover, to soak up the winter sunshine, to rest and to party. Like the big fortieth anniversary bash for the founder of MTV Bob Pittman . . . Crystal chandeliers dangling from trees, bare footed waiters dressed in top hats, tails and black ties,

complemented by a fabulous Jamaican cuisine of baby lobsters, avocado and fruit . . . The men went dressed to kill, in their black ties and sarongs – bare footed. So did the ladies, also bare footed in their splendid evening gowns of silk and satin and their head wraps that gave them a charming Madame Pompadour grace and elegance.[12]

But a few miles away are the notorious Montego Bay ghetto communities of North Gully and Glendevon, mirror images of the far larger and more violent garrison communities like Rema, Concrete Jungle and Tivoli Gardens in Kingston. And, a few miles from these is the even more desperate Riverton City, where thousands of people live literally on the city dump and many survive by a daily schedule of picking through the refuse for spoilt food and saleable junk. One further statistic is, perhaps, of note: According to the UNDP Human Development Index, since 1970 Jamaica, while remaining a 'middle income country' has had the second greatest fall in standard of living of any country in the world (with Romania heading the list).[13]

There has undoubtedly been a long and drawn out economic trauma, the end of which is not yet in sight, but the crisis of the present moment is by no means purely an economic phenomenon. Accompanying it is a crisis of will, of direction, of ideas and of conflicting values, which can be roughly captured under the heading of what can be called 'hegemonic dissolution'.

The Political

Politically, postwar Jamaica has been characterized by the existence of one of the tightest, most impermeable and consistent two-party systems in the hemisphere.[14] There have been twelve general elections, eleven of them seriously contested by both major parties. In 1944, independents as a group actually outvoted the losing PNP. Apart from this, no third party has made any significant inroad. Each party succeeded the other in a two-term, roughly ten-year cycle, with the loser never getting less than 40 percent of the national vote. The system was underwritten by a number of features, including clientelism, extreme Westminster centralization of power, the absence of an effective back bench, the exclusion of third parties, and the absence of a strong, independent civil society. Its success and relative longevity can be said to have derived from a series of unwritten pacts and compromises between the largely brown-skinned and educated upper middle classes[15] who actually controlled state power, and the black working and lower classes who voted for them and occasionally engaged in internecine warfare in the rank and file of either party. These unwritten 'conventions' centred around three main elements: First, access to resources and the use of these resources to consolidate power. Once in power, the government (the patron) was expected to use its position to provide contracts, housing, land, work, access to visas and other scarce benefits to its supporters at all levels of society. Secondly, the acceptance of the principle of succession. This meant that at least every ten years there would be a change which the losing party would accept, despite sharp contestation and rancour, and thus allow the former opposition party a chance to eat from the pie. Thirdly, the existence of accessible and charismatic leadership. The leader, in classic Weberian manner, would not simply rule according to bureaucratic and constitutional norms, but would maintain an extensive level of contact with his supporters – not only to facilitate the distribution of benefits, but to strengthen the notion of a unified and popular party with common national interests.

This led to the consolidation of a tight system, based on the historical and charismatic roles played by the elder Manley and Bustamante, perceived and celebrated as national heroes and co-founders of the nation; the real role of the trade union affiliates of the two parties in improving the lot of the working class; and the significant improvement in the quality of life of the people arising out of the postwar social reforms, which have been felt especially in education, health and housing.[16]

In retrospect, the high point of this system was the year 1980 when, ironically, over 800 died in the lead up to the general election.[17] While there was undoubtedly a cold war dimension to the urban (and increasingly rural) violence as both sides relied to some extent on their international alliances for tactical and political support, on reflection, 1980 was the last election in which the great majority felt that the government was a prize; that the process of supporting a party and winning an election was the vehicle which would bring 'better', whether that better be defined as the mythical future of socialism or the mythical past of plentiful, '1960s' capitalism'. The JLP won that election massively using the slogan of deliverance and promising the people that money would soon "jingle in their pockets". By 1982, however, the polls showed that the government had become a minority[18] – a position it would retain for the entire decade, but for an opportune moment in 1983 when, temporarily boosted by the murder of Maurice Bishop and the invasion of Grenada, it swept back to power in a snap election, boycotted by the opposition PNP.

At the time, sensitive commentators saw this early shift from the JLP as the beginning of a new phenomenon of shorter term governments, with a five, instead of a ten-year cycle. But few, if any, could have recognized it as the beginning of the collapse of the pact of 1944 – the intricate set of rules which developed between the two parties and within the parties, between the leaders and their supporters. This collapse is not yet complete, but all the signs point in that direction. Among the most outstanding are:

- The undermining of the resource base available to successive governments which has enabled them to be effective patrons, distributing largesse to needy clients. The main factor accelerating this has been the IMF inspired structural adjustment agreements which have significantly reduced the size of government and, consequently, its effective role in the wider society

- The natural exhaustion of the two party cycle. Transition from one party to the other, with the accompanying slogans of redemption, has occurred too often without any significant change and the population is no longer willing to listen to promises of 'better' and 'deliverance' which are never fulfilled

- The retirement of Michael Manley from the positions of prime minister and leader of the PNP in 1993 ended the last link in the old charismatic chain which connected him to his father, and to his cousin Bustamante on the other side of the fence. The populist connection never existed for Seaga who, even at the nadir of PNP support in 1981, trailed behind Manley at the polls[19] and it does not seem to be emerging for Patterson.

By the mid eighties, the onset of a sea change was quite evident: The Stone polls showed that compared with 1971 when 87 percent of the electorate were loyal party voters and only 13 percent were issue voters, by 1986, only 48 percent considered themselves loyal to the party and 52 per cent had become issue voters.[20] A poll done in 1994 by Stone's organization a year after his death, suggests that this new configuration is consolidating. Asked 'which party would you vote for?', 26 percent supported the governing PNP, 29 percent were for the opposition while a large bloc of 45 percent remained uncommitted.[21] A further indicator that the two-party system is in mortal crisis has been the failure of the opposition to significantly increase its support out of the dire social and economic difficulties faced currently by the majority of the people. On the first anniversary of the PNP's electoral victory, the JLP declared a 'day of shame' and called on the people to stay away from work in order to protest what it considered the illegitimate 1993 elections and the deteriorating economic situation. Apart from some incidents of gunfire and a few roadblocks in established JLP strongholds, the day passed without any significant popular mobilization.[22]

The failed radical alternative – the WPJ

But if the moment is characterized by the collapse of support for the two traditional parties, it is also one in which a radical alternative has failed to assert itself in the popular imagination. An effective, organized left does not exist in Jamaica today, nor is there any other radical force of a populist, or religious, kind on the immediate horizon.

The Workers Party of Jamaica (WPJ) – the communist left of the seventies and eighties – fell apart towards the end of the latter decade. Indeed, the major debates in the WPJ, influenced by the tragic collapse of the Grenada revolution, preceded the historical collapse of the communist bloc and centred on the broad issues of the role of the market versus central economic control, the legitimacy of democratic centralism as an appropriate policy both within the party and in the state, and the relative stress to be placed on 'national' factors, such as race, as opposed to 'internationalist', purely class factors.

If the specific reasons why the WPJ collapsed in the late eighties were to be isolated, they would include:

- The failure to make any serious headway in elections (despite being in existence for more than a decade) – the decisive benchmark of success in Jamaican politics. No national or local government seat was ever won by the WPJ, a factor which ultimately led to demoralization and inevitably, recrimination. This failure can in turn be accounted for first, in the impermeability of the two-party system, where the fact of fifty years of tradition passed on through families and communities effectively excluded any third force; secondly, in the existence of armed 'garrison' communities inhibiting the possibility of peaceful organization in those poorest communities in which the class-based appeal of the WPJ might have been greatest; thirdly, in the wasted vote syndrome which, in a first-past-the-post electoral system, works against small third parties without significant geographic concentration; fourthly, in the persistent fear of communism among broad cross-sections of the Jamaican population, enhanced by cold war propaganda which provided, perhaps, the most effective inoculation against radical political movements.

- The harbouring of unrealistic notions of imminent revolution which often led to dogmatic, textbook Leninist methods of organization which, on the back of the already daunting list of constraints, served to further isolate the party from mainstream politics.[23]

The Social

In a context where both major parties have lost support, where the two-party project is increasingly discredited, and where there is no clear radical alternative to the system, the third dimension of the crisis seems fairly obvious: that is, the collapse of the social project of 1944. Accompanying the unwritten political pact which surrounded the 1944 electoral arrangements were an entire series of social arrangements which are more visible in their moment of collapse than while they were functioning properly. These would include an acceptance of social cues from the dominantly brown middle classes, including notions of decency in language, dress and manners. To speak English fluently was to be decent; to speak Jamaican 'patois' was not just different, but bad. These arrangements were, of course, welded on to the older plantation hierarchies of colour and class, in a complex structure. Carl Stone, in typically blunt manner, described it thus:

> Jamaica has always been South Africa without apartheid. The brown man and the red man have always assumed social superiority over the blacks in every sphere of activity, and blacks have always played up to these powerful colour and ethnic interests to get by in the society. The red man and the brown man have been taught to believe that they are the natural leaders and that black people's role is really to follow their leadership.[24]

Thus, it was not impossible for a very dark person to be upper class, but this would have to be demonstrated by an overcompensation in manners and language,[25] for the person would have to be on constant guard in case they were mistaken for someone from a lower status position. The converse of this social leadership was that the middle class was expected to play an active role in Jamaica's social and political life. The classic example of this was Norman Manley's Jamaica Welfare[26] of the 1930s, an organization which sought to build community structures in the rural areas, often with tremendous sacrifice from its middle class leadership. The perception today is that the middle class has largely retreated into its suburban enclaves, with houses individually guarded by security guards, cars air-conditioned with tinted windows, effectively insulating them literally and metaphorically from the rest of Jamaica, as captured by this columnist in the *Gleaner*:

> . . . There are certain areas in this country, where a poor, black man cannot walk, without calling attention to himself, and with the risk of being detained and arrested. The only difference between us and South Africa is that our people don't have to carry passes . . . Like South Africa with its sprawling ghettos physically juxtaposed to the affluent white communities, so is Jamaica. The beautiful 'members only' Constant Spring Golf Club elegantly sits next to Cassava Piece 'ghetto' with a mere barbed wire fence separating the two . . .[27]

The economic crisis, the collapse of the political project, the growing psychological independence of the subordinate classes, and the shelving of social leadership by the middle classes are the conditions under which a moment of hegemonic dissolution has emerged. Using hegemony in the Gramscian[28] sense to mean effective leadership and control of the direction of society, we can argue that the social bloc in charge of Jamaican society is no longer ruling over a people convinced of its social superiority and its inherent right to 'run things' – to use the popular Jamaican phrase.

There is sharp contestation[29] over a wide sphere of social and economic issues. At the mercantile level, higglers, formally referred to as informal commercial importers (ICIs) are competing head-on with the traditional Syrian and Chinese merchant classes in the lucrative dry goods trade.

At the level of language there is a practical battle for dominance between English as the lingua franca and 'Jamaican'. This is perhaps most evident in the shift to 'Jamaican' (as opposed to Jamaican English) as the dominant norm in the popular music. If the classical protest reggae music of the seventies – reaching its apogee in the works of Bob Marley – oscillated between standard (if biblical) English appeals against 'Babylon' and more overtly patois statements, the currently popular dance hall form has largely abandoned the tradition of resorting to the occasional refrain in standard English.[30]

In terms of dress and popular fashion, the growing disparity in normative trends is again evident in the dance hall. Unconventional modes of dress, often involving colourful and daring cut-outs and highly unconventional patterns, suggest that the cues as to what is to be considered as high fashion are neither coming from the traditional middle classes nor, for that matter, from a purely North American context. Instead, they are being refracted and reinvented through the lens of the urban ghetto experience into something not only peculiar to that experience, but in an adversarial position to traditional fashion.

In the music itself, an increasingly sharp rift is emerging between 'uptown' and 'downtown', with the latter adhering to dance hall, and the former either completely hostile to reggae or counterposing the more traditional 'classical' forms to the current 'debased' dance hall rhythms. Contestation is sharp and extends beyond the lyrics and rhythms to the actual volume of the music played. In a pointed dance hall piece, popular deejay Shabba Ranks along with the singing group Home T, argue that loud music and the dance hall are the poor people's means of entertainment:

> Some have satellite, some have video
> but poor people have nowhere to go . . .
> Dance hall business is all we know[31]

Then, even more ominously, the verse suggests that the alternative to loud music, if it is suppressed, will be guns and violence:

> If yu nuh wan' dem fi go bus' no shot
> Low di soun' system mek it nice up di spot[32]

The tremendous significance of the dance hall as an alternative space, removed from the restraining confines of (high) society, is captured in this comment from music critic and social observer Jean Fairweather Wilson:

> D.J. Man, a charismatic figure, strides and struts the stage, making periodic leaps
> into the air as if possessed. He dominates the space, ruling his kingdom with a
> microphone, as his subjects hearken unto his voice. The microphone is a rod of

correction. It is a gun. It is a conductor of electricity. It is a symbol of the power his listeners crave, want to identify with or need to affirm in themselves. 'Dance Hall' is about power . . .[33]

At the level of gender, the collapse of the project of 1944 can also be seen as the collapse of a dominant male project. Women, against tremendous odds, and despite continuing resistance, are coming into their own in Jamaican society. They now constitute 38 percent of all private sector executives compared with 21 percent twenty years ago. At the University of the West Indies, in all faculties except Natural Sciences, where they are only slightly outnumbered, women constitute the clear majority. In the critical management studies department, women outnumber men by a ratio of nearly three to one.[34] In the dancehalls, to use that fertile cutting edge example again, women arrive at dances in groups together. They dance together unless one asks a man to dance with her. If any aggressive man tries to enter the group unrequested, he is liable to be attacked by a variety of means, including the use of the weapon of choice – acid – which many revellers carry as protection. Fairweather Wilson again amplifies this dimension:

> Our genuine dance hall women leaders who originate from downtown, typically, have a measure of economic power and independence. Some achieve this through lucrative activities as informal commercial importers. Some have become successful by way of dressmaking and other business concerns. These women can afford to buy themselves the most fabulous finery, successfully competing with the well kept women of the dons. They often go out by themselves, in posses, dressed in their garments of liberation. They can certainly afford to pay their own bar bills. This level of economic independence has implications for the man-woman relationship. It seems to me that the ongoing power struggle between man and woman has taken on some new dimensions in the dance hall culture . . .[35]

In the sphere of manners, there is an almost tangible dissolution of accepted modes and norms. It is felt perhaps most acutely in the increasing failure to form queues of any kind. The Jamaican public has never been particularly sympathetic to the concept of 'lining up', but the little recognition that has been shown in the past is fast disappearing. This example, given by a *Gleaner* columnist, speaks eloquently to the moment:

> Stand in any line, anywhere in Jamaica! Someone will try to push in front of you. If you object it is you who will be berated . . . I remember being in the express line of a corporate area supermarket, under a sign which read 'One to ten items only'. A well dressed woman with a cart full of groceries pushed in front of me. I objected, firstly because she didn't wait behind me and secondly because she had many more than ten items . . . She took a deep breath and treated all those

within earshot to a vocabulary more appropriate to a construction site. Her tirade ended with the trump card: 'Yu t'ink dis a Sout' Africa, white gal?' Even worse, everyone else in the line took her side, suggesting I should join some other line if I didn't like the way this one was being run while the cashier stared off into space.[36]

The example is poignant because it brings so many of the features of the moment into sharp focus. The collapse of middle class hegemony has meant the collapse of the reflexive deference to persons of fairer complexion, but it has also meant the collapse of deeper universalistic norms of respect for other individuals, which are the underpinnings of any functioning civilization. The baby is in danger of being thrown out with the bath water. The glue which held Jamaica together is in a process of terminal meltdown.

The result of all of this is hegemonic dissolution or, as Obika Gray suggests, "dual social power".[37] In some respects, this moment is akin to the dual political power which is one of the definitive features of a mature revolutionary situation. The old hegemonic alliance is unable to rule in the accustomed way, but equally, alternative and competitive modes of hegemony from below are unable to decisively place their stamp on the new and fluid situation. What is definitely absent is an effective populist political organization, which might provide leadership, though, perhaps, also steer the people in the direction of more traditional, hierarchical channels. There is, also, in the new unipolar world order no permissive world context,[38] or international conjuncture which would facilitate the success of a national revolutionary upsurge; so in this critical respect also, the present moment is different.

Three instances

Three case studies help to illuminate the facets of the present conjuncture. In each case, extensive source material from the daily papers is used to suggest the immediacy and poignancy of the situation. All three are incidents which occurred in 1994 and involve sharp, often violent confrontations between the people and authority. In none of the cases is there an outright solution – at least in the short run. People are aggrieved, they fight, and in the end they either lose or arrive at some compromise. Underlying them all though, is a sense of anomie, of drift, and the decay of binding relationships on all sides.

Case One involves the squatter community of Flankers on the outskirts of the tourist city of Montego Bay. The *Gleaner* front page headline of Saturday, March 12 proclaimed: 'Squatter Fury Erupts Out West', and the report reads as follows:

> The depressed community of Flankers erupted in fury yesterday as a result of a pre-dawn demolition raid against squatters. Enraged residents told the *Gleaner* that police were accompanied by armed thugs who began tearing down

houses, vandalizing furniture and stealing money. Residents retaliated with stones until the police and their companions retreated downhill to the main road. Five persons were reportedly shot and several infants were affected by teargas . . . As the disturbances spread, persons started mounting roadblocks with stones, old vehicles and burning tyres. Schools and shops closed and tourists were advised to stay in their hotels. At the eastern exit of town, traffic was backed up all the way to Rosehall and a vociferous crowd surged along the main road by Flankers hurling abuse at the police.

Inspector Steadman Roach, who led the demolition team, was pelted and knocked flat with rocks and wounded. He left the scene in a police car under cover of reinforcements who attempted to disperse the crowd by firing in the air. Burning barricades reappeared as soon as they were removed by the police team, which at one stage included Colonel Trevor Macmillan, Commissioner of Police. Joe Whitter, owner of the property, had his Fort Street office set afire . . . the crowd spotted Mr Whitter in a rental car by a roadblock near Wexford Court. They swarmed the car and almost turned it upside down before Mr Whitter was rescued by the police.

Back at Flankers shortly before noon, the Commissioner of Police arrived and was escorted by a hysterical crowd to the Flankers All Age School . . . Colonel Macmillan, after calling for strict observance of the law, told the people that the information he had received indicated that the police had acted improperly and Inspector Roach had been relieved of his duties with immediate effect, pending the outcome of an investigation which would be done by an independent team from Kingston.

'I want a report by Monday. I give you my word; my word is my bond – that where the police have acted illegally, they will be highly disciplined.'[39]

Case Two involves a shift from the West to the arguably even more beautiful eastern end of the island. Again, it involves a question of right and a clash between vested propertied interests and aggrieved people who invoke traditional rights of access in opposition to the formal right to own property. The *Sunday Gleaner* of April 3, a mere three weeks after the Flankers incident, headlined the following report 'Vandals Wreak Havoc at Blue Lagoon':

Vandals invaded the premises of the Blue Lagoon, Portland, between Friday night and yesterday morning, smashing and destroying five boats. Another boat is reported missing.

The vandals also emptied an undetermined quantity of gasoline into the Blue Lagoon. At least two fishermen lost their boats and equipment in the wave of destruction.

The vandalism followed eviction notices served three weeks ago on twelve squatters who had been occupying the site for some time.

On Friday, a crowd of some 25 persons converged on the Lagoon property shouting death threats at the owner Valerie Marzouca. They also painted the walls and pavements with threats and obscene slogans.

On Friday, police continued with their investigation to determine the identities of persons instigating threats and vandalism.

In a statement to the *Gleaner* on Friday, Mrs Marzouca said that 'It would appear that property owners in Jamaica no longer have any rights to their properties in the face of public indiscipline and anarchy.'[40]

Case Three takes us once more to the West, to the sleepy fishing village of Green Island, and a tragic incident resulting from a common example of excessive force used by members of the Jamaican police force. On September 2 the *Herald* headline read 'Green Island Protest Leaves One Dead', captioning the following report:

Green Island, the fishing town midway between Lucea, Hanover and Negril, the tourist resort in the West, remained calm last night after two days of protest sparked by the police shootings which left one dead, and twenty residents detained by the police.

Dead is Keisha Johnson, 17, a student of Green Island Comprehensive High School . . . She was killed yesterday, the second day of rioting in the town, following an incident on Tuesday between the police and some residents in which an elderly woman was reportedly beaten by two officers . . . Eyewitness [*sic*] told Universal Press Services (UPS) that Miss Johnson was shot fatally when she intervened after the police held her uncle Johnny Whitmore in her yard. The policeman's gun reportedly went off and hit her in the chest and arm . . . The killing sparked protests by residents who described it as 'police brutality'. . . Disorder broke out on Tuesday around noon, residents said, after a number of persons who were seeking medical attention at the local health centre attempted to shelter from heavy rainfall in a building which is under construction. The police were called after an incident developed between the foreman of the construction site and residents . . . The residents said that without warning the police started raining blows on a number of persons on their arrival. It was alleged that a young girl who saw her grandmother being hit by the policeman intervened by using her umbrella to hit the policeman. The scene became a free for all with the police using force and the residents retaliating. By afternoon residents had blocked the main road leading to and from Negril, forcing traffic to divert.[41]

Three common factors are evident in otherwise spatially distinct and unconnected incidents. The first is the willingness of the state – often in close cooperation with vested interests – to resort to force before attempting moral suasion. The second is the complete absence of any fear or respect for the dominant strata, evident in the physical attack on Whitter, the contempt shown for Marzouca, and in a different kind of incident, the willingness of the unnamed young girl to wield an umbrella in defense of her elderly grandmother against the armed forces of the state. The third feature, as previously suggested, is the inability of the aggrieved to prevail. The incident flares up; roads are blocked and tyres burnt; important officers of the state arrive; the incident peters out until the next instance. Those 'above' are losing the moral authority with which they have ruled effectively for five postwar decades. But those 'below' do not have the tools, worldview or organization to present a credible alternative to that rule.

Three Possibilities

There are, perhaps, three broad possibilities: In the first, an authoritarian government comes to power either within or outside the constitution and seeks to reimpose order, good manners and decency via coercive measures. Already, the reintroduction of the long shelved policy of flogging criminals,[42] the strong support across wide sections of the society for the use of the death penalty,[43] and the long tradition of recorded instances of excessive use of force and police brutality in Jamaica,[44] all suggest that an authoritarian solution is not completely out of the question in the future. The second option would entail a process of democratic renewal, which would recognize the potential in the present conjuncture for unleashing the creative energies of the Jamaican people and seek to funnel the present, admittedly chaotic, moment in a positive direction of national consensus and popular inclusion.[45] There is, also, a third alternative, which is Marx and Engels' oft quoted "common ruin of the contending classes". This is an option that no one wishes to contemplate, but the experiences of Yugoslavia, Lebanon, Somalia and, closer home, of Haiti suggest that it is not impossible if the political and social situation continues to drift and no clear social force is able to assert its dominance.[46]

But to address the second and this writer's favoured option, it would have to include:

- First, a democratically constituted constituent assembly to rewrite the constitution. A rewrite is at present under way, but insufficient attempt has been made to include the broadest sections of the population, which would mean, for example, making simplified summaries of the existing document and explaining the implications of various options.[47] Among the issues to be examined in any popular rewrite, would be the overarching powers of the prime minister. A rewrite would require checks and balances – perhaps along presidential lines, while trying to avoid the pitfalls of gridlocked, ineffective government

- Secondly, an element of proportional representation, perhaps in the upper house which is now nominated, in order to avoid the 'do or die' reality of a winner-take-all system inherent in which is the potential for confrontation. At the same time, an element of constituency-based responsibility in the lower house should be maintained

- Thirdly, a system of recall for nonperforming members of parliament, designed to avoid frivolous excesses, yet sufficiently effective to allow greater popular control over representatives

- Fourthly, a concerted, if belated attempt to 'level the economic playing-field' through more transparent means of access to government lands, bank loans and other financial instruments

- Fifthly, a national cultural renewal based on a reappraisal of popular culture and language and its greater acceptance through the public media and other avenues of discourse

- Sixthly, the arrival at a consensus on the economic and social path for the country, with the recognition that certain social services and economic institutions will not be tampered with by successive governments for narrow partisan advantage. This should be coupled with the identification of clear economic priorities, clustered around the things that Jamaican people do well – in the areas of entertainment, sports and services especially.

A case is not being made for the uniqueness of these developments in Jamaica. Politics and the state are under siege throughout the world. Informal economies have grown along with the growth of 'cookie cutter' governments advocating textbook structural adjustment. Poverty is not Jamaican, just as the rebellion in Chiapas[48] cannot be totally isolated from the Venezuelan riots or from the Sendero uprising in Peru. While not adhering to a Wallersteinian[49] interpretation of these events as simply symptoms of one coalescent and coherent world system, it would be simplistic and blind not to see the similarities and underlying causalities which connect them all. The question really is: in a world without sharply differentiated and competitive poles, how to reinvent a notion of popular change which will carry us beyond structural adjustment, lead to a genuine advance in democracy, empower people and ultimately provide a better life.[50] Is change possible? Will it come from above or below? Are there real live persons on the ground able to lead such a renewal? All crises provide the opportunity to look forward and to look back. This sketch of the present Jamaican crisis suggests that the answer is not at all predetermined, but the clues to its possible direction are to be found on the outskirts of Montego Bay, next to the pristine Blue Lagoon of Portland and in the throbbing dancehalls of Kingston and every town in Jamaica on Saturday night.

Notes

1 Dissatisfaction with the elections was substantial. A year after, albeit in a period when the new government's popularity had begun to wane, 44 percent of those polled felt that the election had not been free and fair, compared to 31 percent who answered in the affirmative and 25 percent who were unsure. See Stone Poll in *Daily Gleaner* (March 17, 1994), 3. For almost two decades, until the early nineties, UWI Professor Carl Stone's highly accurate polls have been the definitive indicator of political popularity in Jamaica. Since his death in 1993, the 'Stone Polls' have continued under the direction of his wife, Rosemarie.

2 The 59 percent turnout of registered voters in the 1993 elections was the lowest since the first universal adult suffrage election in 1944. Within this context, however, the PNP had its largest ever majority, breaking the 60 percent mark for the first time. For its part, the Jamaica Labour Party faced its worst defeat since 1955. See *Sunday Gleaner* (March 27, 1994).

3 Statistical Bulletin: Consumer Price Index, June 1994 (Kingston: STATIN, 1994).

4 For a thoughtful and critical examination of the possible models and the prospects for Jamaica's economy, see Donald Harris, "The Jamaican economy in the twenty-first century: challenges to development and requirements of a response", in Patsy Lewis (ed), *Jamaica: Preparing for the Twenty-first Century* (Kingston: Ian Randle Publishers, 1994),13-52. It is of importance to note that Harris recognizes that for the economy to move forward their must be a "workable truce" and a "social pact" (p. 40), precisely what is missing in Jamaica today.

5 When the Jamaican economy is measured against the criteria required prior to 'take off' on the South-East Asian path, it falls badly short. Gerald Tan suggests that among the critical factors necessary before industrialization can be considered are: (i) an efficient agricultural sector; (ii) rapid, prior growth in exports; (iii) a clear prior shift to the manufacturing sector; (iv) little industrial unrest; (v) low rates of inflation; (vi) an efficient public administration; and (vii) a stable political climate. Jamaica's performance on the economic dimensions are bad, or at best anaemic. On the more political criteria, it cannot claim low levels of industrial unrest, the public administration is poor and while parliamentary democracy is entrenched, it is difficult to describe the current political climate as stable. See Gerald Tan, "The next NICs of Asia", *Third World Quarterly* 14, no. 1 (1993), 57-74.

6 In September 1990, the Net International Reserves figure showed a deficit of US$552.3 million. In December 1993, it went into the black and has been on the increase for every month since then. See *Statistical Digest* (Kingston: Bank of Jamaica, March/April 1994), 82.

7 Ibid., 84.

8 Ibid., 90. The irony, of course, is that tourism with its relatively lavish display of wealth and luxury, is expected to perform as the growth industry in a society beset with chronic unemployment and dire poverty. The potential for disruption of the crucial foreign exchange lifeline, as Jamaicans have experienced on many occasions, is enormous.

9 The item 'private transfers' in the official statistics gives some indication of the potential size of the informal economy. In 1993, this item amounted to some US$267.8 million, or roughly a third of the earnings from tourism. This is only the tip of the iceberg, for it

does not include the vast number of private transfers which are not recorded, the earnings from itinerant musicians on the international circuit and of course, the illegal earnings from drug lords and posse members. See *Statistical Digest*, 90.

10 Interest rates, which hovered at around the 19 percent level in 1988-89, shot up to 35 percent in 1992 before reaching the unprecedented level of 52 percent in the early months of 1994. More recently there has been a gradual decline. See *Statistical Digest*, 50 and *Daily Gleaner* (February 2, 1994) for a report of the government's policies to stem the slide of the dollar.

11 See UNDP, *Human Development Report, 1994* (New York and Oxford: Oxford University Press, 1994), 164.

12 *Daily Gleaner* (March 11,1994), 40.

13 See UNDP, *Human Development Report 1993* (New York and Oxford: Oxford University Press, 1993), 103.

14 For a critical assessment of the main features of the Jamaican political system in the mid to late seventies, see Carl Stone, *Democracy and Clientelism in Jamaica* (New Brunswick (USA) and London: Transaction Books, 1983), and for a later critique of Stone's work, Carlene Edie, *Democracy by Default: Dependency and Clientelism in Jamaica* (Boulder: Lynne Rienner, 1991).

15 For an assessment of the path to power of the dominantly 'brown' middle classes, see Trevor Munroe, *The Politics of Constitutional Decolonization: Jamaica, 1944-1962* (UWI, Mona: Institute of Social and Economic Research, 1972).

16 The genuine improvement in the conditions of life of the people, spurred on by British Fabian policies and a booming economy for much of the postwar period, is still being felt although it has been severely undermined in recent times. The 1994 *Human Development Report* (p.102) could still find that among developing countries Jamaica's life expectancy was ranked at eight; its infant mortality rate was fifth in terms of least deaths; its adult literacy rates second; and its access to safe water first.

17 See, for example, Michael Kaufman, *Jamaica Under Manley: Dilemmas of Socialism and Democracy* (London: Zed, 1985), Michael Manley, *Struggle in the Periphery* (London: Writers and Readers, 1982), and Evelyne Huber Stephens and John Stephens, *Democratic Socialism in Jamaica* (Basingstoke and London: Macmillan, 1986).

18 See Carl Stone, *Politics vs Economics: the 1989 Elections in Jamaica* (Kingston: Heinemann Publishers (Caribbean) Ltd, 1989), 27.

19 In his poll of July 1981, Carl Stone asked his sample who was the most outstanding leader in Jamaica. Only 29.2 percent supported then Prime Minister Seaga, while 33.4 percent supported Manley. See Carl Stone, *The Political Opinions of the Jamaican People* (Kingston, Jamaica: Blackett Publishers, 1982).

20 See Stone, *Politics vs Economics*, 108.

21 See *Sunday Gleaner* (March 27, 1994).

22 See *Daily Gleaner* (March 31, 1994). It can be argued with some justification that it is still too early in the PNP's term of office to conclude that the JLP is no longer a viable alternative. Only time will conclusively prove this, but the absence of popular response to the JLP in the face of what are undoubtedly some of the most traumatic developments in the economy, is a telling factor.

23 For a discussion of some of these issues, see Rupert Lewis, "Which way for the Jamaican left?" *Third World Viewpoint* 1, no. 1 (May 1993).

24 Carl Stone, *The Stone Columns: the Last Year's Work* (Kingston: Sangster's, 1993), 96.

25 For a sensitive discussion of the peculiarities of class and colour in Jamaica, see Rex Nettleford's, *Mirror, Mirror: Identity, Race and Protest in Jamaica* (Glasgow: Collins and Sangster, 1970).

26 For a good description of the early welfare and grassroots development movement in Jamaica, see D. T. M. Girvan, *Working Together for Development* (Kingston: Institute of Jamaica, 1993).

27 *Sunday Gleaner* (March 20,1994).

28 See Antonio Gramsci, *Selections from Prison Notebooks* (London: Lawrence and Wishart, 1986). For a more current, less 'economically bound', though controversial reinterpretation of hegemony, see Ernesto Laclau and Chantal Mouffe, *Hegemony and Socialist Strategy: Towards a Radical Democratic Politics* (London, New York: Verso, 1989).

29 It is not that there is not a broad recognition that something is wrong. In February, Patterson's prestige was boosted immensely when he hosted a national conference on values and attitudes. The topics discussed by the large turnout of delegates ranged across the gamut of issues from crime to the family and the question of gender. The real rift probably exists between a trend which imagines that traditional moral and religious values simply need to be reimposed and the society will return to the good old days, and a view closer to that expressed here, which recognizes a more profound conjunctural crisis, requiring more broad based strategies to address it. See *Report on the National Consultation on Values and Attitudes* (Kingston: Jamaica Information Service, April 1994).

30 For a more detailed and technical discussion of the current trends in dance hall or deejay music, see Carolyn Cooper, *Noises in the Blood: Orality, Gender and the 'Vulgar' Body of Jamaican Popular Culture* (London and Basingstoke: Macmillan, 1993).

31 Shabba Ranks, *Mr Maximum* (Pow Wow Records, 1982).

32 Ibid.

33 Jean Fairweather Wilson, "Dance hall: sifting the truths", *Sunday Gleaner* (April 17, 1994).

34 See *Student Registration, Mona, 1993/4 and 1992/3 as at 3/11/93* (UWI Academic Board document AB (M) p.10, 1993/4).

35 Ibid.

36 Diana Macaulay, "Wrong but strong", *Daily Gleaner* (February 2, 1994).

37 See Obika Gray, "Discovering the social power of the poor", *Social and Economic Studies* 43, no. 3 (September 1994).

38 See Walter Goldfrank, "Theories of revolution and revolution without theory", *Theory and Society* 7, nos. 1 & 2 (1979), and Brian Meeks, *Caribbean Revolutions and Revolutionary Theory: an Assessment of Cuba, Nicaragua and Grenada* (London and Basingstoke: Macmillan, 1993).

39 *Daily Gleaner* (12 March 1994). One of the ironies of the 'Flankers rebellion', which is what it has come to be called in the popular domain, is that the landowner, Mr Whitter, far from being an exemplar of the fair-skinned landed élite, is a self made black man who accumulated his wealth as an immigrant in Britain.

40 *Sunday Gleaner* (April 3, 1994).

41 *Friday Herald* (September 2, 1994).

42 See "Flogging is back; judge orders punishment after twenty-year lapse", *Gleaner* (9 August 1994).

43 See "Hang them: KSAC backs call to get tough with convicts", *Gleaner* (10 August 1994).

44 See "Jamaica leads in police brutality", *Gleaner* (June 6, 1994). The position advocating draconian and extra-constitutional measures has by no means triumphed, but is growing. In a recent conference, former deputy governor of the Bank of Jamaica and now World Bank economist Gladstone Bonnick argued that: "The society should be prepared to give up certain freedoms it has enjoyed in the past but which have been abused by criminals . . . The freedom of movement at all hours of night and day from one area to another may have to be reconsidered". See Gladstone Bonnick, "Crime and violence: implications for economic expansion", in *Preparing for the Twenty-first Century*, 158.

45 See for example, Trevor Munroe's call for fundamental institutional change in *Daily Gleaner* (April 10, 1994) and repeatedly in his book *For a New Beginning: Selected Speeches, 1990-1993* (Kingston: Caricom Publishers Ltd., 1994). Munroe, former general secretary of the WPJ is now a member of a loose alliance called the New Beginning Movement (NBM) composed of former (and some standing) members of the two major parties as well as independent individuals. The NBM has made important statements on the need for transparency and greater democracy in national life, but the impression is that even this group, composed as it is of many people who have been tainted by the old politics, may be trailing behind the mood of the people and the current tendency to disconnect from 'official' organizations.

46 The trend towards the 'common ruin' option is perhaps most evident in the crime statistics. If 1980, the year when the country almost descended into civil war and eight hundred people were murdered, is used as a benchmark, then the current picture is frightening. In 1993, the gun was used in 4,385 crimes and 653 people were murdered. The difference with 1980, is that in that year most of the violence could have been attributed to the partisan battle for political power, whereas the shift in 1993 has been to random acts of violence and domestic incidents. This statistic may provide cold comfort to those who have lost members of their family or friends, but it does underline the drift away from an organized state to some notion of anarchy. See *Daily Gleaner* (January 20, 1994).

47 Carl Stone's thoughtful 1992 report to the Jamaican government on the possible reform of parliament touches on most of the critical areas requiring reform, including the examination of proportional representation, the abandonment of the prime ministerial system and the strengthening of constituency representation. Both government and opposition initially met these reform proposals with a lukewarm response, but have warmed to them as the depth of the political decay has become apparent. Despite the acknowledgement of the need for change, the whole process remains largely divorced from the day to day existence of the vast majority of the people. See Carl Stone's *Report of the Stone Committee Appointed to Advise the Jamaican Government on the Performance, Accountability and Responsibilities of Elected Parliamentarians* (Kingston: Bustamante Institute of Public and International Affairs, 1992).

48 Burbach argues that Chiapas is the first 'postmodern' rebellion, not only because it has occurred after the end of the cold war, but because of the particular level of popular involvement and the relationship between leaders and led. To this extent the present political moment in Jamaica might also be considered postmodern. The 'people' are asserting themselves in national life in unprecedented ways without traditional political leadership in a flanking movement around the state apparatus and beyond national boundaries. See Roger Burbach, "Roots of the postmodern rebellion in Chiapas", *New Left Review*, no. 205 (1994).

49 See Immanuel Wallerstein's "The agonies of liberalism: what hope progress?" *New Left Review*, no. 204 (March/April 1994) for a recent attempt to analyse the ideological dimensions of the 'world system'.

50 For an extensive discussion of the possibilities for democratic transition for developing countries in the new world order, see Shahid Qadir, Christopher Clapham and Barry Gills, "Democratisation in the Third World: an introduction", *Third World Quarterly* 14, no. 3 (1993). Indeed, the entire volume is devoted to a discussion of democratic alternatives.

Bibliography

Adamson, Walter. 1980. *Hegemony and Revolution*. Los Angeles and London: University of California Press.

Alavi, H. 1972. "The state in postcolonial societies: Pakistan and Bangladesh", *New Left Review*, no. 74 (July/August).

Ambursley, Fitzroy. 1983. "Grenada: the New Jewel revolution". In *Crisis in the Caribbean*, edited by F. Ambursley and R. Cohen. London: Heinemann.

Ambursley, Fitzroy, and Robin Cohen, eds. 1983. *Crisis in the Caribbean*. Kingston, Port of Spain: Heinemann.

Anderson, Benedict. 1991. *Imagined Communities: Reflections on the Origins and Spread of Nationalism*. London: Verso.

Anderson, Perry. 1980. *Arguments within English Marxism*. London: Verso.

Anderson, Perry. 1992. *A Zone of Engagement*. London: Verso.

Arrighi, G., and J. Saul. 1973. "African socialism in one country: Tanzania". In *Essays on the Political Economy of Africa*, edited by G. Arrighi and J. Saul. New York and London: Monthly Review Press.

Aya, Rod. 1979. "Theories of revolution reconsidered", *Theory and Society* 8, no. 1.

Aya, Rod. 1990. *Rethinking Revolutions and Collective Violence: Studies on Concept, Theory and Method*. Amsterdam: Het Spinhuis.

Bank of Jamaica. 1994. *Statistical Digest, March/April 1994*. Kingston: Bank of Jamaica.

Bayart, Jean François. 1991. "Finishing with the idea of the Third World: the concept of the political trajectory". In *Rethinking Third World Politics*, edited by James Manor. London and New York: Longman.

Best, Lloyd. 1965. "From Chaguaramas to slavery", *New World Quarterly* 2, no. 1.

Best, Lloyd. 1970. "The February revolution: causes and meaning", *Tapia*, no. 12.

Best, Lloyd. 1990. "From Eric Williams to Abu Bakr", *Trinidad and Tobago Review* 12, nos. 11 & 12.

Blackburn, Robin. 1988. *The Overthrow of Colonial Slavery*. London, New York: Verso.

Blackburn, Robin, ed. 1991. *After the Fall*. London: Verso.

Bonnick, Gladstone. 1994. "Crime and violence: implications for economic expansion". In *Jamaica: Preparing for the Twenty-first Century*, edited by Patsy Lewis. Kingston: Ian Rrandle Publishers.

Brenner, Robert. 1986. "The social basis of economic development". In *Analytical Marxism*, edited by J. Roemer. Cambridge: Cambridge University Press.

Brinton, Crane. 1953. *The Anatomy of Revolution*. Great Britain: Jonathan Cape.

Brizan, George. n.d. "The nutmeg industry: Grenada's black gold", St. George's, n.p.

Brutents, K.N. 1977. *National Liberation Revolutions Today*. Moscow: Progress Publishers.

Buhle, Paul. 1988. *C.L.R. James: the Artist as Revolutionary*, London: Verso.

Burbach, Roger. 1994. "Roots of the postmodern rebellion in Chiapas", *New Left Review*, no. 205.

Callinicos, Alex. 1987. *Making History: Agency, Structure and Change in Social Theory*. Cambridge: Polity Press.

Callinicos, Alex. 1989. *Against Postmodernism*. Cambridge: Polity Press.

Camejo, Acton. 1971. "Racial discrimination in employment in the private sector in Trinidad and Tobago: a study of the business élite and the social structure", *Social and Economic Studies* 20, no. 3.

Campbell, Horace. 1994. "Progressive politics and the Jamaican society at home and abroad", *Social and Economic Studies* 43, no. 3.

Cardoso, F.H. 1973. "Associated dependent development: theoretical and practical implications". In *Authoritarian Brazil: Origins, Politics and Future*, edited by A. Stephen. New Haven: Yale University Press.

Coard, Bernard. 1978. *The Role of the State in Agriculture*, Guyana: Institute of Social & Economic Research/ Institute for Development Studies.

Cohen, G.A. 1980. *Karl Marx's Theory of History: a Defence*, Princeton, N.J.: Princeton University Press.

Cohen, G.A. 1991. "The future of a disillusion", *New Left Review*, no. 190.

Cooper, Carolyn. 1993. *Noises in the Blood: Orality, Gender and the 'Vulgar' Body of Jamaican Popular Culture*. London and Basingstoke: Macmillan.

Cornforth, Maurice. 1972. *Historical Materialism*. New York: International Publishers.

Craig, Susan. 1982. "Background to the 1970 confrontation in Trinidad and Tobago". In *Contemporary Caribbean: a Sociological Reader*, Vol. 2, edited by Susan Craig. Port of Spain: The author.

Cudjoe, Selwyn R. 1993. "C.L.R. James misbound", *Transition*, no. 58.

Daily Express. 1990. *Trinidad under Seige: the Muslimeen Uprising.* Port of Spain: The Trinidad Express Newspapers Limited.

Davies, James, ed. 1971. *When Men Revolt and Why: A Reader in Political Violence and Revolution*. New York: Free Press.

DeBoissière, Ralph. 1981. *Crown Jewel*. London: Picador.

Duncan, Neville. 1990. "The Muslimeen revolt", *Caricom Perspective*, no. 49.

Dunn, John. 1989. *Modern Revolutions: an Introduction to the Analysis of a Political Phenomenon*. 2d ed. Cambridge: Cambridge University Press.

Edie, Carlene. 1991. *Democracy by Default: Dependency and Clientelism in Jamaica*. Boulder: Lynne Rienner.

Elster, Jon. 1979. *Ulysses and the Sirens: Studies in Rationality and Irrationality*. Cambridge: Cambridge University Press.

Elster, Jon. 1989. *Making Sense of Marx*. Cambridge: Cambridge University Press.

Engels, Frederick. 1933. *Germany: Revolution and Counter-Revolution*. Moscow: Progress Publishers.

Engels, Frederick. 1974. "On authority". In *Marx and Engels Basic Writings on Politics and Philosophy*, edited by Lewis S. Feuer. Glasgow: Collins.

Engels, Frederick. 1975. "Letter to Joseph Bloch". In *Marx Engels Selected Correspondence*. Moscow: Progress Publishers.

Farhi, Farideh. 1988. "State disintegration and urban based revolutionary crisis: a comparative analysis of Iran and Nicaragua", *Comparative Political Studies* 21, no. 2.

Farhi, Farideh. 1990. *States and Urban-Based Revolutions: Iran and Nicaragua*. Champagne: University of Illinois Press.

Feierabend, Ivo, and Rosalind Feierabend. 1971. "Aggressive behaviour within polities 1948-1962: a cross-national study". In *When Men Revolt and Why: a Reader in Political Violence and Revolution*, edited by James Davies. New York: Free Press.

Feuer, Lewis, S., ed. 1974. *Marx and Engels: Basic Writings on Politics and Philosophy*. Glasgow: Collins.

Fick, Carolyn. 1990. *The Making of Haiti: the St Domingue Revolution from Below*. Knoxville: University of Tennessee Press.

Foucault, Michel. 1990. *The Archaeology of Knowledge*. Great Britain: Routledge.

Foucault, Michel. 1990. *The History of Sexuality*. Vol. 1. Harmondsworth: Penguin.

Fukuyama, Francis. 1989. "The end of history?" *The National Interest* (summer).

Fukuyama, Francis. 1992. *The End of History and the Last Man*. New York: Avon.

Geggus, David. 1982. *Slavery, War and Revolution: the British Occupation of St Domingue, 1793-98*. Oxford: Oxford University Press.

Ghany, Hamid. 1990. "The constitution prevailed", *Caricom Perspective*, no. 49.

Giddens, Anthony. 1986. *Capitalism and Modern Social Theory: an Analysis of the Writings of Marx, Durkheim and Weber*. Cambridge: Cambridge University Press.

Girvan, D.T.M. 1993. *Working Together for Development*. Edited by Norman Girvan. Kingston: Institute of Jamaica.

Girvan, Norman. 1968. "After Rodney: the politics of student protest in Jamaica", *New World Quarterly* 4, no. 3.

Goldfrank, Walter. 1979. "Theories of revolution and revolution without theory", *Theory and Society* 7, nos. 1 & 2.

Goldstone, Jack. 1979. "Theories of revolution: the third generation", *World Politics*, no. 32.

Goodwin, Jeff. 1992. "A theory of persistent insurgency: El Salvador, Guatemala and Peru in Comparative perspective". Paper presented at the 17th International Conference of the Latin American Studies Association (LASA), Los Angeles, California, 24-27 September, 1992.

Goulbourne, Harry, ed. 1983. *Politics and State in the Third World*. London and Basingstoke: Macmillan.

Gramsci, Antonio. 1970. *The Modern Prince and Other Writings*. New York: International.

Gramsci, Antonio. 1986. *Selections from Prison Notebooks*. London: Lawrence and Wishart.

Gray, Obika. 1991. *Radicalism and Social Change in Jamaica 1960-1972*. Knoxville: The University of Tennessee Press.

Gray, Obika. 1994. "Discovering the social power of the poor", *Social and Economic Studies* 43, no. 3.

Grenada. Central Statistical Office. 1979. *Abstract of Statistics*. St George's: CSO.

Grimshaw, Anna, ed. 1993. *The C.L.R. James Reader*. Oxford, UK, Cambridge, USA: Basil Blackwell.

Gurr, Ted. 1971. *Why Men Rebel*. Princeton: Princeton University Press.

Habermas, Jurgen. 1987. *The Philosophical Discourse of Modernity: Twelve Lectures*. Cambridge: Polity Press.

Hall, Stuart. 1992. "C.L.R. James: a portrait". In *C.L.R. James's Caribbean*, edited by P. Henry and P. Buhle. London and Basingstoke: Macmillan Caribbean.

Halliday, Fred. 1990. *Cold War, Third World: an Essay on Soviet-US Relations*. London, Sydney: Hutchinson Radius.

Halliday, Fred. 1992. "An encounter with Fukuyama", *New Left Review*, no. 193.

Harris, Donald. 1994. "The Jamaican economy in the twenty-first century: challenges to development and requirements of a response". In *Jamaica: Preparing for the Twenty-first Century*, edited by Patsy Lewis. Kingston: Ian Randle Publishers.

Harvey, Franklin. 1974. *The Rise and Fall of Party Politics in Trinidad and Tobago*. Toronto: New Beginning.

Hayek, F.A. 1990. *The Constitution of Liberty*. Great Britain: Routledge.

Hermassi, Elbaki. 1976. "Towards a study of revolutions", *Comparative Studies in Society and History* 18, no. 2.

Hill, Errol. 1972. *The Trinidad Carnival: Mandate for a National Theatre*. Austin, Texas: University of Texas Press.

Hobsbawm, Eric. 1981. *Bandits*. Rev. ed. New York: Pantheon Books.

Hobsbawm, Eric. 1992. "Today's crisis of ideologies", *New Left Review*, no. 192.

Jacobs, Ian, and Richard Jacobs. 1980. *Grenada: the Route to Revolution*. Havana: Casa de las Americas.

James, C.L.R. 1980. "Marxism and the intellectuals: a critique of Raymond Williams' *Culture and Society*". In *Spheres of Existence*, edited by C.L.R. James. London: Alison & Busby.

James, C.L.R. 1980. *Notes on Dialectics: Hegel, Marx, Lenin*. Westport: Lawrence, Hill and Co.

James, C.L.R. 1982. "Walter Rodney and the question of power". In *Walter Rodney, Revolutionary and Scholar: a Tribute*, edited by E. Alpers and P.-M. Fontaine. University of California, Los Angeles: Center for Afro-American Studies and African Studies Center.

James, C.L.R. 1985. *Mariners, Renegades and Castaways: the Story of Herman Melville and the World we Live in*. London and New York: Allison & Busby.

James, C.L.R. 1986. *Beyond a Boundary*. London: Stanley Paul.

James, C.L.R. 1986. *State Capitalism and World Revolution*. Chicago, Illinois: Charles H. Kerr.

James, C.L.R. 1989. *The Black Jacobins: Toussaint L'Ouverture and the San Domingo Revolution*. New York: Vintage Books.

James, C.L.R. 1993. "The Black Jacobins". In *The C.L.R. James Reader*, edited by Anna Grimshaw. Oxford, UK and Cambridge, USA: Basil Blackwell.

Johnson, Chalmers. 1966. *Revolutionary Change*. Boston: Little, Brown.

Kaufman, Michael. 1985. *Jamaica Under Manley: Dilemmas of Socialism and Democracy*. London: Zed.

Kelly, Vitruvius, E.T. 1991. *The Silent Victory*. Port of Spain: Golden Eagle Enterprises.

Laclau, Ernesto, ed. 1994. *The Making of Political Identities*. London, New York: Verso.

Laclau, Ernesto, and Chantal Mouffe. 1989. *Hegemony and Socialist Strategy: Towards a Radical Democratic Politics*. London, New York: Verso.

LaGuerre, John Gaffar. 1982. *The Politics of Communalism: the Agony of the Left in Trinidad and Tobago, 1930-1955*. Trinidad: Pan-Caribbean Publications.

Laitin, David, and Carolyn Warner. 1992. "Structure and irony in social revolutions", *Political Theory* 20, no. 1.

Lamming, George. 1984. *The Pleasures of Exile*. 2d ed. London: Allison and Busby.

LeBon, G. 1913. *The Psychology of Revolution*. New York: Putnam.

Lehmann, David. 1990. *Democracy and Development in Latin America: Economics, Politics and Religion in the Post-War Period*. Cambridge: Polity Press.

Lenin, V.I. n.d. *The State and Revolution*. Moscow: Foreign Languages Publishing House.

Lenin, V.I. 1971. "Lecture on the 1905 revolution". In *Lenin: Selected Works*. Vol. 1. Moscow: Progress Publishers.

Lenin, V.I. 1971. "Lessons of the revolution". In *Between the Two Revolutions*. Moscow: Progress Publishers.

Lenin. V.I. 1971. "The proletarian revolution and the renegade Kautsky". In *Lenin Selected Works. Volume Three*. Moscow: Progress Publishers.

Lenin, V.I. 1973. "Marxism and insurrection". In *Guerrilla Warfare and Marxism*, edited by William Pomeroy. New York: International Publishers.

Levin, Michael. 1989. *Marx, Engels and Liberal Democracy*. London and Basingstoke: Macmillan.

Lewis, David. 1984. *Reform and Revolution in Grenada: 1950-1981*. Havana: Casa de las Americas.

Lewis, Gordon. 1968. *The Growth of the Modern West Indies*. London: McGibbon and Kee.

Lewis, Gordon. 1987. *Grenada: The Jewel Despoiled*. Baltimore: The Johns Hopkins University Press.

Lewis, Rupert. 1993. "Which way for the Jamaican left?" *Third World Viewpoint* 1, no. 1.

Lewis, Rupert. 1994. "Walter Rodney: 1968 revisited", Social and Economic Studies 43, no. 3.

Leys, Colin, ed. 1967. *Politics and Change in Developing Countries: Studies in the Theory and Practice of Development.* Sussex, Cambridge: IDS.

Lovelace, Earl. 1981. *The Dragon Can't Dance.* Harlow, Essex: Longman.

Luxemburg, Rosa. 1970. *The Russian Revolution and Leninism or Marxism?* Ann Arbor, Michigan: University of Michigan Press.

Lyotard, Jean François. 1991. *The Postmodern Condition: a Report on Knowledge.* Manchester: Manchester University Press.

MacIntyre, Alasdair. 1973. "Ideology, social science and revolution", *Comparative Politics* 5, no. 3.

Manley, Michael. 1982. *Jamaica: Struggle in the Periphery*, London: Writers and Readers.

Mann, Michael. 1989. *The Sources of Social Power.* Vol. 1. *A History of Power from the Beginning to 1760.* Cambridge: Cambridge University Press.

MAP Position Paper. 1972. Listed in microfiche no. 8559: The Grenada Documents in the National Archives. Washington, D.C.

Marable, Manning. 1987. *African and Caribbean Politics: from Kwame Nkrumah to Maurice Bishop.* London: Verso.

Marx, Karl. 1973. "Critique of the Gotha programme". In *Marx Engels Selected Works.* Vol. 2. Moscow: Progress Publishers.

Marx, Karl. 1974. "The eighteenth Brumaire of Louis Bonaparte", In *Marx and Engels: Basic Writings on Politics and Philosophy*, edited by Lewis S. Feuer. Glasgow: Collins.

Marx, Karl, and Frederick Engels. 1975. *Marx Engels Selected Correspondence.* Moscow: Progress Publishers.

Marx, Karl, and Frederick Engels. 1975. *Marx and Engels Collected Works.* Vol. 5. London: Lawrence and Wishart.

Marx, Karl, and Frederick Engels. 1975. *Karl Marx and Frederick Engels: Selected Works in Three Volumes.* Moscow: Progress Publishers.

McLellan, David. 1989. *Marxism after Marx.* London and Basingstoke: Macmillan.

Meeks, Brian. 1976. "The development of the 1970 revolution in Trinidad and Tobago", MSc thesis, University of the West Indies.

Meeks, Brian. 1986. *Some Reflections on the Grenada Revolution Two Years After its Defeat.* Mona, Jamaica: University of the West Indies. Mimeographed.

Meeks, Brian. 1993. *Caribbean Revolutions and Revolutionary Theory: an Assessment of Cuba, Nicaragua and Grenada.* London and Basingstoke: Macmillan.

Meeks, Brian. Forthcoming. *Social Formation and People's Revolution: A Grenadian Study.* London: Karia.

Miliband, Ralph. 1977. *Marxism and Politics.* Oxford: Oxford University Press,

Miliband, Ralph. 1992. "Fukuyama and the socialist alternative", *New Left Review*, no. 193.

Miliband, Ralph, and Leo Panitch, eds. 1990. *The Retreat of the Intellectuals: Socialist Register, 1990.* London: Merlin.

Moore, Barrington. 1987. *Social Origins of Dictatorship and Democracy: Lord and Peasantry in the Making of the Modern World.* Harmondsworth: Penguin.

Munroe, Trevor. 1972. *The Politics of Constitutional Decolonization: Jamaica: 1944-1962.* Mona, University of the West Indies: Institute of Social and Economic Research.

Munroe, Trevor. 1994. *For a New Beginning: Selected Speeches, 1990-1993.* Kingston: Caricom Publishers Ltd.

Nanton, Phillip. 1983. "The changing patterns of state control in St Vincent and the Grenadines". In *Crisis in the Caribbean*, edited by F. Ambursley and R.Cohen. Kingston, Port of Spain: Heinemann.

N'Zengou-Tayo, Marie-José. 1991. "Re-imagining history: the Caribbean vision of the Haitian revolution and the early independence days". Paper presented at the third annual conference of the Haitian Studies Association, Boston.

National Joint Action Committee (NJAC). 1971. *Conventional Politics or Revolution?* Trinidad: Vanguard Press.

Nettleford, Rex. 1970. *Mirror, Mirror: Identity, Race and Protest in Jamaica*. Glasgow: Collins and Sangster.

Nettleford, Rex. 1993. *Inward Stretch, Outward Reach: a Voice from the Caribbean*. London and Basingstoke: Macmillan (Caribbean).

New World Quarterly. 1971. *Special Issue on Black Power*. NWQ 5, no. 4.

NJM Manifesto for Power to the People and Achieving Real Independence. 1973. St Augustine, UWI: Institute of International Relations.

Nozick, Robert. 1991. *Anarchy, State and Utopia*. Oxford: Basil Blackwell.

Ott, Thomas. 1973. *The Haitian Revolution: 1789-1804*. Knoxville: University of Tennessee Press.

Oxaal, Ivor. 1971. *Race and Revolutionary Consciousness*. Cambridge, MA, London: Schenkman.

Pantin, Dennis. 1992. "IMF/World Bank agreements and the July 27 political crisis in Trinidad and Tobago: cause or coincidence?". Draft paper for *Cimarron*.

Pantin, Raoul. 1990. *Black Power Day*. Trinidad: Hatuey Productions.

Pantin, Raoul. 1990. "The days of wrath: an eyewitness account of the capture of Television House (TTT)". In *Trinidad Under Siege: The Muslimeen Uprising*. Port of Spain: The Trinidad Express Newspapers Limited.

Panton, David. 1993. *Jamaica's Michael Manley: the Great Transformation 1972-1992*. Kingston: Kingston Publishers Ltd.

Payne, Anthony. 1984. *The International Crisis in the Caribbean*. Baltimore: The Johns Hopkins University Press.

Pettee, George. 1913. *The Process of Revolution*. New York: Harper and Brothers.

Pluchon, Pierre. 1982. *Histoire des Antilles et de la Guyanne*. Toulouse: Privat.

Poulantzas, Nicos. 1978. *State, Power, Socialism*. London: NLB.

Premdas, Ralph. 1993. "Ethnic conflict in Trinidad and Tobago: domination and reconciliation". In *Trinidad Ethnicity*, edited by Kevin Yelvington. London and Basingstoke: Macmillan.

Qadir, Shahid, Christopher Clapham and Barry Gills. 1993. "Democratization in the Third World: an introduction", *Third World Quarterly* 14, no. 3.

Ramesar, S. 1972. "A socioeconomic profile of the unemployed in Trinidad and Tobago, 1956- 1968". In *Human Resources in the Commonwealth Caribbean*, edited by Jack Harewood. St Augustine, UWI: ISER.

Report on Human Rights Developments in Grenada. 1982. St George's, n.p.

Report on the National Consultation on Values and Attitudes. 1994. Kingston: Jamaica Information Services.

Riviere, William. 1993. "Reminiscences concerning mass work among farmers in Dominica 1976-1989", *Social and Economic Studies* 42, nos. 2 & 3.

Rohlehr, Gordon. 1990. *Calypso and Society in Pre-Independence Trinidad*. Trinidad: The author.

Rossett, Peter, and John Vandermeer, eds. 1983. *The Nicaragua Reader*. New York: Grove Press.

Runciman, W. G. 1983. *A Treatise on Social Theory*, Cambridge: Cambridge University Press.

Rustin, Michael. 1992. "No exit from capitalism?", *New Left Review*, no. 193.

Ryan, Michael. 1988. "Postmodern politics", *Theory, Culture and Society* 5, nos. 2-3.

Ryan, Selwyn. 1972. *Race and Nationalism in Trinidad and Tobago*. Toronto: University of Toronto Press.

Ryan, Selwyn. 1989. *The Disillusioned Electorate: the Politics of Succession in Trinidad and Tobago*. Port of Spain: Inprint Caribbean Ltd.

Ryan, Selwyn. 1991. *The Muslimeen Grab for Power: Race, Religion and Revolution in Trinidad and Tobago*. Port of Spain: Inprint Caribbean Ltd.

Ryan, Selwyn, and Taimoon Stewart, eds. 1995. *The Black Power Revolution 1970: a Retrospective*. St. Augustine, UWI: ISER.

Searle, Chris. 1984. *Grenada: the Struggle Against Destabilization*. London: Writers and Readers.

Searle, Chris. 1991. "The Muslimeen insurrection in Trinidad", *Race and Class* 33, no. 2.

Searle, Chris, and Merle Hodge. 1981. *Is Freedom We Making*. St George's: Government Information Service.

Shivji, Issa. 1982. *Class Struggles in Tanzania*. London: Heinemann.

Singham, Archie. 1968. *The Hero and the Crowd in a Colonial Polity*. New Haven, Connecticut: Yale University Press.

Skocpol, Theda. 1973. "A critical review of Barrington Moore's *Social Origins of Dictatorship and Democracy*", *Politics and Society* 4, no. 1.

Skocpol, Theda. 1979. *States and Social Revolutions: a Comparative Analysis of France, Russia and China*. Cambridge: Cambridge University Press.

Smelser, Neil. 1961. *Theory of Collective Behaviour*. Great Britain: Routledge and Kegan Paul.

Smith, Anna Marie. 1994. "Rastafari as resistance and the ambiguities of essentialism in the 'New Social Movements'". In *The Making of Political Identities*, edited by Ernesto Laclau. London, New York: Verso.

Smith, Dennis. 1989. *The Rise of Historical Sociology*. Cambridge: Polity Press.

Smith, M. G. 1965. *The Plural Society in the British West Indies*. Berkeley and Los Angeles, California: University of California Press.

St. Cyr, Eric. 1972. *Some Recent Trends in Prices and Wages*. Port of Spain. Mimeographed.

Statistical Institute of Jamaica (STATIN). 1994. *Statistical Bulletin: Consumer Price Index, June 1994*. Kingston: STATIN.

Stepan, A., ed. 1973. *Authoritarian Brazil: Origins, Policies and Future*. New Haven, Connecticut: Yale University Press.

Stephens, Evelyne Huber, and John Stephens. 1986. *Democratic Socialism in Jamaica*. London and Basingstoke: Macmillan.

Stone, Carl. 1980. *Democracy and Clientelism in Jamaica*. New Brunswick and London: Transaction Books.

Stone, Carl 1982. *The Political Opinions of the Jamaican People*. Kingston: Blackett Publishers.

Stone, Carl. 1989. *Politics vs Economics: the 1989 Elections in Jamaica*. Kingston: Heinemann (Caribbean) Ltd.

Stone, Carl. 1992. *Report of the Stone Committee Appointed to Advise the Jamaican Government on the Performance, Accountability and Responsibilities of Elected Parliamentarians*. Kingston: Bustamante Institute of Public and International Affairs.

Stone, Carl. 1993. *The Stone Columns: the Last Year's Work*. Kingston: Sangster.

Student Registration, Mona, 1993/4 and 1992/93 as at 3/11/93. UWI Academic Board document AB (M) p10, 1993/94.

Summit of People's Organizations (SOPO). 1990. *Public Statement on National People's Assembly*. Trinidad. Mimeographed.

Sutton, Paul. 1983. "Black Power in Trinidad and Tobago: the crisis of 1970", *Journal of Commonwealth and Comparative Politics* 21, no. 2 (July 1983).

Tabasuri, Tabiri, Hasani. 1981. "A theory of revolution and a case study of the Haitian revolution", PhD diss., University of Oklahoma.

Tan, Gerald. 1993. "The next NICs of Asia", *Third World Quarterly* 14, no. 1.

Taylor, Stan.1984. *Social Science and Revolutions*. London and Basingstoke: Macmillan.

Therborn, Goran. 1992. "The life and times of socialism", *New Left Review*, no. 194.

Thomas, Clive, Y. 1984. *The Rise of the Authoritarian State in Peripheral Societies*. New York, London: Monthly Review Press.

Thomas, Roy. 1974. *The Adjustment of Displaced Workers in a Labour Surplus Economy*. Mona, UWI: ISER.

Thompson, E. P. 1978. *The Poverty of Theory and Other Essays*. New York and London: Monthly Review Press.

Thompson, E. P. 1980. *The Making of the English Working Class*. Harmondsworth: Penguin.

Tilly, Charles. 1978. *From Mobilization to Revolution*. Reading, Mass.: Addison-Wesley.

Tilly, Charles. 1984. *Big Structures, Large Processes, Huge Comparisons*. New York: Russel Sage Foundation.

Trimberger, Ellen Kay. 1978. *Revolution from Above: Military Bureaucrats and Development in Japan, Turkey, Egypt and Peru*. New Brunswick, New Jersey: Transaction Books.

Ulyanovsky, R. 1974. *Socialism and the Newly Independent Nations*. Moscow: Progress Publishers.

UNDP. 1994. *Human Development Report, 1994*. New York, Oxford: Oxford University Press.

Unger, Roberto Mangabeira. 1987. *False Necessity: Anti-Necessitarian Social Theory in the Service of Radical Democracy*. Cambridge: Cambridge University Press.

Victor, Gary. 1989. "L'utopie de l'envers du temps". In *Nouvelles Interdites*. Port au Prince: Henri Deschamps.

Vilas, Carlos. 1986. *The Sandinista Revolution*. New York: Monthly Review Press.

von Clauswitz, Carl. 1976. *On War*. Princeton: Princeton University Press.

Wallerstein, Immanuel. 1984. *The Politics of the World Economy*. Cambridge: Cambridge University Press.

Wallerstein, Immanuel. 1994. "The agonies of liberalism: what hope progress?" *New Left Review*, no. 204.

Weber, Max. 1978. *Economy and Society*. New York: Bedminster Press.

White, Stephen K. 1991. *Political Theory and Postmodernism*. Cambridge: Cambridge University Press.

Winter, Sylvia. 1992. "Beyond the master conception: the counter-doctrine of the Jamesian poesis". In *C. L. R. James's Caribbean*, edited by P. Henry and P. Buhle. London and Basingstoke: Macmillan Caribbean.

Woddis, Jack. 1974. *New Theories of Revolution*. New York: International Publishers.

Wolf, Eric. 1969. *Peasant Wars of the Twentieth Century*. New York: Harper and Row.

Newspapers

Daily Express
Daily Gleaner
Friday Herald
Motion
Sunday Gleaner
Sunday Guardian
Tapia
TNT Mirror
Trinidad Guardian
Trinidad and Tobago Review
Vanguard

Recordings

Johnson, Linton Kwesi. 1985. "Making history". On Linton Kwesi Johnson: Reggae Greats. Island Records, Island Music.

Marley, Robert N. [Bob]. 1974. "Revolution". On Natty Dread. Island Records, Cayman Music.

Marley, Robert N. [Bob]. 1979. "We and dem". On Uprising. Island Records, Cayman Music.

Shabba Ranks. 1992. "Turn it down". On Mr Maximum. Pow Wow Records.

Index